Year 9, Pupil Book 1

NEW MATHS FRAMEWORKING

Matches the revised KS3 Framework

Kevin Evans, Keith Gordon, Trevor Senior, Brian Speed

Contents

Introduction

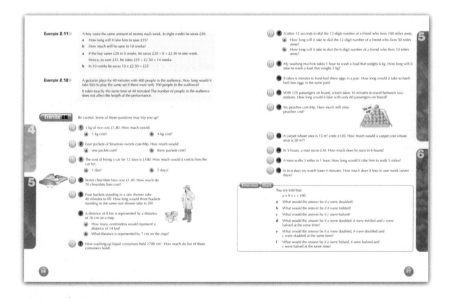

Learning objectives

See what you are going to cover and what you should already know at the start of each chapter. The purple and blue boxes set the topic in context and provide a handy checklist.

National Curriculum levels

Know what level you are working at so you can easily track your progress with the colour-coded levels at the side of the page.

Worked examples

Understand the topic before you start the exercises by reading the examples in blue boxes. These take you through how to answer a question step-by-step.

Functional Maths

Practise your Functional Maths skills to see how people use Maths in everyday life.

(FM) Look out for the Functional Maths icon on the page.

Extension activities

Stretch your thinking and investigative skills by working through the extension activities. By tackling these you are working at a higher level.

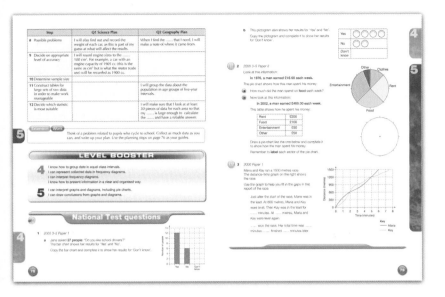

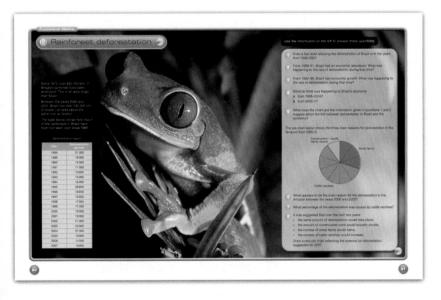

NEW

Hone your Functional Maths skills further by doing the four exciting tasks given in the new chapter – Functional Maths Practice.

Level booster

Progress to the next level by checking the Level boosters at the end of each chapter. These clearly show you what you need to know at each level and how to improve.

National Test questions

Practise the past paper Test questions to feel confident and prepared for your KS3 National Curriculum Tests. The questions are levelled so you can check what level you are working at.

Extra interactive National Test practice

Watch and listen to the audio/visual National Test questions on the separate Interactive Book CD-ROM to help you revise as a class on a whiteboard.

Look out for the computer mouse icon on the page and on the screen.

Functional Maths activities

Put Maths into context with these colourful pages showing real-world situations involving Maths. You are practising your Functional Maths skills by analysing data to solve problems.

Extra interactive Functional Maths questions and video clips

Extend your Functional Maths skills by taking part in the interactive questions on the separate Interactive Book CD-ROM. Your teacher can put these on the whiteboard so the class can answer the questions on the board.

See Maths in action by watching the video clips and doing the related Worksheets on the Interactive Book CD-ROM. The videos bring the Functional Maths activities to life and help you see how Maths is used in the real world.

Look out for the computer mouse icon on the page and on the screen.

CHAPTER 1

Algebra **1** & **2**

This chapter is going to show you	What you should already know
• How to generate and describe whole-number sequences • How to see patterns in practical activities • How to use term-to-term rules to create sequences • How to express simple functions in symbols and to represent mappings algebraically • How to generate points and plot graphs from linear equations	• How to use a flow diagram • The basic rules of arithmetic • How to plot coordinates and draw graphs

Sequences

Follow through the two flow diagrams in Examples 1.1 and 1.2, and write down the **sequence** of numbers each one generates.

Example 1.1

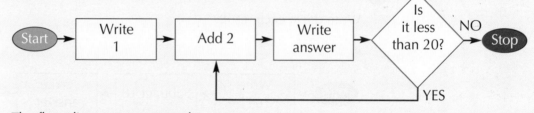

The flow diagram generates the sequence:

    1 3 5 7 9 11 13 15 17 19

These are the odd numbers less than 20.

The term-to-term rule is 'Add 2'.

Example 1.2

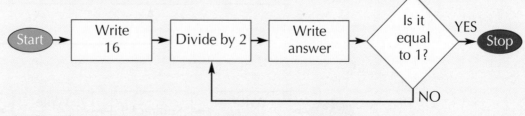

The flow diagram generates the sequence:

    16 8 4 2 1

This sequence of numbers can be described as halving to 1.

Exercise 1A

1 Work through each flow diagram below.

   i   Write down each result.

   ii   Write down a description of the numbers generated.

a

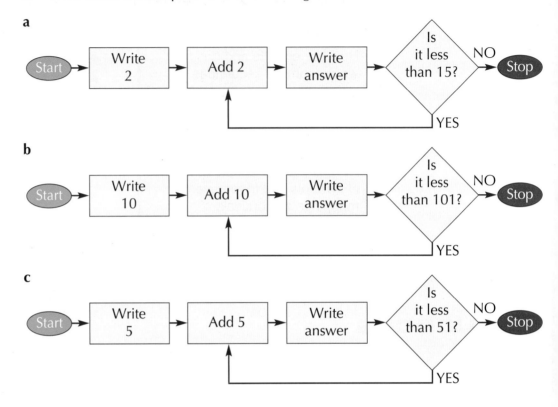

2 Work through each flow diagram below.

Write down each result.

a

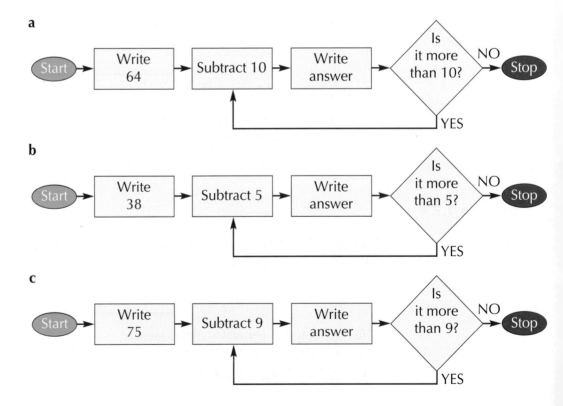

d

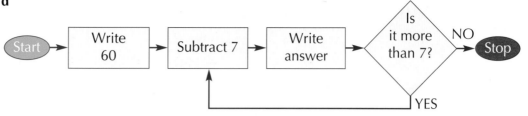

3 Work through each flow diagram below.

Write down each result.

a

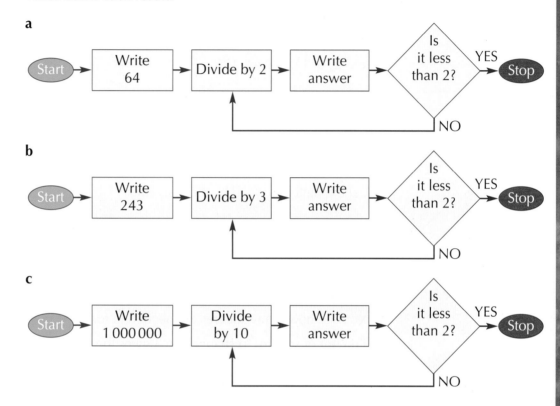

b

c

4 i Write down the next two terms when each of the following sequences is continued.

ii Describe each of the following sequences.

    a 31, 33, 35, 37, ...

    b 35, 40, 45, 50, ...

    c 28, 35, 42, 49, ...

    d 32, 36, 40, 44, ...

5 Draw a flow diagram for each of the following sequences.

    a 3, 6, 9, 12, 15, 18, 21

    b 1, 5, 9, 13, 17, 21, 25

    c 3, 8, 13, 18, 23, 28, 33

    d 31, 29, 27, 25, 23, 21, 19

    e 66, 60, 54, 48, 42, 36, 30

    f 9, 20, 31, 42, 53, 64, 75

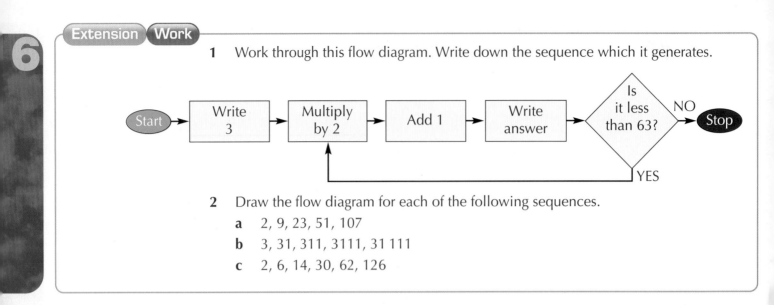

Extension **Work**

1 Work through this flow diagram. Write down the sequence which it generates.

Start → Write 3 → Multiply by 2 → Add 1 → Write answer → Is it less than 63? → NO → Stop

YES (loops back to Multiply by 2)

2 Draw the flow diagram for each of the following sequences.

 a 2, 9, 23, 51, 107

 b 3, 31, 311, 3111, 31 111

 c 2, 6, 14, 30, 62, 126

Sequences from patterns

Look at the pattern formed by these squares.

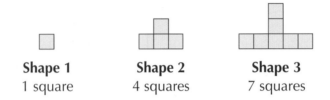

Shape 1
1 square

Shape 2
4 squares

Shape 3
7 squares

Can you see how many squares are needed to form the next two patterns?

The number of squares in shapes 1 to 3 gives the sequence 1, 4, 7, … . So, you will see that the sequence is generated by adding three more squares each time to the last pattern. That is, a square is added each time to each of the three arms of the pattern. Hence, shape 4 will have 7 + 3 = 10 squares and shape 5 will have 10 + 3 = 13 squares.

Shape 4
10 squares

Shape 5
13 squares

Look again at the pattern. Can you tell how many squares shape 10 has? It is too big to draw because that would take too long. So, can you find a rule which gives you the number of squares in any term of the sequence?

You will note that:

 Shape 2 has the first square + 1 × 3 = 4 squares
 Shape 3 has the first square + 2 × 3 = 7 squares
 Shape 4 has the first square + 3 × 3 = 10 squares

That is, the number of threes to add on is one less than the shape number. So, shape 10 has:

 First square + 9 × 3 = 28 squares

1 Look at this sequence of shapes.

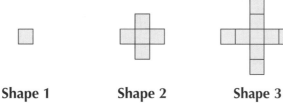

| **Shape 1** | **Shape 2** | **Shape 3** |
| 1 square | 5 squares | 9 squares |

a Draw the next two shapes in the sequence, shape 4 and shape 5.
b Write down the number of squares in each of these shapes.
c Write down the term-to-term rule.
d Find how many squares there are in shape 10 without drawing it.

2 Look at this sequence of shapes.

Shape 1 **Shape 2** **Shape 3**

a Draw the next two shapes in the sequence, shape 4 and shape 5.
b Write down the number of squares in each of these shapes.
c Write down the term-to-term rule.
d Find how many squares there are in shape 10 without drawing it.

3 Look at the following sequences of lines (blue) and crosses (green).

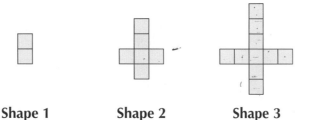

| **Shape 1** | **Shape 2** | **Shape 3** |
| 2 lines | 4 lines | 6 lines |

a Draw the next two shapes in the sequence, shape 4 and shape 5.
b Write down the number of lines in each of these shapes.
c Write down the term-to-term rule for the crosses.
d Write down how many lines and crosses there are in shape 11 without drawing it.

4 Look at this sequence of shapes.

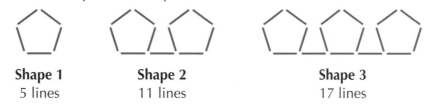

| **Shape 1** | **Shape 2** | **Shape 3** |
| 5 lines | 11 lines | 17 lines |

a Draw the next two shapes in the sequence, shape 4 and shape 5.
b Write down the number of lines in each of these shapes.
c Write down the term-to-term rule.
d Find how many lines there are in shape 21 without drawing it.

5 Look at this sequence of shapes.

Shape 1
1 grey square
8 white squares

Shape 2
2 grey squares
10 white squares

Shape 3
3 grey squares
12 white squares

a Draw the next two shapes in this sequence, shape 4 and shape 5.
b Write down the number of grey squares in each of these shapes.
c Write down the number of white squares in each of these shapes.
d Without drawing the shapes:
   i find how many grey squares there are in shape 10.
   ii find how many white squares there are in shape 20.
   iii find the total number of squares in shape 30.

6 Look at this sequence of shapes.

Shape 1   **Shape 2**   **Shape 3**

a Draw the next two shapes in this sequence, shape 4 and shape 5.
b Write down the number of grey squares in each of these shapes.
c Write down the number of white squares in each of these shapes.
d Without drawing the shapes:
   i find how many grey squares there are in shape 10.
   ii find how many white squares there are in shape 20.
   iii find out the total number of squares in shape 30.

Extension Work

Look at this sequence of shapes.

Answer the following without drawing the shapes.

 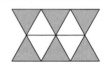

a Find how many grey triangles there are in shape 50.

b Find how many white triangles there are in shape 100.

c Find the total number of triangles in shape 500.

d Suppose you continue this pattern and in one shape you use 28 grey triangles. How many white ones would you need?

e Suppose you continue this pattern and in one shape you use 100 white triangles. How many grey ones would you need?

f What is the number of the shape which has 998 triangles?

The *n*th term of a sequence

The position of a term in a sequence can sometimes be used to find its value. The idea is to find a general term, called the **nth term**, from which the value of any term can be found. Look at Examples 1.3 and 1.4 to see how this works.

Example 1.3 ▸ Find the *n*th term for the sequence given below.

Position number, *n*	1	2	3	4	5
Value of term		5	6	7	8	9

Each term can be found by adding 4 to its position number, *n*. So, the *n*th term is given by $n + 4$.

Example 1.4 ▸ Write down the first five terms of a sequence where the *n*th term is given by $2n + 3$.

To find each term, give the position number, *n*, the value 1 to 5, in order, as shown below.

$$n \longrightarrow 2n + 3$$

or $\qquad n \longrightarrow \boxed{\times 2} \longrightarrow \boxed{+ 3} \longrightarrow$ Value of term

The 1st term is:	1	$\longrightarrow$	2 $\longrightarrow$	5
The 2nd term is:	2	$\longrightarrow$	4 $\longrightarrow$	7
The 3rd term is:	3	$\longrightarrow$	6 $\longrightarrow$	9
The 4th term is:	4	$\longrightarrow$	8 $\longrightarrow$	11
The 5th term is:	5	$\longrightarrow$	10 $\longrightarrow$	13

Hence, the sequence is 5, 7, 9, 11, 13, … .

When you are given a rule like this, you can use it to find a term well into the sequence. For example, the 50th term in the above sequence is found by putting $n = 50$ into $n \longrightarrow 2n + 3$, which gives:

$$n \longrightarrow \boxed{\times 2} \longrightarrow \boxed{+ 3} \longrightarrow \text{Value of term}$$

$$50 \longrightarrow 100 \longrightarrow 103$$

Exercise 1C

1. The *n*th term of a sequence is given by $n \longrightarrow 5n + 2$.

    a Find the first five terms of the sequence.

    b Find the 20th term of the sequence.

    c Find the 50th term of the sequence.

2. The *n*th term of a sequence is given by $n \longrightarrow 7n - 1$.

    a Find the first five terms of the sequence.

    b Find the 10th term of the sequence.

    c Find the 100th term of the sequence.

$4 \times \not{1}\not{p} + 9$

3 The nth term of a sequence is given by $n \longrightarrow 4n + 9$.

    a   Find the first five terms of the sequence.

    b   Find the 30th term of the sequence.

    c   Find the 150th term of the sequence.

4 The nth term of a sequence is given by $n \longrightarrow 100 + 2n$.

    a   Find the first five terms of the sequence.

    b   Find the 10th term of the sequence.

    c   Find the 50th term of the sequence.

5 The nth term of a sequence is given by $n \longrightarrow 100 - 2n$.

    a   Find the first five terms of the sequence.

    b   Find the 20th term of the sequence.

    c   Find the 50th term of the sequence.

6 Look at the pattern below.

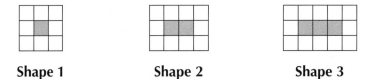

Shape 1	**Shape 2**	**Shape 3**
1 grey square	2 grey squares	3 grey squares
8 white squares	10 white squares	12 white squares

Matty, the mathematician, worked out the following details.

- The number of grey squares in the nth shape is simply n.
- The number of white squares in the nth shape is $2n + 6$.
- The total number of squares in the nth shape is $3n + 6$.

    a   Show that Matty was correct for the three shapes shown.

    b   How many grey squares are in shape 17?

    c   How many white squares are in shape 40?

    d   How many squares altogether are in shape 60?

7 Look at the pattern below.

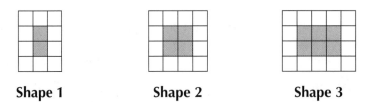

    Shape 1   **Shape 2**   **Shape 3**

Lesley, another mathematician, worked out the following details.

- The number of grey squares in the nth shape is $2n$.
- The number of white squares in the nth shape is $2n + 8$.
- The total number of squares in the nth shape is $4n + 8$.

    a   Show that Lesley was correct for the three shapes shown.

    b   How many grey squares are in shape 13?

    c   How many white squares are in shape 20?

    d   How many squares altogether are in shape 100?

1 Create a series of shapes, whose *n*th shape has 4*n* + 1 squares.

2 Create a series of shapes, whose *n*th shape has 3*n* + 1 squares.

3 Create a series of shapes, whose *n*th shape has:
   a *n* grey squares.   **b** 4*n* white squares.

4 Create a series of shapes, whose *n*th shape has:
   a 2*n* grey squares   **b** 3*n* white squares.

5 Create a series of shapes, whose *n*th shape has:
   a 3*n* grey squares   **b** 6*n* white squares.

Combined functions and mappings

A **function** is a rule which changes one number, called the **input**, to another number, called the **output**. It involves any one or more of the following operations: addition, subtraction, multiplication, division.

A function can also be defined as a mapping which has *only one* output number for every input. Example 1.5 shows how this works.

Example 1.5 Draw a mapping diagram to illustrate the following.

Input $\longrightarrow$ | Multiply by 2 | $\longmapsto$ | Add 3 | $\longrightarrow$ Output

Start with any set of numbers as the input. Each input maps with the function to the output. So, for the function:

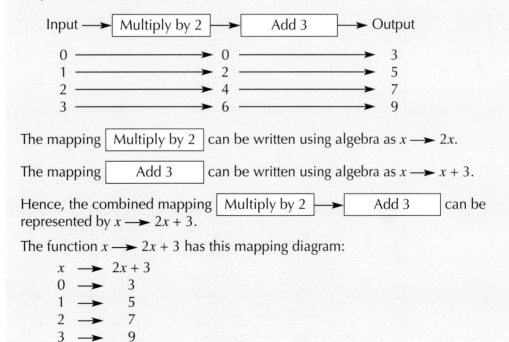

The mapping | Multiply by 2 | can be written using algebra as $x \longrightarrow 2x$.

The mapping | Add 3 | can be written using algebra as $x \longrightarrow x + 3$.

Hence, the combined mapping | Multiply by 2 | $\longmapsto$ | Add 3 | can be represented by $x \longrightarrow 2x + 3$.

The function $x \longrightarrow 2x + 3$ has this mapping diagram:

$x \longrightarrow 2x + 3$
$0 \longrightarrow 3$
$1 \longrightarrow 5$
$2 \longrightarrow 7$
$3 \longrightarrow 9$

From this, you can see that a function may be thought of as a machine which processes numbers. Take as an example $x \rightarrow 2x + 3$:

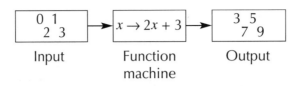

Input   Function   Output
machine

5

Exercise 1D

1 Copy and complete each of the following mapping diagrams for the functions shown.

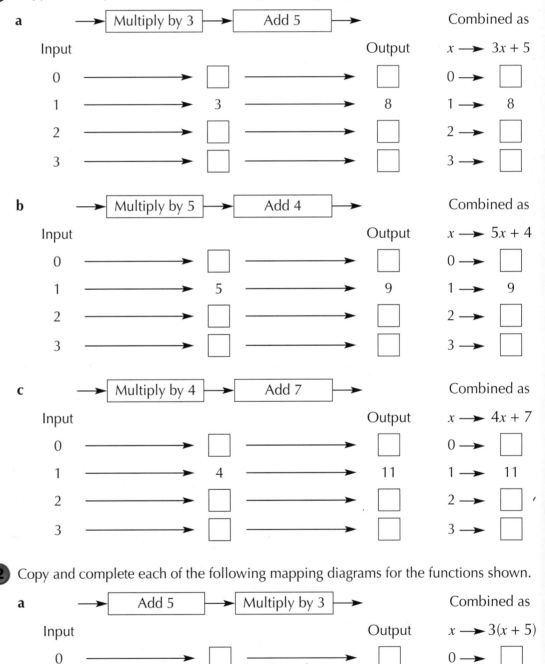

2 Copy and complete each of the following mapping diagrams for the functions shown.

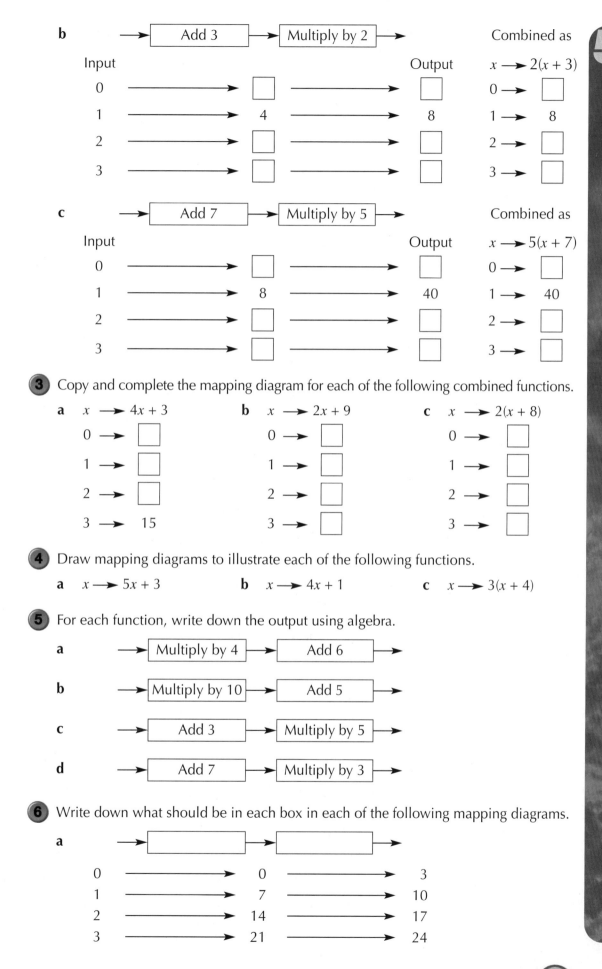

b → | Add 3 | → | Multiply by 2 | →   Combined as

Input			Output	$x \longrightarrow 2(x+3)$
0	→ ☐	→	☐	0 → ☐
1	→ 4	→	8	1 → 8
2	→ ☐	→	☐	2 → ☐
3	→ ☐	→	☐	3 → ☐

c → | Add 7 | → | Multiply by 5 | →   Combined as

Input			Output	$x \longrightarrow 5(x+7)$
0	→ ☐	→	☐	0 → ☐
1	→ 8	→	40	1 → 40
2	→ ☐	→	☐	2 → ☐
3	→ ☐	→	☐	3 → ☐

3 Copy and complete the mapping diagram for each of the following combined functions.

a $x \longrightarrow 4x + 3$
0 → ☐
1 → ☐
2 → ☐
3 → 15

b $x \longrightarrow 2x + 9$
0 → ☐
1 → ☐
2 → ☐
3 → ☐

c $x \longrightarrow 2(x + 8)$
0 → ☐
1 → ☐
2 → ☐
3 → ☐

4 Draw mapping diagrams to illustrate each of the following functions.

a $x \longrightarrow 5x + 3$ **b** $x \longrightarrow 4x + 1$ **c** $x \longrightarrow 3(x + 4)$

5 For each function, write down the output using algebra.

a → | Multiply by 4 | → | Add 6 | →

b → | Multiply by 10 | → | Add 5 | →

c → | Add 3 | → | Multiply by 5 | →

d → | Add 7 | → | Multiply by 3 | →

6 Write down what should be in each box in each of the following mapping diagrams.

a → | ☐ | → | ☐ | →

0	→ 0	→ 3
1	→ 7	→ 10
2	→ 14	→ 17
3	→ 21	→ 24

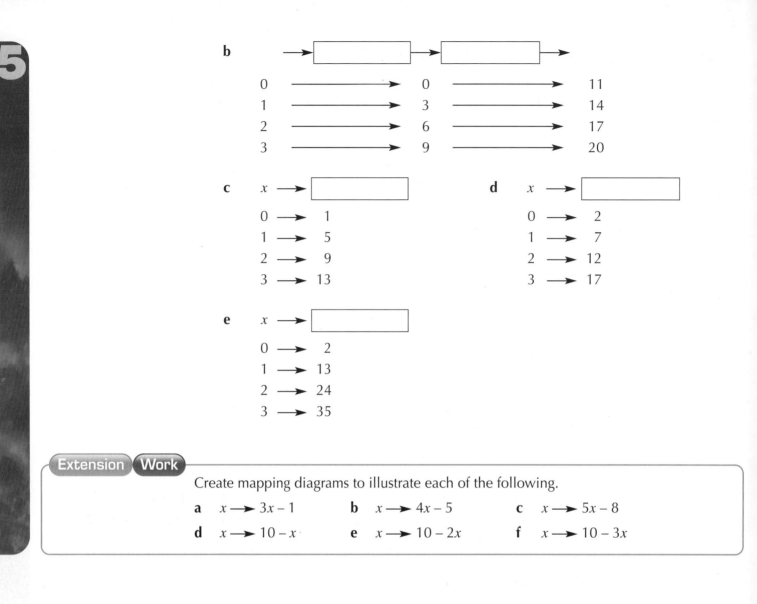

b

0	→		→	0	→		→	11
1	→		→	3	→		→	14
2	→		→	6	→		→	17
3	→		→	9	→		→	20

c x →

0	→	1
1	→	5
2	→	9
3	→	13

d x →

0	→	2
1	→	7
2	→	12
3	→	17

e x →

0	→	2
1	→	13
2	→	24
3	→	35

Extension   Work

Create mapping diagrams to illustrate each of the following.

a $x \longrightarrow 3x - 1$ **b** $x \longrightarrow 4x - 5$ **c** $x \longrightarrow 5x - 8$

d $x \longrightarrow 10 - x$ **e** $x \longrightarrow 10 - 2x$ **f** $x \longrightarrow 10 - 3x$

Graphs of functions

There are different ways to write functions. For example, the function:

$x \rightarrow 3x + 1$

can also be written as:

$y = 3x + 1$

with the inputs as x and the outputs as y.

This alternative way of writing functions simplifies the drawing of graphs. Every function has its own graph which is produced by finding ordered pairs of numbers, or coordinates, from the function, and plotting them.

Note: The graph of any linear function is a straight line.

Example 1.6 Draw a graph of the function $y = 3x + 1$.

First, make a table of easy values for the x-coordinates. Then calculate the corresponding values of y, using $y = 3x + 1$. These y-coordinates are also put in the table.

x	−1	0	1	2	3
$y = 3x + 1$	−2	1	4	7	10

Then, either construct a grid or use suitably graduated graph paper, marking the x-axis from −1 to 3 and the y-axis from −2 to 10. Next, plot the coordinates and join them to give a straight line graph.

Note that this graph passes through countless other coordinates, all of which obey the same rule of the function: that is, $y = 3x + 1$. You can choose any point on the line which has not been plotted to show that this is true.

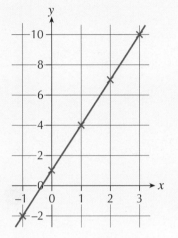

 1 **a** Copy and complete the table below for the function $y = x + 2$.

x	−1	0	1	2	3
$y = x + 2$	1	2			

b Draw a grid with its x-axis from −1 to 3 and y-axis from −1 to 5.
c Use the table to construct, on the grid, the graph of the function $y = x + 2$.

2 **a** Copy and complete the table below for the function $y = 2x + 3$.

x	−1	0	1	2	3
$y = 2x + 3$	1	3			

b Draw a grid with its x-axis from −1 to 3 and y-axis from −1 to 9.
c Use the table to construct, on the grid, the graph of the function $y = 2x + 3$.

 3 **a** Copy and complete the table below for the function $y = 4x + 2$.

x	−1	0	1	2	3
$y = 4x + 2$	−2	2			

b Draw a grid with its x-axis from −1 to 3 and y-axis from −2 to 14.
c Use the table to construct, on the grid, the graph of the function $y = 4x + 2$.

4 **a** Copy and complete the table below for the function $y = 5x + 1$.

x	−1	0	1	2	3
$y = 5x + 1$	−4	1			

b Draw a grid with its x-axis from −1 to 3 and y-axis from −4 to 16.
c Use the table to construct, on the grid, the graph of the function $y = 5x + 1$.

5 a Copy and complete the table below for the functions shown.

x	−1	0	1	2	3
y = 2x + 1	−1				7
y = 2x + 2	0			6	
y = 2x + 3	1	3	5		
y = 2x	−2	0	2		

b Draw a grid with its x-axis from −1 to 3 and y-axis from −2 to 11.

c Draw the graph for each function in the table above.

d What two properties do you notice about each line?

e Use the properties you have noticed to draw the graph of each of the following functions.

　i y = 2x + 4　　　　**ii** y = 2x + 5

6 a Copy and complete the table below for the functions shown.

x	−1	0	1	2	3
y = 3x + 1					10
y = 3x + 2	−1			8	
y = 3x + 3		3			
y = 3x + 4			7		

b Draw a grid with its x-axis from −1 to 3 and y-axis from −2 to 13.

c Draw the graph for each function in the table above.

d What two properties do you notice about each line?

e Use the properties you have noticed to draw the graph of each of the functions.

　i y = 3x + 5　　**ii** y = 3x + 6　　**iii** y = 3x

Extension Work

1 Draw the graph of y = 4x + 1 and of y = 4x + 5.

2 Now draw, without any further calculations, the graph of y = 4x + 3 and of y = 4x + 7.

LEVEL BOOSTER

I can generate sequences, given the first term and the term-to-term rule. For example, first term 7 and term-to-term rule 'multiply by 2' give 7, 14, 28, 56, 112, …

I can predict the next terms in a linear sequence of numbers.

I can find any term in a sequence, given the first term, say 5, and the term-to-term rule such as 'goes up by 6 each time', that is the 20th term is 119.

I can find any term in a sequence, given the algebraic rule for the nth term, e.g. a sequence with an nth term of $6n - 5$ has a 10th term of 55.

I can draw the graph of a function such as y = 2x + 3 by setting up a table of values.

I can use algebra to write down a function, given the operations that create the function, for example:

1 *2005 3–5 Paper 2*

Here is a sequence of shapes made with grey and white tiles.

The number of grey tiles = 2 × the shape number
The number of white tiles = 2 × the shape number

shape number 1   shape number 2   shape number 3   shape number 4

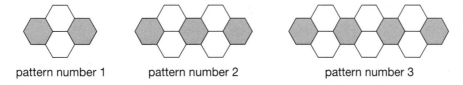

a Altogether, how many tiles will there be in shape number **5**?

b Altogether, how many tiles will there be in shape number **15**?

c Write down the missing number from this sentence:

The **total** number of tiles = ... × the shape number.

2 *2006 3–5 Paper 2*

a The following rules show how to get from one number to the next in these sequences.

Use the rules to write the next **two** numbers in each sequence:

Rule: **Add 8**

      4   12   ....

Rule: **Multiply by 3**

      4   12   ....

Rule: **Divide by 4 then add 11**

      4   12   ....

b A sequence of numbers starts like this:

      30   22   18

Could the rule be **Subtract 8?**

Explain your answer.

3 *2006 3–5 Paper 1*

Look at this sequence of patterns made with hexagons:

pattern number 1   pattern number 2   pattern number 3

To find the number of hexagons in pattern number n you can use these rules:

Number of **grey** hexagons = $n + 1$
Number of **white** hexagons = $2n$

Altogether, what is the total number of hexagons in **pattern number 20**?

FM Mobile phone tariffs

Pick your plan

Mix & match plans	Inclusive UK minutes and texts	Free 3 to 3 minutes	Free voicemail	Free Instant Messaging	Free Skype
£12 a month	£12 Promotional tariff	**100** Anytime any network minutes or texts or any mix of the two	**300** 3 to 3 minutes	✔	✔	✔
£15 a month	Mix & match 300	**300** Anytime any network minutes or texts or any mix of the two	**300** 3 to 3 minutes	✔	✔	✔
£18 a month	Mix & match 500	**500** Anytime any network minutes or texts or any mix of the two	**300** 3 to 3 minutes	✔	✔	✔
£21 a month	Mix & match 700	**700** Anytime any network minutes or texts or any mix of the two	**300** 3 to 3 minutes	✔	✔	✔
£24 a month	Mix & match 900	**900** Anytime any network minutes or texts or any mix of the two	**300** 3 to 3 minutes	✔	✔	✔
£27 a month	Mix & match 1100	**1100** Anytime any network minutes or texts or any mix of the two	**300** 3 to 3 minutes	✔	✔	✔

- Pay by voucher or direct debit
- If you pay by voucher, service is suspended once the monthly allowance is reached
- If you pay by direct debit, any minutes or texts over the allowance are charged at 15p per minute or 15p per text
- 10% discount if you pay by direct debit
- All tariffs do not include VAT which is charged at $17\frac{1}{2}$%

Use the information on Mobile phone tariffs to help you answer these questions.

1. How many hours is 900 minutes?

2. How many hours and minutes is 700 minutes?

3. Janis has the '£12 Promotional tariff'. She pays by voucher. She does not use her phone for voice calls. So far in a month she has sent 43 texts. How many more can she send that month before service is suspended?

4. Andy has the '£12 Promotional tariff'. He pays by direct debit. How much will this cost per month after the 10% discount?

5. Ben has the 'Mix and match 300' tariff. Before any discounts or VAT how much would this cost for a 12-month contract?

6. Gordon has the '£12 Promotional tariff'. So far he has used 24 minutes on voice calls and sent 19 texts. How many more minutes or texts can he send before he gets charged extra?

7. Shaun has the 'Mix and match 900' tariff and pays by direct debit each month. In one month he makes an extra 50 minutes of voice calls and sends an extra 30 texts.

   a. How much extra will he pay before any discounts are taken off?

   b. What will his bill for that month be after the 10% discount?

8. a. The 'Mix and match 300' tariff allows 300 minutes or texts for £15. How much does each minute or text cost on average?

   b. The 'Mix and match 500' tariff allows 500 minutes or texts for £18. How much does each minute or text cost on average?

The table shows two tariffs for people who send a lot of texts.

Pick your plan

Texter plans		Texts	Minutes	Free voicemail	One-Off Cost	Unlimited Skype
£15 a month	£15 Texter	600	75 Anytime, any network			
£20 a month	£20 Texter	1000	100 Anytime, any network			

- If you pay by direct debit, any extra voice minutes are charged at 15p per minute and extra texts are charged at 10p per text

- 10% discount if you pay by direct debit

- All tariffs do not include VAT which is charged at $17\frac{1}{2}$%

Sony Ericsson K850i   MOTORAZR² V9

9. Mel has the 'Mix and match 500' tariff. She pays by direct debit. In one month she uses all of her allowed anytime, any network voice minutes and makes some more minutes of voice calls. Her bill for the month is £24 before any discount is given. How many minutes of calls over the 500 allowed minutes did she make?

10. Dave has the '£15 Texter' tariff. He pays by direct debit. In one month he uses 750 texts and 100 minutes of voice calls.

What is his bill for that month before the discount is given?

11. Andy has the '£20 texter' tariff. He pays by direct debit. In one month he uses all of his 100 anytime, any network voice calls and sends over 1000 texts. His bill for the month before discount and VAT is £23. How many more texts than the 1000 allowed did he send?

12. Lucy has the '£15 Texter' tariff. She pays by direct debit. In one month she makes over 75 minutes of voice calls and sends 540 texts. Her bill for the month is £24.90 before any discount is given. How many minutes of calls over the allowed 75 minutes did she make?

13. Coryn has a 'Mix and match 300' tariff. He pays by voucher. Coryn knows that his average voice calls per month are 220 minutes and he sends an average of 40 texts. He sees this advertisement.

> Special offer for existing customers
> 'Mix and match 250'
> 250 anytime any network minutes or texts
> or any mix of the two.
> Only £13.00 per month *including* VAT.
> Extra minutes or texts 15p.

If Coryn changes to the 'Mix and match 250' tariff, will he save money in an average month?

You must show your working to justify your answer.

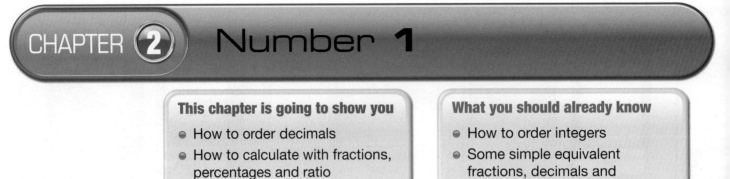

This chapter is going to show you	What you should already know
<ul><li>How to order decimals</li><li>How to calculate with fractions, percentages and ratio</li><li>How to round numbers to two decimal places</li></ul>	<ul><li>How to order integers</li><li>Some simple equivalent fractions, decimals and percentages</li><li>How to find simple equivalent fractions</li></ul>

Ordering whole numbers and decimals

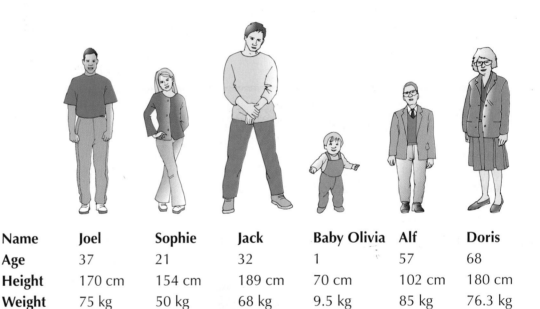

Name	Joel	Sophie	Jack	Baby Olivia	Alf	Doris
Age	37	21	32	1	57	68
Height	170 cm	154 cm	189 cm	70 cm	102 cm	180 cm
Weight	75 kg	50 kg	68 kg	9.5 kg	85 kg	76.3 kg

Look at the people in the picture. How would you put them in order?

When you compare the size of numbers, you have to consider the **place value** of each digit. This is the value given to a digit because of the position the digit has in the number relative to the units place.

It helps if you fill in the numbers in a table like the one shown on the right.

The decimal point separates the whole-number part of the number from the decimal-fraction part.

Example 2.1 explains how the table works.

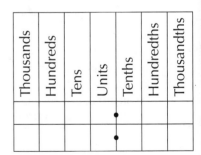

Example 2.1 ▸ Put the numbers 254, 245, 164 and 352 in order from smallest to largest.

We can write the numbers in the table like this:

Working across the table from the left, you can see that the smallest digit in the hundreds column is a 1. So 164 is the smallest number.

Two numbers have a 2 in the hundreds column, but the first number then has 5 in the tens column and the second number has a 4 in the tens column, so the second number is smaller. 245 is smaller than 254.

This leaves the largest number as 352.

So, the order is: 164, 245, 254, 352

Thousands	Hundreds	Tens	Units
	2	5	4
	2	4	5
	1	6	4
	3	5	2

Example 2.2 ▸ Put the numbers 56, 57, 56.4 and 55.607 in order from smallest to largest.

Writing the numbers in the table, filling in any missing decimal places with zeros, gives:

Working across the table from the left, you can see that all the tens digits are the same. The smallest units digit is in the number 55.607, so this is the smallest number.

Two numbers have a 6 in the units column – 56.000 and 56.400 – but the first number then has 0 in the tenths column, so 56 is the next number and then 56.4. Finally, the largest number is 57.

So, the order is: 55.607, 56, 56.4, 57

Thousands	Hundreds	Tens	Units	Tenths	Hundredths	Thousandths
		5	6	0	0	0
		5	7	0	0	0
		5	6	4	0	0
		5	5	6	0	7

Exercise 2A

1 Write each of these sets of number in order from smallest to largest.

    a   24, 42, 28, 33, 43

    b   84, 175, 157, 48, 62

    c   1025, 1100, 1502, 1102, 1052

2 Put the following amounts of money in order, smallest first.

    a   108p, £0.80, 78p, £0.65, £0.09

    b   £0.90, 89p, £9, 10p, £0.68

    c   £19.99, £25, 84p, £18.75, £0.90

3 Put these times in order: 1 hour 10 minutes, 25 minutes, 1.25 hours, 0.5 hours.

6

4 For each part, copy the table (but not the numbers) in Example 2.2.

Write the sets of numbers in your table, placing each digit in the appropriate column. Then write the numbers in order from smallest to largest.

a 7.5, 6.1, 6.3, 6.8, 7.0
b 2.5, 5.2, 2.7, 2.3, 5.1
c 9.13, 9.01, 8.99, 8.75, 9.10
d 10, 9.5, 11.2, 9.75, 9.8
e 5.68, 56, 5.6, 0.056, 0.6, 5.06
f 0.63, 0.063, 0.7, 0.609, 0.6
g 1.607, 1.7, 1.809, 1.808, 1.8
h 23, 2.3, 0.23, 1.23, 0.023

5 One metre is 100 cm. Change all the lengths below to metres and then put them in order from smallest to largest.

4.45 m, 349 cm, 20 cm, 3.5 m, 0.24 m

6 One kilogram is 1000 g. Change all the weights below to kilograms and then put them in order from smallest to largest.

37 g, 1.370 kg, 37 kg, 0.4 kg, 0.036 kg

Extension Work

Choose a set of six consecutive whole numbers, such as 3, 4, 5, 6, 7 and 8.

Use a calculator to work out the first number divided by the second number as a decimal (3 ÷ 4), the second number divided by the third number (4 ÷ 5) and so on.

Put your five answers in order from smallest to largest.

What do you notice?

Now repeat for any six numbers written in order, such as 1, 5, 8, 14, 15 and 20.

What do you notice?

Adding and subtracting fractions

This section will give you more practice with adding and subtracting fractions.

Here is a multiplication table you can use to find equivalent fractions.

This is how it works: to cancel down the fraction $\frac{21}{35}$, find 21 and 35 in the same column. Then look at the numbers in the left hand column of the same rows.

So, $\frac{21}{35} = \frac{3}{5}$

All the fractions made from those two rows are equivalent, so $\frac{3}{5} = \frac{6}{10} = \frac{9}{15} = \frac{12}{20}$ and so on.

×	1	2	3	4	5	6	7	8	9	10
1	1	2	3	4	5	6	7	8	9	10
2	2	4	6	8	10	12	14	16	18	20
3	3	6	9	12	15	18	21	24	27	30
4	4	8	12	16	20	24	28	32	36	40
5	5	10	15	20	25	30	35	40	45	50
6	6	12	18	24	30	36	42	48	54	60
7	7	14	21	28	35	42	49	56	63	70
8	8	16	24	32	40	48	56	64	72	80
9	9	18	27	36	45	54	63	72	81	90
10	10	20	30	40	50	60	70	80	90	100

Example 2.3 ▷ Use the multiplication table to complete the following.

a $\frac{6}{8} = \frac{}{4}$ b $\frac{2}{5} = \frac{}{10}$ c $\frac{2}{7} = \frac{}{21}$

a $\frac{6}{8} = \frac{3}{4}$ b $\frac{2}{5} = \frac{4}{10}$ c $\frac{2}{7} = \frac{6}{21}$

When the denominators of the fractions are not the same, they must be made the same before numerators are added or subtracted. To do this, we find the lowest common multiple (LCM) of the denominators.

Example 2.4 ▷ a Complete the following.

i $\frac{4}{5} = \frac{}{10}$ ii $\frac{3}{7} = \frac{}{14}$

b Work out the answers to these calculations.

i $\frac{4}{5} + \frac{1}{10}$ ii $\frac{3}{7} - \frac{1}{14}$

a i $\frac{4}{5} = \frac{8}{10}$ ii $\frac{3}{7} = \frac{6}{14}$

b i $\frac{4}{5} + \frac{1}{10} = \frac{8}{10} + \frac{1}{10} = \frac{9}{10}$

   ii $\frac{3}{7} - \frac{1}{14} = \frac{6}{14} - \frac{1}{14} = \frac{5}{14}$

Exercise 2B

1 Use the multiplication table to copy and complete the following.

a $\frac{3}{4} = \frac{}{12}$ b $\frac{1}{5} = \frac{}{10}$ c $\frac{2}{3} = \frac{}{9}$ d $\frac{1}{2} = \frac{}{10}$

e $\frac{9}{10} = \frac{}{40}$ f $\frac{6}{7} = \frac{}{28}$ g $\frac{1}{8} = \frac{}{32}$ h $\frac{7}{9} = \frac{}{63}$

2 Copy and complete each of the following.

a $\frac{1}{7} + \frac{1}{7} = \frac{}{7}$ b $\frac{1}{9} + \frac{1}{9} = \frac{}{9}$ c $\frac{1}{5} + \frac{2}{5} = \frac{}{5}$

d $\frac{1}{3} + \frac{1}{3} = \frac{}{3}$ e $\frac{3}{10} + \frac{3}{10} = \frac{}{10} = \frac{}{5}$ f $\frac{1}{8} + \frac{3}{8} = \frac{}{8} = \frac{}{2}$

g $\frac{2}{9} + \frac{4}{9} = \frac{}{9} = \frac{}{3}$ h $\frac{1}{12} + \frac{5}{12} = \frac{}{12} = \frac{}{2}$

3 Copy and complete each of the following.

a $\frac{5}{7} - \frac{1}{7} = \frac{}{7}$ b $\frac{8}{9} - \frac{4}{9} = \frac{}{9}$ c $\frac{4}{5} - \frac{2}{5} = \frac{}{5}$

d $\frac{2}{3} - \frac{1}{3} = \frac{}{3}$ e $\frac{7}{10} - \frac{3}{10} = \frac{}{10} = \frac{}{5}$ f $\frac{5}{8} - \frac{3}{8} = \frac{}{8} = \frac{}{4}$

g $\frac{7}{9} - \frac{4}{9} = \frac{}{9} = \frac{}{3}$ h $\frac{11}{12} - \frac{5}{12} = \frac{}{12} = \frac{}{2}$

4 Copy and complete each of the following.

a $\frac{1}{10} + \frac{1}{5} = \frac{1}{10} + \frac{2}{10} = \frac{}{10}$ b $\frac{1}{2} + \frac{1}{6} = \frac{}{6} + \frac{1}{6} = \frac{}{6}$ c $\frac{1}{8} + \frac{1}{2} = \frac{1}{8} + \frac{}{8} = \frac{}{8}$

d $\frac{1}{2} + \frac{1}{4} = \frac{}{4} + \frac{1}{4} = \frac{}{4}$ e $\frac{3}{4} + \frac{1}{8} = \frac{}{8} + \frac{1}{8} = \frac{}{8}$ f $\frac{3}{5} + \frac{1}{10} = \frac{}{10} + \frac{1}{10} = \frac{}{10}$

g $\frac{5}{12} + \frac{1}{6} = \frac{5}{12} + \frac{}{12} = \frac{}{12}$ h $\frac{1}{7} + \frac{1}{14} = \frac{}{14} + \frac{1}{14} = \frac{}{14}$

5 Copy and complete each of the following.

a $\frac{9}{10} - \frac{1}{5} = \frac{9}{10} - \frac{}{10} = \frac{}{10}$ b $\frac{1}{3} - \frac{1}{6} = \frac{}{6} - \frac{1}{6} = \frac{}{6}$ c $\frac{1}{2} - \frac{1}{8} = \frac{}{8} - \frac{1}{8} = \frac{}{8}$

d $\frac{1}{2} - \frac{1}{4} = \frac{}{4} - \frac{1}{4} = \frac{}{4}$ e $\frac{3}{4} - \frac{1}{8} = \frac{}{8} - \frac{1}{8} = \frac{}{8}$ f $\frac{4}{5} - \frac{1}{10} = \frac{}{10} - \frac{1}{10} = \frac{}{10}$

g $\frac{11}{12} - \frac{5}{6} = \frac{11}{12} - \frac{}{12} = \frac{}{12}$ h $\frac{1}{7} - \frac{1}{14} = \frac{}{14} - \frac{1}{14} = \frac{}{14}$

6 Firstly, convert the following fractions to equivalent fractions with a common denominator, then work out the answer.

a $\frac{1}{5} + \frac{1}{4}$ b $\frac{1}{8} + \frac{1}{2}$ c $\frac{3}{4} + \frac{1}{5}$ d $\frac{1}{6} + \frac{2}{9}$

e $\frac{1}{4} - \frac{1}{5}$ f $\frac{5}{8} - \frac{1}{3}$ g $\frac{3}{4} - \frac{1}{5}$ h $\frac{5}{6} - \frac{2}{3}$

FM **7** A magazine has $\frac{1}{4}$ of its pages for advertising, $\frac{1}{12}$ for letters and the rest for articles.

a What fraction of the pages is for articles?

b If the magazine has 150 pages, how many are used for articles?

FM **8** A survey of pupils showed that $\frac{1}{5}$ of them walked to school, $\frac{1}{3}$ came by bus and the rest came by car.

a What fraction came by car?

b If there were 1200 pupils in the school, how many came by car?

Extension Work

You may use a calculator for this work.

1 Work out $\frac{1}{2} + \frac{1}{4}$, $\frac{1}{4} + \frac{1}{8}$, $\frac{1}{8} + \frac{1}{16}$ and $\frac{1}{16} + \frac{1}{32}$.

What do you notice about the answers?

2 Now work out $\frac{1}{3} + \frac{1}{9}$, $\frac{1}{9} + \frac{1}{27}$ and $\frac{1}{27} + \frac{1}{81}$.

What do you notice about the answers?

Whole numbers and fractions

Example 2.5 ▷

Work out each of the following.

a $\frac{1}{2}$ of 24   b $\frac{2}{3}$ of 15

a $\frac{1}{2}$ of 24 = 24 ÷ 2 = 12

b $\frac{1}{3}$ of 15 = 15 ÷ 3 = 5

So $\frac{2}{32}$ of 15 = 5 × 2 = 10

Example 2.6 ▷

Work out each of the following.

a $\frac{1}{4} \times 60$ b $\frac{2}{5} \times 15$

a $\frac{1}{4} \times 60$ is the same as $\frac{1}{4}$ of 60

$\frac{1}{4}$ of 60 = 60 ÷ 4 = 15

$\frac{1}{4} \times 60 = 15$

b $\frac{2}{5} \times 15$ is the same as $\frac{2}{5}$ of 15

$\frac{1}{5}$ of 15 = 15 ÷ 3 = 3

So $\frac{2}{5}$ of 15 = 3 × 2 = 6

$\frac{2}{5} \times 15 = 6$

Exercise 2C

1 Work these out.

   a $\frac{1}{2}$ of 18   **b** $\frac{1}{2}$ of 46   **c** $\frac{1}{2}$ of 60   **d** $\frac{1}{3}$ of 21

   e $\frac{1}{3}$ of 33   **f** $\frac{1}{4}$ of 28   **g** $\frac{1}{4}$ of 36   **h** $\frac{1}{5}$ of 35

2 Use the answers to parts **d** to **h** of question 1 to work out the following.

   a $\frac{2}{3}$ of 21   **b** $\frac{2}{3}$ of 33   **c** $\frac{3}{4}$ of 28   **d** $\frac{3}{4}$ of 36   **e** $\frac{2}{5}$ of 35

3 Match these cards in pairs.

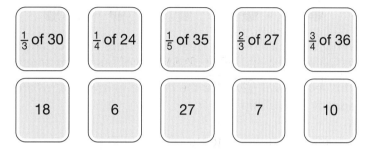

4 Match these cards in pairs.

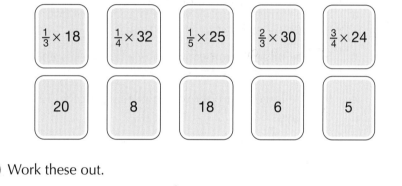

5 Work these out.

   a $\frac{1}{3} \times 12$ **b** $\frac{2}{3} \times 12$ **c** $\frac{1}{4} \times 40$ **d** $\frac{3}{4} \times 40$

   e $\frac{1}{8} \times 16$ **f** $\frac{5}{8} \times 16$ **g** $\frac{1}{12} \times 24$ **h** $\frac{7}{12} \times 24$

FM **6** A man earns £300. He pays out two-thirds on his rent. How much rent does he pay?

FM **7** Betty has 36 pairs of shoes. Three-quarters of them are black. How many pairs of black shoes she does she have?

Extension **Work**

Copy and fill in each of the missing numbers.

$\frac{1}{5} \times 2 = \frac{2}{5}$ $\frac{4}{5} \times 2 = \frac{8}{5}$ $\frac{1}{5} \times 3 = \frac{3}{5}$

$\frac{4}{5} \times 3 = \ldots\ldots$ $\frac{3}{7} \times 2 = \ldots\ldots$ $\frac{1}{5} \times 4 = \ldots\ldots$

$\frac{4}{5} \times 4 = \ldots\ldots$ $\frac{4}{7} \times 5 = \ldots\ldots$ $\frac{1}{5} \times 8 = \ldots\ldots$

$\frac{4}{5} \times 8 = \ldots\ldots$ $\frac{5}{7} \times 3 = \ldots\ldots$ $\ldots\ldots \times 10 = 2$

$\ldots\ldots \times 20 = 8$ $\ldots\ldots \times 4 = \frac{24}{7}$ $\frac{1}{5} \times \ldots\ldots = 200$

$\frac{4}{5} \times \ldots\ldots = 800$ $\frac{?}{7} \times 35 = 50$

Ratio

What is the ratio of blue bugs to red bugs to black bugs? What is the ratio of four-legged to six-legged bugs? What is the ratio of bugs with antennae to bugs without antennae?

This section will give you the chance to revise ratios and take the ideas that you have arleady met, a step further.

Example 2.7 ▷ Cancel each of the following ratios to its simplest form.

 a 14 : 16   **b** 25 : 20   **c** 6 : 12 : 24

 a 2 is the largest number which is a factor of both 14 and 16. Dividing each number by 2 gives 14 : 16 = 7 : 8

 b 5 is the largest number which is a factor of both 25 and 20. Dividing each number by 5 gives 25 : 20 = 5 : 4

 c 6 is the largest number which is a factor of 6, 12 and 24. Dividing each number by 6 gives 6 : 12 : 24 = 1 : 2 : 4

Example 2.8 ▷ One day, a bread shop sells brown loaves and white loaves in the ratio 4 : 1. If the shop sells 30 white loaves, how many brown loaves does it sell?

The ratio 4 : 1 means 4 parts to 1 part, so for every 4 brown loaves sold, 1 white loaf is sold.

So if 30 white loaves are sold, 1 part = 30 loaves

So 4 parts = 4 × 30 loaves = 120 loaves

The shop sells 120 brown loaves.

Example 2.9 ▷ Divide £150 in the ratio 2 : 3.

The ratio 2 : 3 means that £150 is first divided into 2 + 3 equal parts. That is, 5 parts = £150, which gives 1 part = £150 ÷ 5 = £30

Hence, you have:

   2 parts = £60
   3 parts = £90

which give the ratio £60 : £90.

Exercise 2D

1 Cancel each of the following ratios to its simplest form.

a	4 : 12	**b**	10 : 15	**c**	8 : 16	**d**	5 : 15
e	25 : 40	**f**	4 : 16	**g**	15 : 50	**h**	9 : 27
i	8 : 20	**j**	6 : 15	**k**	5 : 40	**l**	4 : 10
m	16 : 2	**n**	10 : 2	**o**	8 : 10	**p**	25 : 10
q	5 : 10	**r**	9 : 12	**s**	6 : 12	**t**	15 : 25
u	4 : 16 : 20	**v**	10 : 15 : 25				

FM **2** **a** Pink paint is mixed from red and white paint in the ratio 1 : 3
If 6 litres of red paint is used, how much white paint is needed?

b Green paint is mixed from blue and yellow paint in the ratio 1 : 4
If 20 litres of yellow paint is used, how much blue paint is needed?

c Purple is mixed from red and blue paint in the ratio 2 : 3
If 18 litres of red paint is used, how much blue paint is needed?

3 Mr & Mrs Smith have savings in the ratio 3 : 1. If Mr Smith has £600, how much does Mrs Smith have?

4 Work these out.

a Divide £30 in the ratio 4 : 1
b Divide £60 in the ratio 1 : 2
c Divide £100 in the ratio 9 : 1
d Divide £45 in the ratio 2 : 1
e Divide £36 in the ratio 1 : 8
f Divide £49 in the ratio 6 : 1

5 Work these out.

a Divide 50 kg in the ratio 3 : 2
b Divide 45 litres in the ratio 2 : 7
c Divide 30 cm in the ratio 2 : 3
d Divide 35 tonnes in the ratio 5 : 2
e Divide 26 miles in the ratio 6 : 7
f Divide 40 grams in the ratio 5 : 3

FM **6** A concrete mix is made from one part cement, two parts sand and three parts gravel by weight. How much cement and gravel will I need to mix with 40 kg of sand?

Extension **Work**

To make dark green paint two parts of yellow paint are mixed with five parts of blue. I have 250 ml of yellow and 1 litre of blue. What is the maximum amount of dark green paint I can make?

Direct proportion

Example 2.10 ▷ Six tubes of toothpaste have a total mass of 900 g.
What is the mass of:

a one tube?   **b** five tubes?

a If six tubes have a mass of 900 g, one tube has a mass of 900 ÷ 6 = 150 g

b Five tubes have a mass of 5 × 150 = 750 g

Example 2.11 ▷ A boy saves the same amount of money each week. In eight weeks he saves £20.

    a   How long will it take him to save £35?

    b   How much will he save in 10 weeks?

    a   If the boy saves £20 in 8 weeks, he saves £20 ÷ 8 = £2.50 in one week.

          Hence, to save £35, he takes £35 ÷ £2.50 = 14 weeks.

    b   In 10 weeks he saves 10 × £2.50 = £25

Example 2.12 ▷ A guitarist plays for 40 minutes with 400 people in the audience. How long would it take him to play the same set if there were only 300 people in the audience?

It takes exactly the same time of 40 minutes! The number of people in the audience does not affect the length of the performance.

Exercise 2E Be careful. Some of these questions may trip you up!

FM **1** 3 kg of rice cost £1.80. How much would:

    a 1 kg cost?   **b** 4 kg cost?

FM **2** Four packets of Smartoes sweets cost 88p. How much would:

    a one packet cost?   **b** three packets cost?

FM **3** The cost of hiring a car for 12 days is £180. How much would it cost to hire the car for:

    a 1 day?   **b** 5 days?

FM **4** Seven chocolate bars cost £1.40. How much do 10 chocolate bars cost?

FM **5** Four buckets standing in a rain shower take 40 minutes to fill. How long would three buckets standing in the same rain shower take to fill?

6 A distance of 8 km is represented by a distance of 16 cm on a map.

    a How many centimetres would represent a distance of 14 km?

    b What distance is represented by 7 cm on the map?

FM **7** Nine washing-up liquid containers hold 2700 cm³. How much do five of these containers hold?

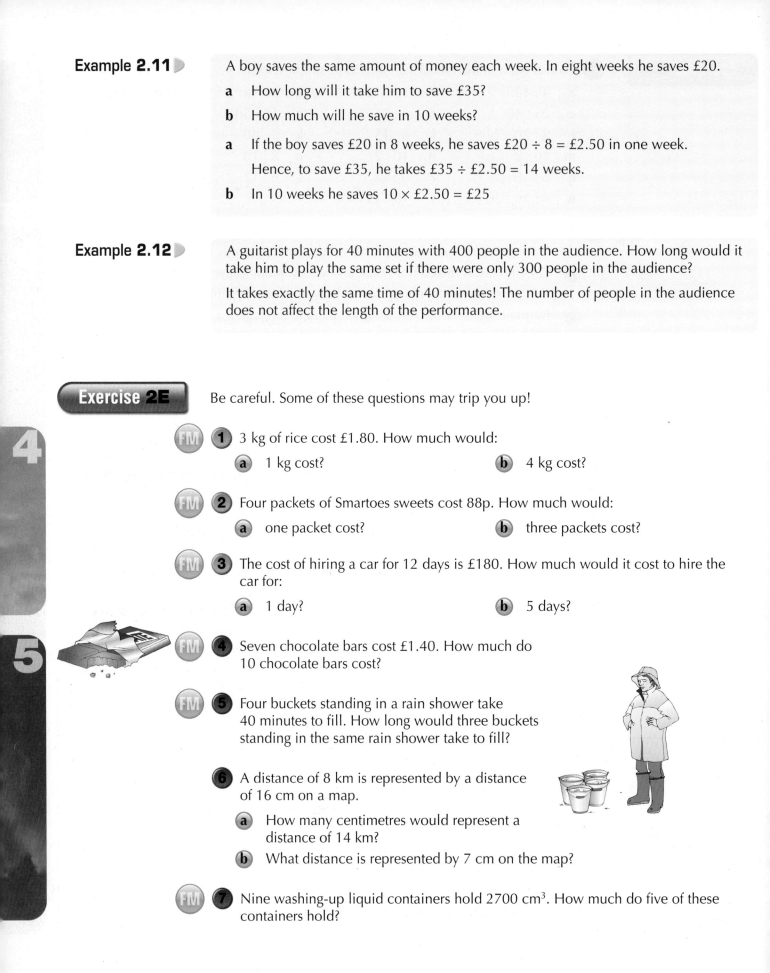

8 It takes 12 seconds to dial the 12-digit number of a friend who lives 100 miles away.

     a How long will it take to dial the 12-digit number of a friend who lives 50 miles away?

     b How long will it take to dial the 6-digit number of a friend who lives 10 miles away?

 9 My washing machine takes 1 hour to wash a load that weighs 6 kg. How long will it take to wash a load that weighs 5 kg?

10 It takes 6 minutes to hard-boil three eggs in a pan. How long would it take to hard-boil two eggs in the same pan?

 11 With 120 passengers on board, a train takes 16 minutes to travel between two stations. How long would it take with only 60 passengers on board?

 12 Six peaches cost 84p. How much will nine peaches cost?

'Six for 84p'

 13 A carpet whose area is 15 m² costs £120. How much would a carpet cost whose area is 20 m²?

 14 In 5 hours, a man earns £30. How much does he earn in 6 hours?

 15 A man walks 3 miles in 1 hour. How long would it take him to walk 5 miles?

16 In two days my watch loses 4 minutes. How much does it lose in one week (seven days)?

6

Extension Work

You are told that:

$$a \times b \times c = 100$$

a What would the answer be if a were doubled?

b What would the answer be if b were trebled?

c What would the answer be if c were halved?

d What would the answer be if a were doubled, b were trebled and c were halved at the same time?

e What would the answer be if a were doubled, b were doubled and c were doubled at the same time?

f What would the answer be if a were halved, b were halved and c were halved at the same time?

Inverse proportion

Example 2.13

Six teenagers take four days to paint a fence.

How long will it take:

a one teenager?

b eight teenagers?

a One teenager would take six times longer, so one teenager takes 6 × 4 = 24 days

b Eight teenagers would be eight times quicker than one teenager, so eight teenagers would take 24 ÷ 8 = 3 days

Example 2.14

At 40 mph, it takes a train 3 hours to cover a certain distance.

How long would it take at 80 mph?

At 80 mph it would be twice as quick, so it takes 1 hour 30 minutes.

Example 2.15

Six shirts hanging on a washing line take 2 hours to dry.

How long would it take three shirts to dry?

It would take the same time! The number of shirts on the line does not make any difference.

Exercise 2F

Be careful. Some of these questions may trip you up!

Use of a calculator is allowed for this exercise.

1 Five people lay a pipeline in 5 days. How long would one person take?

2 Two decorators can paint a room in 6 hours. How long would one decorator take?

3 From the top of a hill, two walkers can see 20 miles. How far would one walker be able to see from the top of the same hill?

4 It takes two people 10 minutes to hang out a load of washing. How long would it take one person?

5 Two taps fill a bath in 20 minutes. How long would it take one tap to fill the same bath?

6 Travelling at 8 miles per hour, a man takes 5 hours for a cycling trip. How long would he take at a speed of 16 miles per hour?

7 A box of emergency rations can feed 12 people for 6 days. How long would the box of rations last 6 people?

FM **8** My cat eats a bag of cat food every six days. If I get another cat, how long would the bag of cat food last now?

FM **9** Nine people build a wall in 20 days. How long will the job take 18 people?

FM **10** One man went to mow a meadow. It took him 15 minutes to walk there. If two men went to mow a meadow, how long would it take them to walk there?

FM **11** A lorry takes 4 hours to do a journey at 30 mph.

  a How long would the same journey take at 60 mph?

  b How fast would the lorry be travelling if the journey took 8 hours?

Extension Work

1 Two fences posts are 10 m apart.

If three posts are spaced equally between them, the gap between each post will be 2.5 m.

  a How large will the gap be between each post if five posts are equally spaced between the two outer posts?

  b How large will the gap be between each post if nine posts are equally spaced between the two outer posts?

$\leftarrow$ 10 m $\rightarrow$

2.5 m

2 Two posts are 12 m apart. How many posts would need to be placed between them so that they end up 2 m apart?

LEVEL BOOSTER

4
I can order whole numbers.
I can order decimals with one decimal place.
I can put simple quantities in order of size.

5
I can order decimals with more than one decimal place.
I can work out least common multiples.
I can add and subtract simple fractions.
I can reduce a fraction to its simplest form by cancelling common factors.
I can solve simple ratio problems.

6
I can change fractions to decimals.
I can add and subtract fractions with different denominators.
I can solve problems involving ratio.

1 *2007 4–6 Paper 1*

Here are six number cards:

a Choose two of these six cards to make a fraction that is equivalent to $\frac{1}{3}$.

b Choose two of these six cards to make a fraction that is **greater than** $\frac{1}{2}$ but **less than 1**.

2 *2006 4–6 Paper 1*

Add **three** to the number on each number line.

The first one is done for you.

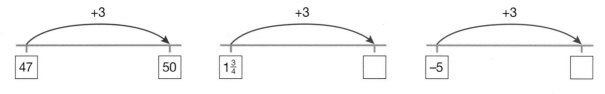

3 *2005 4–6 Paper 1*

Copy these number lines and write in the missing numbers:

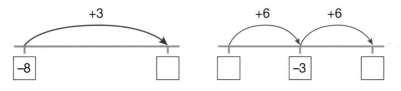

4 *2005 4–6 Paper 1*

Here are four fractions.

$$\frac{3}{4} \qquad \frac{1}{8} \qquad \frac{1}{3} \qquad \frac{3}{5}$$

Copy the number line and write each fraction in the correct box.

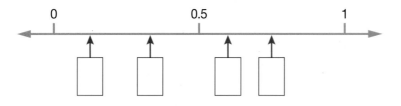

5 *2006 5–7 Paper 2*

Three different kinds of woodpecker live in Britain.

The pictogram shows information about the numbers of each type.

a Copy and complete the table below to show the **percentages** of each type of woodpecker:

Type A	Type B	Type C

| Type A great spotted woodpecker | Type B lesser spotted woodpecker | Type C green woodpecker |

Key

represents 10 000 woodpeckers

b The ratio of **Type A : Type B** woodpeckers is 6 : 1

What is the ratio of **Type B : Type C** woodpeckers?

6 *2007 5–7 Paper 1*

a In this design, the ratio of **grey to black** is **3 : 1**

What **percentage** of the design is **black**?

b In this design, **60%** is **grey** and the rest is black.

What is the ratio of **grey to black?**

Write your ratio in its simplest form.

7 *2005 5–7 Paper 1*

a Look at this information.

> Two numbers **multiply** to make zero.

One of the statements below is true.

Write it down.

- Both numbers must be zero.
- At least one number must be zero.
- Exactly one number must be zero.
- Neither number can be zero.

b Now look at this information.

> Two numbers **add** to make zero.

If **one** number is **zero**, what is the other number?

If **neither** number is **zero**, give an example of what the numbers could be.

The London Olympics 2012

Olympic village

Beds provided for 17 320 athletes and officials during Olympics.

Beds provided for 8756 athletes and officials during Paralympics.

The dining hall will cater for 5500 athletes at a time.

After the Games, the village will provide 4000 homes.

Tickets

Number of tickets for sale

- 8 million for the Olympics
- 1.6 million for the Paralympics

Tickets include free travel on London Transport.

Cost

75% of tickets will cost less than £50.

Organisers expect to sell 82% of all Olympic tickets and 63% of all Paralympics tickets.

Athletics

Ticket prices start from £15.

20 000 big screen tickets available for £10.

Travel

90% of venues will have three or more forms of public transport including:

- Docklands light railway
- 'Javelin' rail link from St Pancras to Olympic park
- London Underground
- New rail links
- Buses – The iBus: an automatic vehicle location system
- Cycle lanes and footpaths
- Two major park and ride sites off the M25 with a combined capacity of 12 000 cars

During the Games, up to 120 000 passengers will arrive and depart through Stratford station each day.

1 How many beds are there for athletes and officials during the Olympics? Give your answer to the nearest thousand.

2 The Olympic stadium will have 80 000 seats. If for an event the stadium is three-quarters full, how many seats will be empty?

3
a How many passengers will arrive and depart through Stratford station:
   i   on 1 day?   ii   over the 17 days?
b 45% of all spectators visiting the games each day will arrive and depart through Stratford station.
   What percentage will travel by other routes?

4 Boccia is a Paralympic sport.

The aim of the game is to throw red or blue leather balls as close as possible to a white target ball.

At the end of every round, the competitor whose ball is closest to the target ball scores one point for every one of his balls that is closer than his opponent's.

a At the end of a game, the blue team has 8 points and the red team has 4 points. Write the number of points as a ratio in its simplest form.

b At the end of another game 15 points have been scored altogether but the blue team has scored twice as many points as the red team.
   How many points does each team have?

5 Here are some men's long jump world record distances and the years in which they occurred.

8.90 metres   8.95 metres   7.98 metres   8.13 metres   8.21 metres

      1991   1968   1931   1960   1935

Copy and complete the table by putting the distances and years in the correct order. Two of the answers have already been filled in.

Name	Year	World record
Mike Powell	1991	
Bob Beamon		
Ralph Boston		
Jesse Owens		
Chuhei Nambu		7.98 metres

6 How many tickets for the Olympics will cost less than £50?

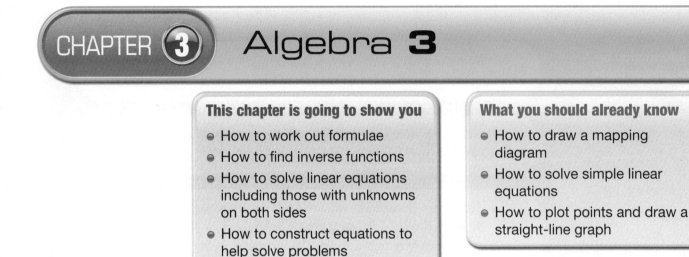

This chapter is going to show you

- How to work out formulae
- How to find inverse functions
- How to solve linear equations including those with unknowns on both sides
- How to construct equations to help solve problems
- How graphs can be used to help solve problems

What you should already know

- How to draw a mapping diagram
- How to solve simple linear equations
- How to plot points and draw a straight-line graph

Formulae

A **formula** is a rule used to work out a value from one or more values (called **variables** or **inputs**). For example, $A = ab$ is a rule, or formula, used to calculate the area, A, of a rectangle from the lengths, a and b, of two adjacent sides.

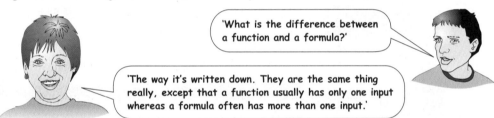

'What is the difference between a function and a formula?'

'The way it's written down. They are the same thing really, except that a function usually has only one input whereas a formula often has more than one input.'

A formula also always has a **subject** (an output), which is usually written on the left-hand side of the equals sign. For example:

$$P = 2a + 2b$$

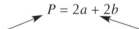

The output is P. Inputs are a and b.

This is also called the subject of the formula.

When a is 3 cm and b is 5 cm, the formula becomes:

$P = 2 \times 3 + 2 \times 5$
$= 16$ cm

Exercise 3A

1. The formula $C = 3D$ is used to calculate approximately the circumference, C, of a circle from its diameter, D. Use the formula to calculate the approximate circumference of each circle shown below.

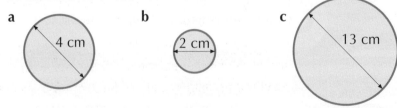

a 4 cm   b 2 cm   c 13 cm

5

2 The formula $A = 180n - 360$ is used to calculate the sum of the angles inside a polygon with n sides. Use the formula to calculate the sum of the angles inside each polygon shown below.

a Pentagon, five sides

b Hexagon, six sides

 3 The cost, C, of placing an advertisement in a local newspaper is given by:

$C = £20 + £2N$

where N is the number of words used in the advertisement.

What is the cost of placing advertisements with the following number of words?

a 12 words

b 25 words

 4 Lennie, the driving instructor, used the following formula to charge learner drivers:

$C = £4 + £13H$

where H is the number of hours in the driving lesson.

What is the cost of driving lessons with the following durations?

a Lasting 2 hours

b Lasting from 1 pm to 4 pm

 5 The amount of money, M, expected to be collected for a charity was approximated by the following formula:

$M = £5000T + £20C$

where T is the number of TV advertisements appearing the day before a charity event was held, and C is the number of collectors.

Approximately, how much is expected to be collected by each of the following charities?

a NCS had three TV advertisements and 100 collectors.

b TTU had two TV advertisements and 300 collectors.

c BCB had no TV advertisements and 500 collectors.

 6 The speed, S m/s, of a rocket can be found from the formula $S = AT$, where the rocket has acceleration, A m/s², for a number of seconds, T.

Find the speed of a rocket in each of the following cases.

a The rocket has an acceleration of 25 m/s² for 8 seconds.

b The rocket has an acceleration of 55 m/s² for 6 seconds.

7 The formula $a = \frac{1}{2}bh$ is used to calculate the area, a, of a triangle from its base length, b, and its height, h. Use the formula to calculate the area of each triangle shown below.

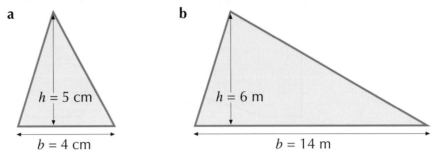

a

$h = 5$ cm

$b = 4$ cm

b

$h = 6$ m

$b = 14$ m

FM **8** MC Dave used the following formula to calculate the cost, C, of his gigs:

$C = £55 + £3N + £5T + £10E$

where:

    N is the number of people attending the gig.

    T is the number of hours worked before midnight.

    E is the number of hours worked after midnight.

Calculate the cost of each of the following gigs.

a 60 people attending from 9 pm to 2 am

b 40 people from 7 pm to 1 am

Extension **Work**

The function $x \rightarrow \dfrac{3x + 5}{4}$ can be worked through with the following flow chart.

| Write any number as x | → | Multiply by 3 | → | Add 5 | → | Divide by 4 |

Write the value of x

a Show that starting with $x = 9$, the flow chart gives the following results after working through twice:

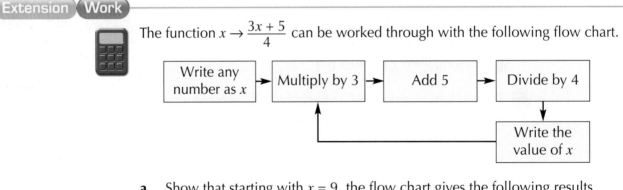

9 → 27 → 32 → 8 → Write 8

24 → 29 → 7.25 → Write 7.25

b Continue to work through the flow chart at least 8 more times.

c What do you notice?

d Does the value of the starting number make any difference?

Inverse flow diagrams

Every operation has an **inverse** operation. The inverse of addition is subtraction and vice versa. The inverse of multiplication is division. Equations can be solved by inverse flow diagrams.

Example 3.1 ▷ Solve the equation $3x = 15$

Step 1: Set up the flow diagram.

Step 2: Set up the inverse flow diagram.

Step 3: Put 15 through the inverse flow diagram.

Hence the answer to $3x = 15$ is $x = 5$

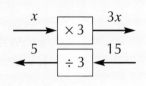

When an equation is built up from two or more operations, you have to use the inverse function of each operation and work back through them to find the answer.

Example 3.2 ▷ Solve the equation $4x + 3 = 13$

Step 1: Set up the flow diagram.

Step 2: Set up the inverse flow diagram.

Step 3: Put 13 through the inverse flow diagram.

Hence the answer to $4x + 3 = 13$ is $x = 2.5$

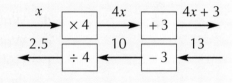

Example 3.3 ▷ Solve the equation $\frac{x}{2} - 1 = 3$

Step 1: Set up the flow diagram

Step 2: Set up the inverse flow diagram

Step 3: Put 3 through the inverse flow diagram

Hence the answer to $\frac{x}{2} - 1 = 3$ is $x = 8$

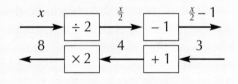

Exercise 3B

1 Write down the inverse operation of the following.

  a $\times 2$ **b** $\times 5$ **c** $+ 1$
  d $- 7$ **e** $\div 3$ **f** $\div 8$

2 Draw the flow diagram and the inverse flow diagram for these expressions.

  a $2x$ **b** $x - 7$ **c** $2x + 3$
  d $3x - 5$ **e** $\frac{x}{3} + 2$ **f** $\frac{x}{4} - 1$

3 Using your answers from question 2 solve the following equations.

  a $2x = 7$ **b** $x - 7 = 12$ **c** $2x + 3 = 10$
  d $3x - 5 = 10$ **e** $\frac{x}{2} + 2 = 5$ **f** $\frac{x}{4} - 1 = 4$

4 Using inverse flow diagrams solve the following equations.

a $3x + 5 = 11$　　　　**b** $3x - 1 = 11$　　　　**c** $4x + 7 = 23$

d $4x - 1 = 9$　　　　　**e** $\frac{x}{4} + 5 = 1$　　　　**f** $\frac{x}{3} - 2 = 5$

5

'I have a rule for any number they give me. It's multiply by 5 and add on 3.'

a Write down Joy's rule as a function.

b Write down the inverse function of Joy's function.

c Use the inverse function to find what number was given to Joy when she gave the reply '43'.

'I have a rule for any number they give me. It's add on 4 then multiply by 3.'

d Write down Dave's rule as a function.

e Write down the inverse function of Dave's function.

f Use the inverse function to find what number was given to Dave when he gave the reply '36'.

Extension　Work

Solve the following equations using inverse flow diagrams.

Remember when setting up the flow diagram the operation inside the bracket has to be done first.

a $3(x + 4) = 21$　　　　**b** $5(x - 3) = 20$

c $4(y + 1) = 28$　　　　**d** $2(m - 5) = 6$

Doing the same thing to both sides

You have already met a few different types of equation, which were solved by using a flow diagram. Here, you are going to be shown how to solve them by adding, subtracting, multiplying or dividing both sides of an equation by the same number. The aim is to get the variable (usually x) on its own.

Example 3.4 ▷　Solve the equation $2x = 16$

Divide both sides by 2, to give: $\dfrac{2x}{2} = \dfrac{16}{2}$

which gives: $x = 8$

So, the solution is $x = 8$

Example 3.5 ▶

Solve the equation $4t + 3 = 23$

Subtract 3 from both sides, to give: $4t + 3 - 3 = 23 - 3$

which gives: $4t = 20$

Divide both sides by 4, to give: $t = 5$

So, the solution is $t = 5$

Example 3.6 ▶

Solve the equation $\frac{x}{3} - 4 = 2$

Add 4 to both sides to give $\frac{x}{3} - 4 + 4 = 2 + 4$

which gives $\frac{x}{3} = 6$

Multiply both sides by 3 to give $x = 18$

So, the solution is $x = 18$

Exercise 3C

In each of the following questions, show your working. Write each step on a new line.

1 Solve each of the following equations.

   a $2x = 10$ **b** $3x = 12$ **c** $\frac{x}{5} = 6$ **d** $4x = 28$

   e $\frac{t}{5} = 12$ **f** $7m = 21$ **g** $\frac{k}{3} = 6$ **h** $\frac{p}{2} = 18$

2 Solve each of the following equations.

   a $3x + 5 = 11$ **b** $\frac{x}{2} + 3 = 11$ **c** $4x + 7 = 15$

   d $\frac{x}{5} + 3 = 8$ **e** $3x + 4 = 19$ **f** $\frac{x}{6} + 1 = 5$

   g $2x + 7 = 15$ **h** $\frac{x}{4} + 3 = 13$ **i** $3x + 6 = 27$

3 Solve each of the following equations.

   a $5x - 2 = 13$ **b** $\frac{x}{3} - 4 = 1$ **c** $6x - 1 = 23$

   d $\frac{x}{2} - 3 = 5$ **e** $4x - 3 = 25$ **f** $\frac{x}{3} - 2 = 2$

   g $4x - 5 = 3$ **h** $\frac{x}{6} - 1 = 3$ **i** $5x - 3 = 17$

4 Solve each of the following equations.

   a $4x + 3 = 23$ **b** $\frac{x}{3} + 2 = 4$ **c** $5x + 4 = 19$

   d $\frac{x}{4} - 1 = 19$ **e** $2x - 3 = 17$ **f** $\frac{x}{5} - 4 = 21$

   g $3m - 5 = 7$ **h** $\frac{b}{4} + 5 = 7$ **i** $6q + 1 = 31$

5 Nazia has made a mistake somewhere in her working for each of the equations shown below. Can you spot the line on which the error occurs and work out the correct solution?

a

$$3x + 8 = 23$$

$$3x + 8 - 8 = 23 - 8$$

$$3x = 18$$

$$\frac{3x}{3} = \frac{18}{3}$$

$$x = 6 \ ✗$$

b

$$\frac{x}{5} - 3 = 2$$

$$3 - \frac{x}{5} - 3 = 2 + 3$$

$$\frac{x}{5} = 5$$

$$5 \times \frac{x}{5} = 5 \times 5$$

$$x = -25 \ ✗$$

c

$$9 - \frac{x}{2} = 24$$

$$9 + \frac{x}{2} - 9 = 24 - 9$$

$$\frac{x}{2} = 15$$

$$2 \times \frac{x}{2} = 15 \times 2$$

$$x = 30 \ ✗$$

d

$$2x - 5 = 17$$

$$2x - 5 + 5 = 17 + 5$$

$$2x = 12$$

$$\frac{2x}{2} = \frac{12}{2}$$

$$x = 6 \ ✗$$

Extension **Work**

1 Solve each of the following equations. (All of the answers are negative numbers.)

    a $2x + 10 = 4$ **b** $\frac{x}{3} + 9 = 3$ **c** $4x + 15 = 7$

    d $3x + 11 = 2$ **e** $\frac{x}{5} + 21 = 6$ **f** $\frac{x}{2} + 17 = 5$

2 Solve each of the following equations. (All of the answers are decimal or negative numbers.)

    a $\frac{x}{4} + 13 = 3$ **b** $5x + 2 = 8$ **c** $\frac{x}{2} + 8 = 1$

    d $5x - 4 = 8$ **e** $\frac{x}{2} + 12 = 5$ **f** $4x - 3 = 11$

Constructing equations to solve problems

The first step to solve a problem using algebra is to write down an equation. This is called constructing an equation. To do this, you must choose a letter to stand for the simplest variable (unknown) in the problem. This might be x or the first letter of a suitable word. For example, n is often used to stand for the number.

Example 3.7 ▷

My son is 25 years younger than I am. Our ages add up to 81. How old are we?

Construct the equation using x as my son's age. (Since this is the lower age.)

So, my age is $x + 25$.

The total of our ages is 81, which gives:

$$x + x + 25 = 81$$

This simplifies to:

$$2x + 25 = 81$$

Subtract 25 from both sides, to give:

$$2x = 56$$
$$x = 28 \quad \text{(Divide through by 2.)}$$

So, my son's age is 28 years, and I am 25 years older, aged 53.

Exercise 3D

1. Tom has 10 more marbles than Jeff.
   Together they have 56.
   Let the number of marbles that Jeff has be x.
   a   Write down an equation which this gives.
   b   Solve the equation to find the number of marbles each boy has.

2. Sanjay has 35 more CDs than Surjit. Together they have 89 CDs.
   Let Surjit have x CDs.
   a   Write down an equation which this gives.
   b   Solve the equation to find the number of CDs they each have.

3. Gavin has 13 more DVDs than Michelle. Together they have 129 DVDs.
   Let Michelle have x DVDs.
   a   Write down an equation which this gives.
   b   Solve the equation to find the number of DVDs they each have.

4. Joy thinks of a number rule.
   a   When Paul gives Joy a number, she replies, '23'. Write down the equation this gives and solve it to find the number which Paul gave to Joy.

   'Multiply the number by 3 and add 5.'

   b   When Billie gives Joy a number, she replies, '38'. Write down the equation this gives and solve it to find the number which Billie gave to Joy.

5. Paula is three times as old as Angus. Their ages add up to 52.
   Let Angus be x years old.
   a   Write down an equation which this gives.
   b   Solve the equation to find both ages.

6 David scored twice as many goals in a season as Mark. Together, they scored 36 goals. Let Mark score x goals.

    a Write down an equation which this gives.

    b Solve the equation to find how many goals each player scored.

7 Alan spent four times as many minutes on his maths homework as he did on the rest of his homework. He spent two hours on his homework altogether.

Let Alan spend x minutes on the rest of his homework.

    a Write down an equation which this gives.

    b Solve the equation to find out how much time Alan spent on his maths homework.

8 Farmer Giles keeps only sheep and cows on his farm. He has 55 more sheep than cows and has 207 animals altogether.

Let the number of cows be x.

    a Write down an equation which this gives.

    b Solve the equation to find the number of sheep and the number of cows on Farmer Giles' farm.

9 In a school of 845 pupils, there are 29 more girls than boys.

Let there be x boys.

    a Write down an equation which this gives.

    b Solve the equation to find the number of girls and the number of boys in the school.

10 On an aircraft carrying 528 passengers, there were 410 more adults than children. Let there be x children.

    a Write down an equation which this gives.

    b Solve the equation to find the number of children on this aircraft.

Extension Work

1 Two consecutive numbers add up to 77. What are the two numbers?
Let the smallest number be n.

2 Two consecutive numbers add up to 135. What is the product of the two numbers?
Let the smallest number be n.

3 What is the product of three consecutive numbers which add up to 402?
Let the smallest number be n.

Equations with unknown quantities on both sides

When x is on both sides of the equals sign, your first step is to get rid of x from one side. You do this by adding or subtracting terms.

Example 3.8 ▶

Solve the equation $4x = 12 + x$

Subtract x from both sides, to give:

$$4x - x = 12 + x - x$$

which simplifies to:

$$3x = 12$$
$$\frac{3x}{3} = \frac{12}{3} \quad \text{(Divide through by 3.)}$$
$$x = 4$$

So, the solution is $x = 4$

Example 3.9 ▶

Solve the equation $6x + 5 = 2x + 33$

Subtract $2x$ from both sides, to give:

$$6x + 5 - 2x = 2x + 33 - 2x$$

which simplifies to:

$$4x + 5 = 33$$

Now subtract 5 from both sides, to obtain:

$$4x = 28$$
$$\frac{4x}{4} = \frac{28}{4} \quad \text{(Divide through by 4.)}$$
$$x = 7$$

So, the solution is $x = 7$

Example 3.10 ▶

Solve the equation $4x + 3 = 13 - x$

Add x to both both sides, to give:

$$4x + 3 + x = 13 - x + x$$

which simplifies to:

$$5x + 3 = 13$$

Subtract 3 from both sides, to obtain:

$$5x = 10$$
$$\frac{5x}{5} = \frac{10}{5} \quad \text{(Divide through by 5.)}$$
$$x = 2$$

So, the solution is $x = 2$

6

Exercise 3E

1 Solve each of the following equations.

    a $3x = 8 + x$ **b** $4x = 15 + x$ **c** $5x = 20 + x$ **d** $6x = 25 + x$

    e $4x = 20 + 2x$ **f** $6x = 12 + 2x$ **g** $5x = 21 + 2x$ **h** $6x = 32 + 2x$

    i $8x = 12 + 4x$ **j** $5x = 16 + 3x$ **k** $4x = 10 + 2x$ **l** $8x = 30 + 5x$

2 Solve each of the following equations.

    a $4x + 3 = x + 15$ **b** $3x + 4 = x + 20$ **c** $5x + 3 = x + 19$

    d $5x - 2 = 2x + 10$ **e** $6x - 3 = 2x + 9$ **f** $5x - 6 = 3x + 14$

    g $7x - 19 = 2x - 4$ **h** $6x - 10 = 3x - 1$ **i** $7x + 2 = 4x + 8$

3 Solve each of the following equations.

    a $5x + 2 = 10 + x$ **b** $7x + 5 = 17 + x$ **c** $4x + 1 = 10 + x$

    d $7x - 3 = 12 + 2x$ **e** $6x - 2 = 18 + 2x$ **f** $5x - 5 = 7 + 2x$

    g $7 + 4x = 13 + 2x$ **h** $7 + 4x = 11 + 2x$ **i** $8 + 5x = 14 + 3x$

4 Solve each of the following equations.

    a $2x + 3 = 15 - x$ **b** $3x + 5 = 25 - x$ **c** $5x - 4 = 10 - 2x$

    d $5x - 10 = 6 - 3x$ **e** $7x + 3 = 21 - 2x$ **f** $9x - 10 = 23 - 2x$

    g $5x + 7 = 37 - x$ **h** $7 + 4x = 49 - 2x$ **i** $7x - 6 = 34 - 3x$

Extension Work

1 Solve each of the following equations. (All the answers are negative numbers.)

    a $3x + 8 = 4 + x$ **b** $5x + 19 = 3 + x$ **c** $6x + 11 = 1 + x$

    d $5x + 11 = 2 + 2x$ **e** $6x + 21 = 5 - 2x$ **f** $3x + 17 = 2 - 2x$

2 Solve each of the following equations. (All the answers are decimal numbers.)

    a $5x + 3 = 9 + x$ **b** $4x + 2 = 7 + 2x$ **c** $7x + 1 = 8 + 2x$

    d $3x - 4 = 7 - 2x$ **e** $x - 5 = 14 - 3x$ **f** $4x - 7 = 12 - 6x$

Problems involving straight-line graphs

When a car is being filled with petrol, both the amount and the cost of the petrol are displayed on the pump. One litre of petrol costs 80p. So, 2 litres cost 160p (£1.60) and 5 litres cost 400p (£4).

The table below shows the costs of different quantities of petrol as displayed on the pump.

Amount of petrol (litres)	5	10	15	20	25	30
Cost (£)	4.00	8.00	12.00	16.00	20.00	24.00

The information can be graphed, as shown on the right. Notice that for every 5 litres across the graph, the graph rises by £4. This is the reason why the graph is a straight line.

This idea can be used to solve a number of different types of problem.

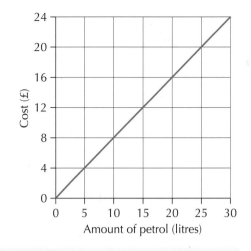

Example 3.11 ▷ Mr Evans wanted to convert all pupils' scores in a French test to percentages. He used the facts given on the right to help him to draw a conversion graph.

French score	0	60
Percentage	0	100

He used the above two points to draw a straight-line graph, as shown on the right.

Stephanie scored 30. Mr Evans used the graph to convert this score to 50%. Joe scored 38. Again using the graph, Mr Evans converted this to 63%.

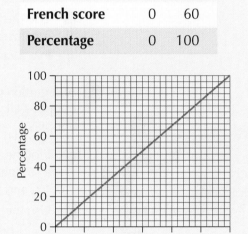

FM **1** Jenny sold apples on a market stall. She was told just the following two prices.

Number of apples	0	12
Cost	£0	£1.50

a Plot the two points on a graph and join them with a straight line. Use the horizontal axis for the number of apples, going up to 20, and the vertical axis for the cost of apples, going up to £3.

b Use the graph to find the cost of each of the following.
  i 4 apples **ii** 10 apples **iii** 20 apples

c Use the graph to find how many apples you could buy for:
  i 75p **ii** £1.75 **iii** £2.75

FM **2** At a Joe King concert, fans can get posters of Joe from one of the stalls. Benny sells the posters and knows these facts about the costs.

Number of posters	0	20
Cost	£0	£17

a Plot the two points on a graph and join them with a straight line. Use the horizontal axis for the number of posters, and the vertical axis for the cost of posters, going up to £17.

b Use the graph to find the cost of each of the following.
   i   6 posters   **ii**   12 posters   **iii**   16 posters

c Use the graph to find how many posters you could buy for:
   i   £6.80   **ii**   £11.90   **iii**   £15.30

FM **3** Tom put a weight on the end of a spring to see how much it was stretched. After this, he knew these facts:

Weight (g)	0	900
Stretch (cm)	0	18

a Plot the two points on a graph and join them with a straight line. Use the horizontal axis for the weights added, going up to 1000 g, and the vertical axis for the stretch of the spring, going up to 20 cm.

b Use the graph to find the stretch of each of the following.
   i   200 g   **ii**   300 g   **iii**   1 kg

c Use the graph to find the weight needed to stretch the spring to the following lengths.
   i   2 cm   **ii**   5 cm   **iii**   14 cm

FM **4** At a garden party, Kim looked after the hoopla stall. She knew two costs of the hooplas.

Number of hooplas	0	10
Cost	£0	£2.20

a Plot the two points on a graph and join them with a straight line. Use the horizontal axis for the numbers of hooplas, going up to 12, and the vertical axis for the cost of hooplas, going up to £3.

b Use the graph to find the cost of each of the following.
   i   3 hooplas   **ii**   8 hooplas   **iii**   12 hooplas

c Use the graph to find how many hooplas you get for the following amounts.
   i   88p   **ii**   £1.10   **iii**   £2.42

FM **5** Sue went to France for her holiday and knew the following facts about British money and Euros.

British £	£0	£100
Euros €	€0	€160

a Plot the two points on a graph and join them with a straight line. Use the horizontal axis for British pounds, going up to £150, and the vertical axis for Euros, going up to €250.

b Use the graph to find the value in Euros of each of the following.
   i   £20   **ii**   £70   **iii**   £130

c Use the graph to find the value in British pounds of each of the following.
   i   €40   **ii**   €80   **iii**   €232

Extension Work

FM Try to solve this problem by drawing a graph.

Two women are walking on the same long, straight road towards each other. One sets off at 9.00 am at a speed of 4 km/h. The other also sets off at 9.00 am, 15 km away, at a speed of 5 km/h.

a At what time do the women meet?

b How far will the first woman have walked when they meet?

5 I can substitute numbers into formulae such as P = 2w + 2l.

I can solve equations of the type $3x - 8 = 13$, for example, using inverse flow diagrams where the solution may be fractional or negative.

I can solve equations of the type $\frac{x}{5} - 1 = 3$, for example, by doing the same thing to both sides.

6 I can solve equations where the variable appears on both sides, such as $4x + 3 = x + 6$.

I can use algebra to set up an equation to represent a practical situation.

I can draw and interpret graphs that show direct proportion.

National Test questions

FM *2007 3–5 Paper 1*

The lengths of babies are measured at different ages.

The graph shows the longest and shortest a baby boy is likely to be.

a Write down the numbers missing from the following statements:

A baby boy is **8 weeks old**.

The **longest** he is likely to be is about ...... cm.

The **shortest** he is likely to be is about ...... cm.

b A **34 week old** baby boy is **72 cm** long.

Copy the graph and put a cross on it to show this information.

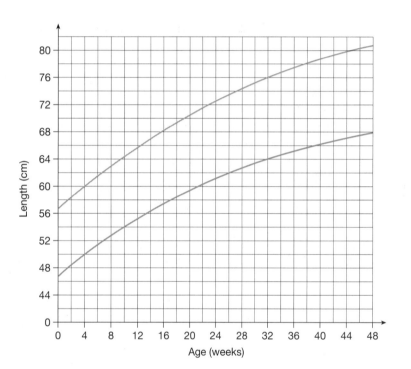

2 *2005 3–5 Paper 1*

Solve these equations:

$3y + 1 = 16$ $\qquad$ $18 = 4k + 6$

3 *2007 3–5 Paper 1*

Look at this equation: $\quad y = 2x + 10$

a When **x = 4**, what is the value of **y**?

b When **x = –4**, what is the value of **y**?

c Which of the equations below gives the **same** value for both **x = 4** and **x = –4**?

$y = 2x$ $\qquad$ $y = 2 + x$ $\qquad$ $y = x^2$ $\qquad$ $y = \frac{x}{2}$

<table>
<tr><td>

This chapter is going to show you

- How to identify alternate and corresponding angles
- How to calculate angles in triangles and quadrilaterals
- How to calculate the interior angles of polygons
- How regular polygons tesselate
- How to construct perpendicular bisectors and angle bisectors
- Names of the different parts of a circle

</td><td>

What you should already know

- How to identify parallel and perpendicular lines
- How to measure and draw angles
- Interior angles of a triangle add up to 180°
- Names of polygons
- Be able to draw a circle given its radius

</td></tr>
</table>

Alternate and corresponding angles

The diagram shows two parallel lines with another straight line cutting across them.

The line that cuts across a pair of parallel lines is called a **transversal**.

Notice that the transversal forms eight angles.

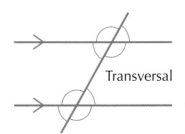

Transversal

Alternate angles

Trace angle x on the diagram. Rotate your tracing paper through 180° and place angle x over angle y. What do you notice?

You should find that the two angles are the same size.

The two angles x and y are called **alternate angles**. (This is because they are on alternate sides of the transversal.) They are sometimes called Z-angles.

This shows that alternate angles are equal.

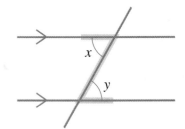

Example 4.1 ▷

Find the size of angle a on the diagram.

Alternate angles are equal, so $a = 120°$.

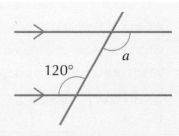

120°

Trace angle x on the diagram. Slide your tracing paper along the transversal and place angle x over angle y. What do you notice?

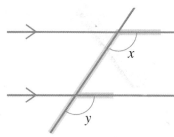

You should find that the two angles are the same size.

The two angles, x and y, are called **corresponding angles**. (This is because the position of one angle corresponds to the position of the other.) They are sometimes called F-angles.

This shows that corresponding angles are equal.

Example 4.2

Find the size of angle b and angle c on the diagram.

Corresponding angles are equal, so $b = 125°$.

Angles on a straight line add up to 180°.
Therefore, c is $180° - b$, which gives:

$$c = 180° - 125° = 55°$$

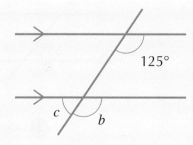

Exercise 4A

1. Which diagrams show a pair of alternate angles?

2. Which diagrams show a pair of corresponding angles?

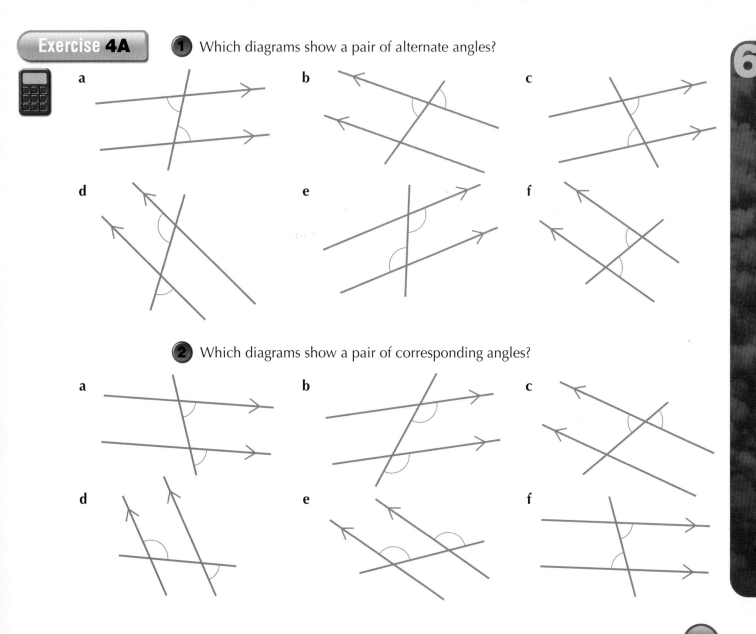

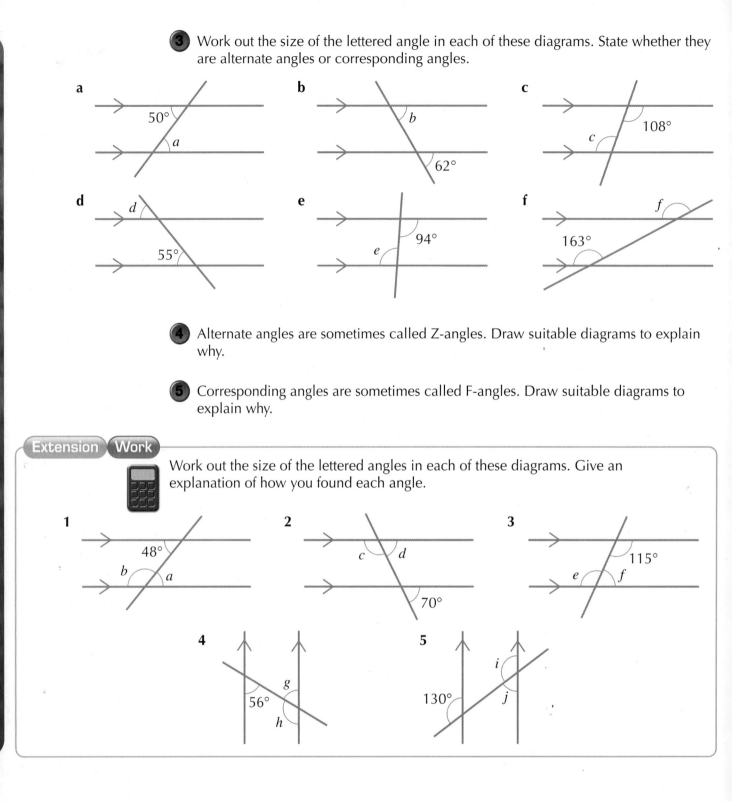

3 Work out the size of the lettered angle in each of these diagrams. State whether they are alternate angles or corresponding angles.

a   50°   a

b   b   62°

c   c   108°

d   d   55°

e   94°   e

f   f   163°

4 Alternate angles are sometimes called Z-angles. Draw suitable diagrams to explain why.

5 Corresponding angles are sometimes called F-angles. Draw suitable diagrams to explain why.

Extension Work

Work out the size of the lettered angles in each of these diagrams. Give an explanation of how you found each angle.

1   48°   b   a

2   c   d   70°

3   115°   e   f

4   56°   g   h

5   130°   i   j

Angles of a triangle

You already know that the sum of the interior angles of a triangle is 180°. In the diagram:

$a + b + c = 180°$

Example 4.3 shows you how to find an **exterior angle** of a triangle.

Example 4.3 ▶ Work out the size of the angles marked *x* and *y* on the diagram, where *y* is an exterior angle of the triangle.

The angles in a triangle add up to 180°. Therefore:

$$x = 180° - 48° - 110°$$
$$= 22°$$

The angles on a straight line add up to 180°. This gives:

$$y = 180° - 22°$$
$$= 158°$$

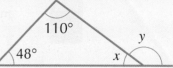

Exercise 4B

1. Find the size of the angle marked by a letter in each scalene or right-angled triangle.

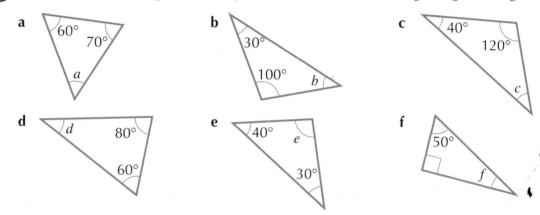

a
60°
70°
a

b
30°
100°
b

c
40°
120°
c

d
d
80°
60°

e
40°
e
30°

f
50°
f

2. Find the size of the unknown angles in each isosceles triangle.

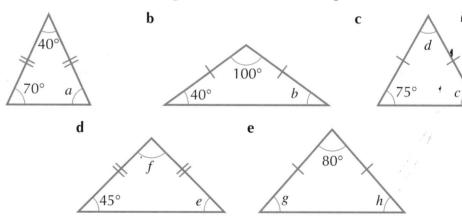

a
40°
70° *a*

b
100°
40° *b*

c
d
75° *c*

d
f
45° *e*

e
80°
g *h*

3. Calculate the size of the lettered angles in each of these triangles.

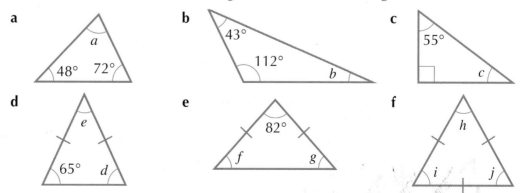

a
a
48° 72°

b
43°
112°
b

c
55°
c

d
e
65° *d*

e
82°
f *g*

f
h
i *j*

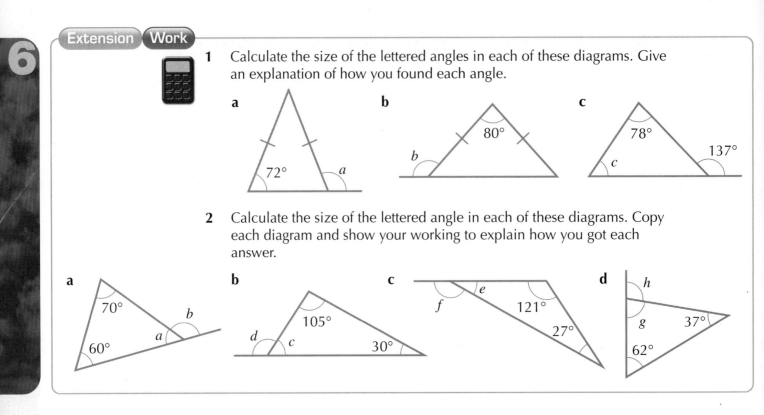

1   Calculate the size of the lettered angles in each of these diagrams. Give an explanation of how you found each angle.

a

b

c

2   Calculate the size of the lettered angle in each of these diagrams. Copy each diagram and show your working to explain how you got each answer.

a

b

c

d

Angles of a quadrilateral

An investigation

Draw a large quadrilateral similar to the one on the right.

Measure each interior angle as accurately as you can, using a protractor. Now add up the four angles. What do you notice?

You should find that your answer is close to 360°.

Now draw a different quadrilateral and find the sum of the angles. How close were you to 360°?

For any quadrilateral, the sum of the interior angles is 360°.
So, in the diagram:

$$a + b + c + d = 360°$$

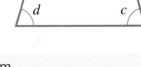

Example 4.4

Work out the sizes of the angles marked p and q on the diagram.

The angles in a quadrilateral add up to 360°, which gives:

$$p = 360° - 135° - 78° - 83°$$
$$= 64°$$

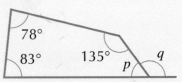

The angles on a straight line add up to 180°, so:

$$q = 180° - 64°$$
$$= 116°$$

Angle q is an **exterior angle** of the quadrilateral.

Exercise 4C

1 Find the size of the angle marked by a letter in each quadrilateral.

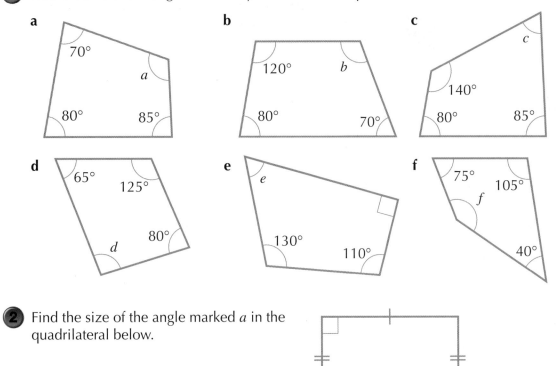

a 70° 80° 85° a

b 120° b 80° 70°

c c 140° 80° 85°

d 65° 125° 80° d

e e 130° 110°

f 75° 105° f 40°

2 Find the size of the angle marked *a* in the quadrilateral below.

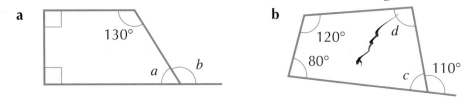

a

3 Calculate the size of the lettered angle in each of these quadrilaterals.

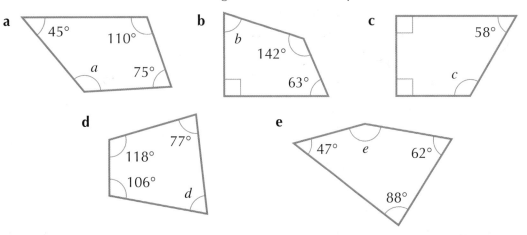

a 45° 110° a 75°

b b 142° 63°

c 58° c

d 77° 118° 106° d

e 47° e 62° 88°

4 Calculate the size of the lettered angles in each of these diagrams. Give an explanation of how you found each angle.

a 130° a b

b 120° d 80° c 110°

6

1   ABCD is a parallelogram with ∠ADC = 60°.

   a   What do you know about a parallelogram?
   b   Explain how you could find ∠BAD.
   c   Write down the size of ∠ABC and ∠BCD.

2   ABCD is a kite with ∠DAB = 80° and ∠BCD = 50°.

   a   Make a sketch of the kite and draw its line of symmetry.
   b   What do you know about angles *p* and *q*?
   c   Use this information to work out angles *p* and *q*.

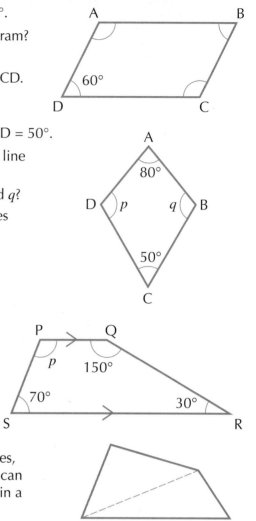

3   PQRS is a trapezium.

   a   Work out the size of the angle marked *p*.
   b   Write down anything you notice about the angles in the trapezium.

4   A quadrilateral can be split into two triangles, as shown in the diagram. Explain how you can use this to show that the sum of the angles in a quadrilateral is 360°.

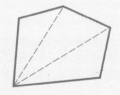

Interior angles of polygons

The angles inside a polygon are known as **interior angles**.

Example 4.5 ▷   Find the sum of the interior angles of a pentagon.

The diagram shows how a pentagon can be split into three triangles from one of its vertices. The sum of the interior angles for each triangle is 180°.

So, the sum of the interior angles of a pentagon is given by:

$$3 \times 180° = 540°$$

Exercise 4D

1 a Copy each polygon below.

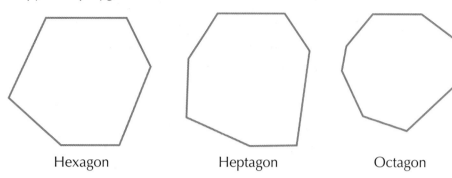

Hexagon   Heptagon   Octagon

b Split each polygon into triangles.

c Split each polygon into triangles and find the sum of the interior angles of:

   i a hexagon.   **ii** an octagon.

d Copy and complete the table below. The pentagon has been done for you.

Name of polygon	Number of sides	Number of triangles inside polygon	Sum of interior angles
Triangle			
Quadrilateral			
Pentagon	5	3	540°
Hexagon			
Heptagon			
Octagon			

2 Calculate the unknown angle in each of the following polygons.

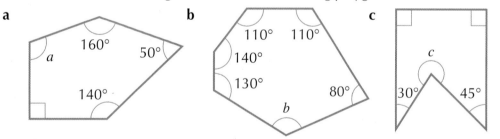

a 160° 50° a 140°

b 110° 110° 140° 130° 80° b

c c 30° 45°

Extension **Work**

1 a A polygon is regular when all its interior angles are equal and all its sides have the same length.

The shape on the right is a regular pentagon. The sum of its interior angles is 540°. So, the size of each interior angle is:

540° ÷ 5 = 108°

b Copy and complete the table below for regular polygons. The regular pentagon has been done for you.

Regular polygon	Number of sides	Sum of interior angles	Size of each interior angle
Equilateral triangle			
Square			
Regular pentagon	5	540°	108°
Regular hexagon			
Regular octagon			
Regular decagon			

2 Find angle x in the pentagon on the right.

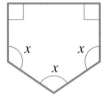

Tessellations and regular polygons

A **tessellation** is a repeating pattern made on a plane (flat) surface with identical shapes which fit together exactly, leaving no gaps.

This section will show you how some of the regular polygons tessellate.

Remember: To show how a shape tessellates, draw up to about ten repeating shapes.

Example 4.6 ▷ The diagrams below show how equilateral triangles and squares tessellate.

Exercise 4E

1 On an isometric grid, show how a regular hexagon tessellates.

2 Trace this regular pentagon onto card and cut it out to make a template.

a Use your template to show that a regular pentagon does not tessellate.

b Explain why a regular pentagon does not tessellate.

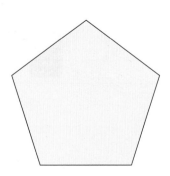

3 Trace this regular octagon onto card and cut it out to make a template.

    a Use your template to show that a regular octagon does not tessellate.

    b Explain why a regular octagon does not tessellate.

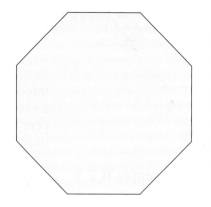

4 **a** Copy and complete the table below for regular polygons.

Regular polygon	Size of each interior angle	Does this polygon tessellate?
Equilateral triangle		
Square		
Regular pentagon		
Regular hexagon		
Regular octagon		

    b Use the table to explain why only some of the regular polygons tessellate.

    c Do you think that a regular nonagon tessellates? Explain your reasoning.

 **Extension** **Work**

Polygons can be combined to form a **semi-tessellation**. Two examples are shown below.

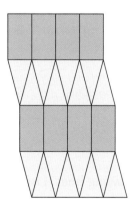

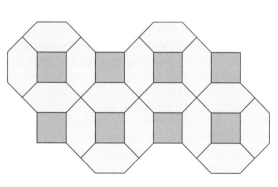

Rectangles and isosceles triangles   **Squares and hexagons**

Invent your own semi-tessellations and make a poster to display in your classroom.

Constructions

Two important geometric constructions are given in examples 4.7 and 4.8. Carefully work through them yourself. They are important because they produce exact measurements, and are therefore used by architects and in design and technology. You will need a sharp pencil, a straight edge (or ruler), compasses and a protractor. Leave all your construction lines on the diagrams.

Example 4.7 ▷   *To construct the mid-point and the perpendicular bisector of a line AB*

- Draw a line segment AB of any length.
- Set your compasses to any radius greater than half the length of AB.
- Draw two arcs with their centre at A, one above and one below AB.
- With your compasses set at the same radius, draw two arcs with their centre at B, to intersect the first two arcs at C and D.
- Join C and D to intersect AB at X. X is the mid-point of the line AB.
- The line CD is the perpendicular bisector of the line AB.

Example 4.8 ▷   *To construct the bisector of the angle ABC*

- Draw an angle ABC of any size.
- Set your compasses to any radius and, with its centre at B, draw an arc to intersect BC at X and AB at Y.
- With your compasses set to any radius, draw two arcs with their centres at X and Y, to intersect at Z.
- Join BZ.
- BZ is the bisector of the angle ABC.
- Then ∠ABZ = ∠CBZ

Exercise 4F

1 Use a ruler to draw each of the following lines. Using compasses, construct the perpendicular bisector for each line.

   a   6 cm   **b**   10 cm   **c**   7 cm   **d**   8.4 cm   **e**   5.5 cm

2 Use a protractor to draw each of the following angles. Using compasses, construct the angle bisector for each angle.

   a   40°   **b**   70°   **c**   90°   **d**   55°   **e**   140°

The isosceles triangle ABC on the right has a base of 4 cm and a perpendicular height of 5 cm.

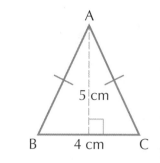

a By constructing the perpendicular bisector of BC, draw an accurate copy of the triangle.

b Measure the length of the sides AB and AC.

Extension **Work**

1 To construct an angle of 60°

Draw a line AB of any length. Set your compasses to a radius of about 4 cm. With its centre at A, draw a large arc to intersect the line at X. Using the same radius and, with its centre at X, draw an arc to intersect the first arc at Y. Join A and Y. Angle YAX is 60°.

Explain how you could use this construction to make angles of 30° and 15°.

2 To construct the inscribed circle of a triangle

Draw a triangle ABC with sides of any length. Construct the angle bisectors for each of the three angles. The three angle bisectors will meet at a point O, in the centre of the triangle. Using O as its centre, draw a circle to touch the three sides of the triangle.

The circle is known as the **inscribed circle** of the triangle.

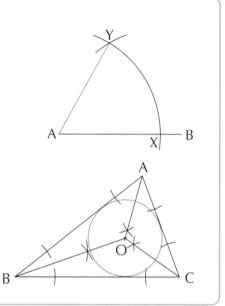

The circle and its parts

A circle is a set of points equidistant from a fixed point, called the **centre**, designated here by O.

You must learn all of the following terms for the different parts of a circle.

Circumference   The length round a circle. It is a special name for the perimeter of a circle.

Arc   One of the two parts between two points on a circumference.

Radius   The distance from the centre of a circle to its circumference. The plural of the term is 'radii'.

Diameter	The distance across a circle through its centre. The diameter d of a circle is twice its radius r, so $d = 2r$.

Chord	A straight line which joins two points on the circumference of a circle.
Tangent	A straight line that touches a circle at one point only on its circumference. This point is called the **point of contact**.
Segment	The region of a circle enclosed by a chord and an arc. Any chord encloses two segments, which have different areas.
Sector	A portion of a circle enclosed by two radii and one of the arcs between them.
Semicircle	One half of a circle: either of the parts cut off by a diameter.

Exercise 4G

1. Measure the radius of each of the following circles, giving your answer in centimetres. Write down the diameter of each circle.

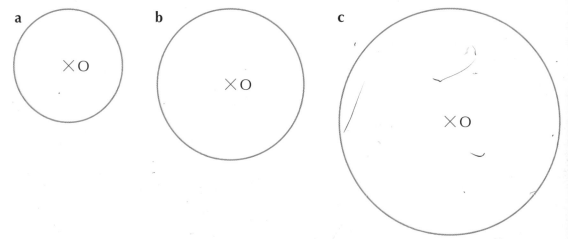

a   b   c

2. Draw circles with the following measurements.

   a   Radius = 2.5 cm   b   Radius = 3.6 cm
   c   Diameter = 8 cm   d   Diameter = 6.8 cm

3 Draw each of the following shapes accurately.

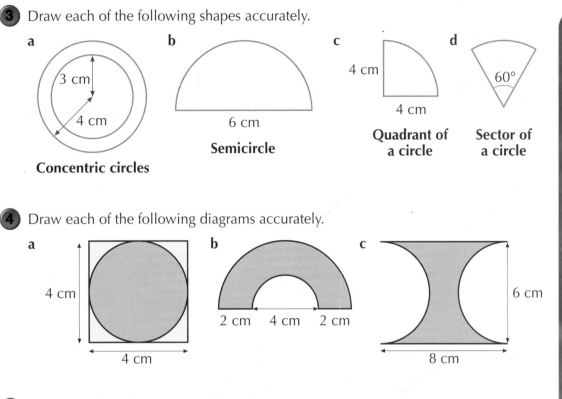

a

3 cm

4 cm

Concentric circles

b

6 cm

Semicircle

c

4 cm

4 cm

Quadrant of a circle

d

60°

Sector of a circle

4 Draw each of the following diagrams accurately.

a

4 cm

4 cm

b

2 cm 4 cm 2 cm

c

6 cm

8 cm

5 Draw a circle with centre O and with a radius of 4 cm. Draw six radii that are 60° apart, as shown in the diagram on the right. Join the points on the circumference to make an inscribed regular hexagon.

a Explain why the radii must be 60° apart.

b Use this method to draw each of these.
  i An inscribed regular pentagon
  ii An inscribed regular octagon

Extension Work

To find the centre of a circle

Draw a circle around a circular object so that the centre is not known.

Draw any two chords on the circle, as shown in the diagram. Then draw the perpendicular bisector for each chord.

The two perpendicular bisectors will intersect at the centre of the circle.

Repeat for circles of various radii.

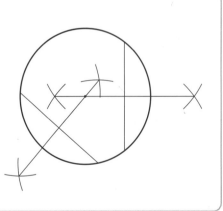

4   I know the names of the different types of quadrilaterals and polygons.

5   I know the interior angles of a triangle add up to 180°.
       I can tessellate a shape.
       I can draw shapes from circles.

6   I can construct the perpendicular bisector of a line and the bisector of an angle.
       I can recognise alternate and corresponding angles.
       I can find the exterior angle of a triangle.
       I know the interior angles of a quadrilateral add up to 360°.
       I can find interior angles of polygons.

National Test questions

1   *1997 Paper 2*

Here is a rough sketch of a sector of a circle.

Make an accurate, full-size drawing of this sector.

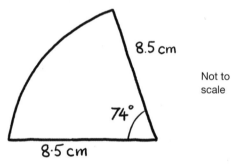

8.5 cm

Not to scale

74°

8·5 cm

2   *2003 Paper 2*

Look at the diagram. Triangle ABD is the reflection of triangle ABC in the line AB.

Copy the statements below and fill in the gaps to explain how to find angle x.

The length of AC is ..12.. cm.

The length of AD is ...... cm.

The length of CD is ...... cm.

ACD is an equilateral triangle because ....

so angle y is ......° because ....

so angle x is ......° because ....

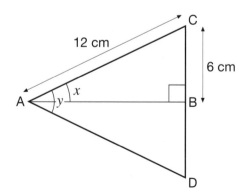

C

12 cm

6 cm

x

A y B

D

3 *2006 4–6 Paper 2*

Look at this diagram, made from straight lines:

Work out the sizes of the angles marked with letters.

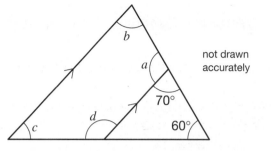

not drawn accurately

4 *2000 4–6 Paper 2*

a Any quadrilateral can be split into two triangles.

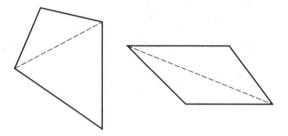

Explain how you know that the angles inside a quadrilateral add up to 360°.

b What do the angles inside a pentagon add up to?

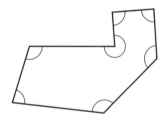

c What do the angles inside a heptagon (seven-sided shape) add up to?

Show your working.

FM Garden design

Greg has just moved house and is designing his new garden.

To work out the questions related to Greg's garden, you will need a copy of the Activity Worksheet on page 231.

1 Greg wants to make a trellis to grow some climbing plants on.
On the activity worksheet there is a sketch of the trellis.
Write down the other angles Greg needs to know.

2 A 1-metre wide path is to be laid around the BBQ area.
a Draw the path on activity worksheet.
b What is the area of the path?
c The path will be made using square paving slabs which are 50 cm by 50 cm. How many paving slabs will be needed?
You can draw in some of the slabs – this may help you.

3 A large semi-circular table will be placed in front of the BBQ area, as shown here.
Draw the table accurately on the activity worksheet.

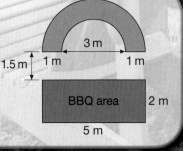

3 m

1.5 m | 1 m | 1 m

BBQ area | 2 m

5 m

4 The hexagonal seat that goes around the tree is to be made from planks of wood. Each of the six sections are identical.
Work out the angles, (shown in the diagram), that each section needs to be cut at.

5 There is going to be a circular pond of radius 3 m at the end of the garden. The centre of the pond will be 6 m from the corner where the west fence meets the north fence. The pond will be equidistant from the two fences.

a Bisect the angle made by the two fences

b Draw the pond accurately on the activity worksheet.
Leave in your construction lines.

6 A rotary washing line is to be placed exactly halfway along and 4 m from the northeast fence.

a Draw the perpendicular bisector of the northeast fence.

b Show the position of the rotary washing line on the activity worksheet with a cross (X).
Leave in your construction lines.

7 Paving slabs are going to be put underneath the rotary washing line.

a Which of the following slabs tessellate around a point?
Explain how you know.
Draw a sketch if it will help you explain more fully.

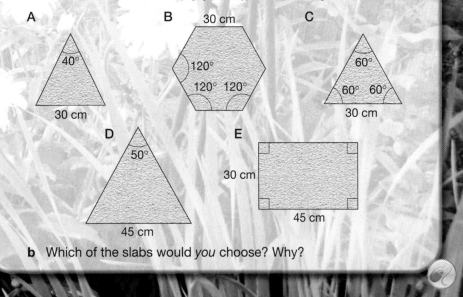

b Which of the slabs would *you* choose? Why?

Pie charts

This section will remind you about ten-sector pie charts, which you looked at in Year 8. It will also show you how to construct pie charts for more complex data.

Example 5.1 ▷

Eight-sector pie charts

A travel agent recorded the types of holiday that 200 people booked on one weekend. Draw a pie chart to represent this information.

Type of holiday	Tour	Flight Abroad	Short Break	Other
Frequency	25	100	50	25

We can see that:
- the 'Flight abroad' is half of the people (100 is half of 200)
- the 'Short break' is a quarter of the people (50 is a quarter of 200)

So each of the other two will be half of a quarter, which is one eighth.

So, completing the 8-sector pie chart gives us the chart shown on the right.

Example 5.2 ▷

Ten-sector pie charts

Draw a pie chart to represent the following set of data, which shows the favourite ice-creams of a group of pupils.

Ice-cream	Vanilla	Strawberry	Chocolate	Other
Number of pupils	9	6	12	3

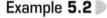

The data adds up to 30 pupils. Therefore, each sector on the ten-sector pie chart represents 3 pupils.

So, vanilla gets 3 sectors, strawberry gets 2 sectors, chocolate gets 4 sectors and 'other' gets 1 sector.

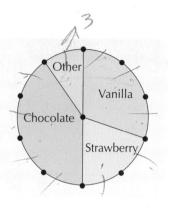

Exercise 5A

1. Draw eight-sector pie charts to represent each of the following tables of data.

   a   The sports chosen by a group of 80 pupils

Sport	Football	Netball	Basketball	Fitness
Frequency	40	20	10	10

   b   The meals taken by 60 teachers

Meal	School dinner	Packed lunch	Eat out
Frequency	15	30	15

   c   The favourite music of 48 Year 9 pupils

Type of music	Pop	Classical	Rap	Rock	Other
Frequency	12	6	6	18	6

2. Draw ten-sector pie charts to represent each of the following tables of data.

   a   The sports chosen by a group of 100 pupils

Sport	Gymnastics	Netball	Basketball	Swimming
Frequency	40	20	10	30

   b   The colour of car owned by 50 teachers

Colour	Blue	Red	Black	Other
Frequency	20	15	10	5

   c   The favourite music of 100 Year 9 pupils

Type of music	Pop	Classical	Rap	Rock	Jazz
Frequency	40	10	10	30	10

3. A survey about the cost of visiting a theme park is carried out. The results from 800 visitors are shown in the table below.

Cost	Expensive	Quite Expensive	Fair	Cheap	Very Cheap
Frequency	300	100	200	100	100

   Draw a pie chart to represent this data.

Use ten-sector pie charts to represent the following data (you will need to use fractions of the sectors).

1	Meals	Chinese	Indian	Italian	Other
	Frequency	35	15	45	5

2	Computer	PC	Apple	Laptop
	Frequency	55	5	40

Interpreting graphs and diagrams

In this section you will learn how to **interpret** graphs and diagrams, and how to **criticise** statements made about the data which they contain.

Example 5.3 ▷ The diagram shows how a group of pupils say they spend their time per week.

Matt says: 'The diagram shows that pupils spend too much time at school and doing homework.'
Give two arguments to suggest that this is not true.

The diagram represents a group of pupils, so the data may vary for individual pupils. It could also be argued, for example, that pupils spend longer watching TV than doing homework.

Watching TV 10%   Homework 8%   Eating 7%   School 20%   Other 20%   Sleeping 35%

4

FM ① A journey is shown on the distance–time graph. There are three stages to the journey and two stops.

a How far is travelled in the first stage of the journey?

b How long is the first stop?

c Chris says that the total distance travelled is 60 km. Explain why Chris is incorrect.

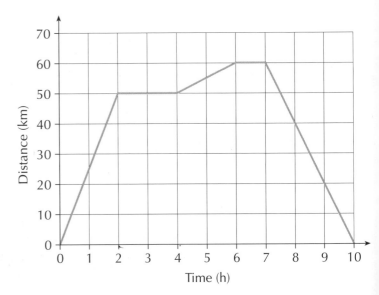

FM **2** The results of a junior school throwing competition are shown in the bar chart.

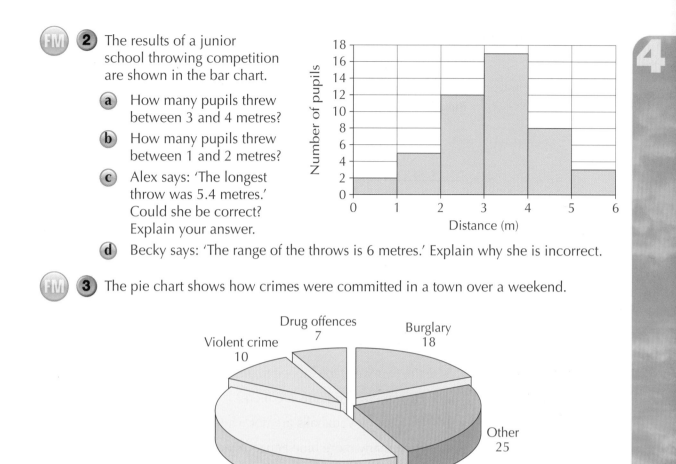

a How many pupils threw between 3 and 4 metres?

b How many pupils threw between 1 and 2 metres?

c Alex says: 'The longest throw was 5.4 metres.' Could she be correct? Explain your answer.

d Becky says: 'The range of the throws is 6 metres.' Explain why she is incorrect.

FM **3** The pie chart shows how crimes were committed in a town over a weekend.

Drug offences 7
Violent crime 10
Burglary 18
Other 25
Theft 40

a How many drug offences were committed?

b How many offences were committed altogether?

c It is claimed that most crime involves theft. Explain why this is incorrect.

FM **4** The table shows information about the animal populations on four small farms in the years 2000 and 2005.

Farm	Animal population 2000	Animal population 2005
A	275	529
B	241	205
C	75	65
D	63	40
Total	654	839

a Which farm has increased the number of animals between 2000 and 2005?

b Which farm has shown the largest decrease in animal population from 2000 to 2005?

c A newspaper headline says that farm animal populations are increasing. Using the information in the table, criticise this headline.

Extension Work

FM Find a graph or chart from a newspaper. Write down the facts that the newspaper article is claiming that the graph or chart shows. Use different arguments, referring to the graph or chart, to cast doubt on the facts given.

Two-way tables

Jeff and Catherine go to the school car park and record data about the 80 cars parked there. Here is their record.

		Colour of cars				
		Red	**White**	**Blue**	**Black**	**Other**
	Peugeot	8	1	4	1	4
	Ford	11	2	4	2	6
Make of cars	**Vauxhall**	5	4	0	0	2
	Citroen	1	2	2	0	3
	Other	6	3	3	4	2

This is called a **two-way table**.

Example 5.4 ▷ Use the two-way table above to answer the questions about the cars in the car park.

   a How many red Fords are there?

   b How many Vauxhalls are not white?

   c How many more blue Peugeots are there than white Citroens?

   a There are 11 red Fords.

   b There are 11 Vauxhalls but 4 are white, so 7 are not white.

   c There are 4 blue Peugeots and 2 white Citroens, so there are 2 more blue Peugeots than white Citroens.

Example 5.5 ▷ An Internet company charges delivery for goods based on the type of delivery – normal delivery (taking 3 to 5 days) or next-day delivery – and also on the cost of the order. The table shows how it is calculated.

Cost of order	Normal delivery (3 to 5 days)	Next-day delivery
£0–£10	£1.95	£4.95
£10.01–£30	£2.95	£4.95
£30.01–£50	£3.95	£6.95
£50.01–£75	£2.95	£4.95
Over £75	Free	£3.00

   a Comment on the difference in delivery charges for normal and next-day delivery.

   b Two items cost £5 and £29. How much would you save by ordering them together using: **i** normal delivery? **ii** next-day delivery?

Example 5.5
continued

a It always costs more using next-day delivery but for goods costing between £10.01 and £30, or between £50.01 and £75, it is only £2 more. It is £3 more for all other orders.

b Using normal delivery and ordering the items separately, it would cost £1.95 + £2.95 = £4.90, but ordering them together would cost £3.95. The saving would be £4.90 – £3.95 = 95p

Using next-day delivery and ordering the items separately, it would cost £4.95 + £4.95 = £9.90, but ordering them together would cost £6.95. The saving would be £9.90 – £6.95 = £2.95

Exercise 5C

1 Ali and Padmini go to their local supermarket and record data on the cars parked there.

		Colour of cars				
		Blue	**White**	**Red**	**Black**	**Other**
Make of cars	**Toyota**	6	2	6	2	3
	Peugeot	8	1	3	3	1
	Vauxhall	4	2	5	1	2
	Ford	9	0	4	3	1
	Other	5	2	3	4	2

a How many blue Toyotas are there?
b How many Peugeots are not blue?
c How many more blue Fords are there than red Vauxhalls?
d Which make of car is the most common at this car park?

2 Reha, Jake, Colin and Celina had a games competition.
They played two games, 'Noughts and Crosses' and 'Boxes'.
Each played each of the others at both games.
Colin recorded how many games each person won:

Reha	I I I
Jake	I I I
Colin	I I
Celina	I I I I

Celina recorded who won each game:

Noughts and Crosses	Jake, Colin, Jake, Celina, Reha, Jake
Boxes	Celina, Celina, Reha, Celina, Colin

a Celina has missed one name out from her table. Use Colin's table to say which name is missing.
b Who won most games of Noughts and Crosses?
c Give a reason why Colin's table is a good way of recording the results.
d Give a reason why Celina's table is a good way of recording the results.

FM **3** The table shows the number of pupils who have school lunches in Years 7, 8 and 9.

	Have school lunch	Do not have school lunch
Year 7	120	64
Year 8	97	87
Year 9	80	104

a How does the number of pupils who have school lunch change as they get older?

b Between which two years are the greatest changes? Explain your answer.

c By looking at the changes in the table, approximately how many pupils would you expect to not have a school lunch in Year 10?

FM **4** The table shows the percentage of boys and girls by age group who have mobile phones.

a Work out the differences in the percentages for boys and girls at ages 10 to 15.

b Write down what you notice about the differences in the percentages for boys and girls.

Age	Boys	Girls
10	18%	14%
11	21%	18%
12	42%	39%
13	53%	56%
14	56%	59%
15	62%	64%

Extension Work

FM The heights of 70 Year 9 pupils were recorded. The results are given in the table below:

a Put this information onto a dual bar chart to show clearly the differences between the boys and the girls.

b Use the chart to see if the boys are taller than girls in Year 9. Explain your answer.

Height	Boys	Girls
130–139	3	3
140–149	2	4
150–159	10	12
160–169	14	11
170–179	6	5

Drawing and using frequency diagrams

Look at the picture. How does the shopkeeper know how many clothes of each size he will sell the most of?

Example 5.6 ▷ Construct a bar chart, for the given data, about the months in which a Year 9 group had their birthdays.

Birthday month	Frequency
January or February	18
March or April	21
May or June	26
July or August	24
September or October	16
November or December	17

It is important that the diagram has a title and labels as shown.

Example 5.7 ▷ Construct a frequency diagram to show how lawn-mower sales at a shop vary throughout a year.

Jan	Feb	Mar	Apr	May	Jun	Jul	Aug	Sep	Oct	Nov	Dec
0	25	63	75	92	68	53	32	76	15	0	12

Write down why you think the sales are high in September and why there are some sales in December.

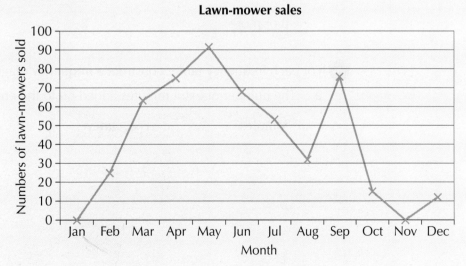

The reasons for the sales in September could be that the shop reduces the prices in an attempt to sell off stock before winter. The December sales could be Christmas presents.

1 For each frequency table, construct a bar chart.

a The number of restaurants in a particular town

Meal	Frequency
Chinese	3
Italian	7
Indian	15
Turkish	12
Greek	5
English	2

b The number of types of worker at a factory

Type of worker	Frequency
Trainee	38
Skilled	20
Managers	5
Directors	1

c The number of tomatoes on a truss

Number of tomatoes	Frequency
1	3
2	5
3	12
4	18
5	4
6 or more	2

2 For each frequency table, construct a frequency diagram.

a The number of extra minutes added on to the end of 44 football matches

Minutes	Frequency
0	1
1	7
2	15
3	12
4	6
5 or more	3

b The salary band of workers at a factory

Salary Band (£)	Frequency
1 – 10,000	38
10,001 – 20,000	20
20,001 – 30,000	5
30,001 – 40,000	2

c The shoe sizes sold by a shop in one week

Shoe size	Frequency
3 or smaller	8
4 or 5	19
6 or 7	12
8 or 9	6
10 or larger	2

FM **3** The following table shows the rainfall, in millimetres, for a town in the north of England.

Month	Jan	Feb	Mar	Apr	May	Jun	Jul	Aug	Sep	Oct	Nov	Dec
Rainfall (mm)	45	36	44	47	51	54	49	55	50	44	51	50

a Construct a line graph of this data.
b Which month had the greatest rainfall?
c Which month had the least rainfall?
d For how many months was the amount of rainfall below 45 mm?
e What is the difference between the amount of rainfall in July and the amount of rainfall in August?
f Between which two consecutive months is there the greatest difference in rainfall?

Extension **Work**

FM The table shows population forecasts for the UK and Afghanistan.

Year	2005	2010	2015	2020	2025	2030	2035	2040	2045	2050
Population of UK (millions)	60	61	62	63	64	64	65	65	64	64
Population of Afghanistan (millions)	29	33	37	40	44	48	53	58	61	66

a Construct a line graph for each country using the same axes.

b Estimate the year when the populations of the two countries will be equal.

c Estimate the year when the population of the UK is at its maximum. State what this maximum population could be.

Statistical investigations

Investigating a problem will involve several steps. An example from PE is given together with an example of how to write a report.

	Step	Plan
1	Decide which general topic to study	For this investigation, I am going to find out how to improve pupils' performance in sport.
2	Specify in more detail	In particular, I am going to investigate the ability of pupils to throw a cricket ball.
3	Guess what you think could happen (This is called 'Stating your hypotheses')	I will consider whether a run-up improves performance. I will also compare pupils of similar heights, as it is possible that height would also affect performance.
4	Conjectures	I think that the distance thrown will improve using a run-up but if the run-up is too long it might then fail to improve performance. I think that Year 11 pupils of the same height may be physically stronger and would therefore throw further.
5	Sources of information required	I will carry out a survey of the distance thrown with different lengths of run-up.
6	Relevant data	I am going to choose pupils from Year 9 and Year 11, arranged in three groups according to height: short, medium height and tall. I will use 5 boys and 5 girls in each group. I will try to use pupils of different sporting abilities. Each pupil will have 3 throws, one with no run-up, one with a 5 metre run-up and one with a 10 metre run-up.
7	Possible problems	I will allow each pupil the same length of time, 5 minutes, to warm up. I will organise the event so that the throws are always taken in the same order. For example, the first throw for every pupil has no run-up. This should produce more reliable results.
8	Possible problems	I will put each pupil into a category according to their height and Year group. I will then record the distance for each throw.
9	Decide on appropriate level of accuracy	I will round off all measurements to the nearest 10 cm.
10	Determine sample size	In order to collect all this information effectively, I will ask a group of friends to help me.
11	Construct tables for large sets of raw data in order to make work manageable	I will create a two-way table to record my results for each group.
12	Decide which statistic is most suitable	I will calculate the mean for each group of results and then compare its value with my predictions.

Here is an example of a recording sheet for Year 9 pupilss of medium height.

Year 9 Medium height	Pupil 1	Pupil 2	Pupil 3	Pupil 4	Pupil 5
No run-up					
5 m run-up					
10 m run-up					

1 List in order the missing words in each plan given below.

Missing words for Science Plan are:

car	bias	not	books
petrol	nearest	investigate	engine

Missing words for Geography Plan are:

mean	incomes	information	compare
sample	average	Internet	housing

	Step	Q1 Science Plan	Q2 Geography Plan
1	Decide which general topic to study	I am going to …… the effect of engine size on a car's acceleration.	I am going to …… life expectancy against the cost of housing.
2	Specify in more detail	I will begin by studying only one make of ……. .	I will compare house prices in Yorkshire with those in the South-east.
3	Guess what you think could happen. (This is called 'Stating your hypotheses')	I am going to try to find out if a bigger …… always means that a car can accelerate faster.	I am going to investigate whether people in expensive …… tend to live longer.
4	Conjectures	It may be that more powerful engines tend to be in heavier cars and therefore the acceleration is …… affected. I am sure that larger engines in the same model of car will improve acceleration.	As people in expensive housing have greater …… , they may also have a longer life expectancy.
5	Sources of information required	I am going to use car magazines and …… to find information on engine sizes and the acceleration times for 0–60 mph.	I am going to use the library and search the …… for census data for each area.
6	Relevant data	I am using 0–60 mph because the government requires car manufacturers to publish the time taken to accelerate from 0–60 mph.	I will record the …… cost of housing for each area and also the life expectancy for each area.
7	Possible problems	I will keep a record of the make of car, the engine size and the acceleration time. I will only compare petrol engines with other …… engines and not with diesel engines to avoid …… in my results.	

Step	Q1 Science Plan	Q2 Geography Plan
8 Possible problems	I will also find out and record the weight of each car, as this is part of my guess at what will affect the results.	When I find the …… that I need, I will make a note of where it came from.
9 Decide on appropriate level of accuracy	I will round engine sizes to the …… 100 cm³. For example, a car with an engine capacity of 1905 cc (this is the same as cm³ but is what the motor trade use) will be recorded as 1900 cc.	
10 Determine sample size		
11 Construct tables for large sets of raw data in order to make work manageable		I will group the data about the population in age groups of five-year intervals.
12 Decide which statistic is most suitable		I will make sure that I look at at least 30 pieces of data for each area so that my …… is large enough to calculate the …… and have a reliable answer.

Extension Work

Think of a problem related to pupils who cycle to school. Collect as much data as you can, and write up your plan. Use the planning steps on page 76 as your guides.

LEVEL BOOSTER

4
I know how to group data in equal class intervals.
I can represent collected data in frequency diagrams.
I can interpret frequency diagrams.
I know how to present information in a clear and organised way.

5
I can interpret graphs and diagrams, including pie charts.
I can draw conclusions from graphs and diagrams.

National Test questions

1   *2005 3–5 Paper 1*

a   Jane asked **27 people**: "Do you like school dinners?"
The bar chart shows her results for 'Yes' and 'No'.

Copy the bar chart and complete it to show her results for 'Don't know'.

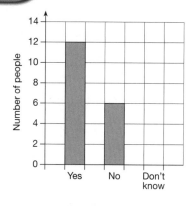

b This pictogram also shows her results for 'Yes' and 'No'.

Copy the pictogram and complete it to show her results for 'Don't know'.

Yes	◯ ◯ ◯ ◯
No	◯ ◯
Don't know	

FM **2** *2005 3–5 Paper 2*

Look at this information:

In 1976, a man earned £16.00 each week.

The pie chart shows how this man spent his money:

a How much did the man spend on **food** each week?

b Now look at this information:

In 2002, a man earned £400.00 each week.

This table shows how he spent his money:

Rent	£200
Food	£100
Entertainment	£50
Other	£50

Draw a pie chart like the one below and complete it to show how the man spent his money.

Remember to **label** each sector of the pie chart.

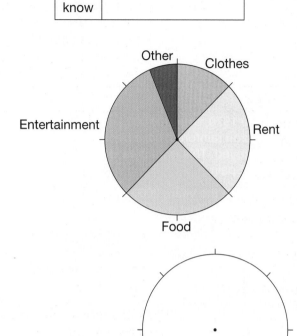

FM **3** *2000 Paper 1*

Maria and Kay ran a 1500 metres race.
The distance–time graph on the right shows the race.

Use the graph to help you fill in the gaps in this report of the race.

Just after the start of the race, Maria was in the lead. At 600 metres, Maria and Kay were level. Then Kay was in the lead for …… minutes. At …… metres, Maria and Kay were level again.

…… won the race. Her total time was …… minutes. …… finished …… minutes later.

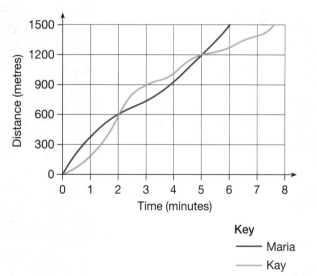

Key
— Maria
— Kay

FM Rainforest deforestation

Since 1970, over 600 000 km^2 of Amazon rainforest have been destroyed. This is an area larger than Spain.

Between the years 2000 and 2005, Brazil lost over 132 000 km^2 of forest – an area about the same size as Greece.

The table below shows how much of the rainforests in Brazil have been lost each year since 1988.

Deforestation figure

Year	Deforestation (sq km)
1988	21 000
1989	18 000
1990	14 000
1991	11 000
1992	14 000
1993	15 000
1994	15 000
1995	29 000
1996	18 000
1997	13 000
1998	17 000
1999	17 000
2000	18 000
2001	18 000
2002	21 000
2003	25 000
2004	27 000
2005	19 000
2006	14 000
2007	10 000

Use the information on the left to answer these questions.

1 Draw a bar chart showing the deforestation of Brazil over the years from 1988–2007.

2 From 1988–91, Brazil had an economic slowdown. What was happening to the rate of deforestation during that time?

3 From 1992–95, Brazil had economic growth. What was happening to the rate of deforestation during that time?

4 What do think was happening to Brazil's economy:
  a from 1998–2004?
  b from 2005–7?

5 What does the chart and the information given in questions 1 and 2 suggest about the link between deforestation in Brazil and the economy?

The pie chart below shows the three main reasons for deforestation in the Amazon from 2000–5.

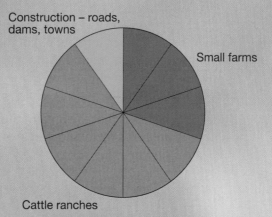

Construction – roads, dams, towns

Small farms

Cattle ranches

6 What appears to be the main reason for the deforestation in the Amazon between the years 2000 and 2005?

7 What percentage of the deforestation was caused by cattle ranches?

8 It was suggested that over the next two years:
  ○ the same amount of deforestation would take place.
  ○ the amount of construction work would actually double.
  ○ the number of small farms would halve.
  ○ the number of cattle ranches would increase.

Draw a new pie chart reflecting the reasons for deforestation suggested for 2007.

This chapter is going to show you

- How to calculate the area of a triangle, a parallelogram and a trapezium
- How to calculate the area of a compound shape
- How to calculate the volume of a cuboid
- How to convert imperial units to metric units
- How to find the mid-point of a line segment

What you should already know

- How to find the area of a rectangle
- How to calculate the surface area of a cuboid
- How to convert one metric unit to another
- How to plot points in all four quadrants

Area of a triangle

To find the area, A, of a triangle, you need to know the length of its base, b, and its height, h. The height of the triangle is sometimes known as its **perpendicular height**.

The diagram shows that the area of the triangle is half of the area of a rectangle, the length of whose sides are b and h:

Area 1 = Area 2

and

Area 3 = Area 4

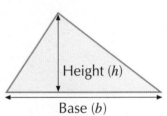

So, the area of a triangle is $\frac{1}{2}$ × base × height. That is:

$$A = \frac{1}{2} \times b \times h = \frac{1}{2}bh = \frac{b \times h}{2}$$

Remember that the metric units of area in common use are:

- Square millimetre (mm^2)
- Square centimetre (cm^2)
- Square metre (m^2)

Example 6.1

Find the area of the right-angled triangle shown on the right.

Area of rectangle = 6 × 4 = 24 cm^2

So area of triangle = $\frac{24}{2}$ = 12 cm^2

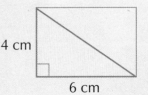

Example 6.2 ▷ Find the area of the triangle shown on the right.

$$A = \frac{6 \times 3}{2} = 9 \text{ cm}^2$$

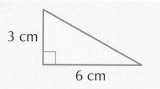

3 cm

6 cm

Example 6.3 ▷ Find the area of the triangle shown on the right.

$$A = \frac{8 \times 5}{2} = \frac{40}{2} = 20 \text{ cm}^2$$

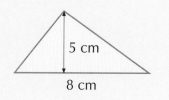

5 cm

8 cm

1 Find the area of each triangle by first finding the area of the rectangle that encloses it. Each square represents 1 square centimetre.

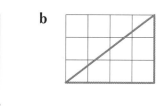

a   b   c   d

2 Use the formula to find the area of each right-angled triangle.

$$A = \frac{b \times h}{2}$$

h

b

a

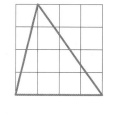

4 cm

5 cm

b

6 cm

8 cm

c

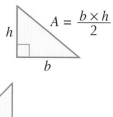

8 cm

8 cm

d

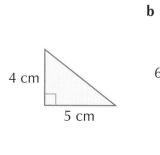

7 cm

10 cm

e

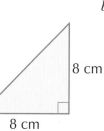

7 cm

2 cm

f

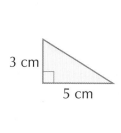

3 cm

5 cm

3 Find the area of each of the right-angled triangles drawn on the centimetre-square grid below.

Use the formula: $A = \dfrac{b \times h}{2}$

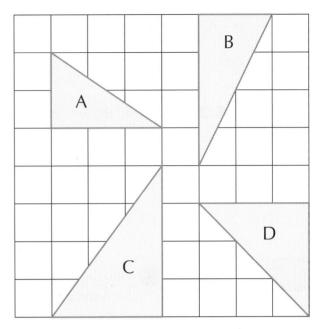

4 Find the area of each of the following triangles.

Use the formula: $A = \dfrac{b \times h}{2}$

a

5 cm

6 cm

b

8 cm

7 cm

c

12 m

18 m

d

25 mm

20 mm

5 Copy and complete the table for triangles **a** to **d**.

Use the formula: $A = \dfrac{b \times h}{2}$

Triangle	Base	Height	Area
a	3 cm	4 cm	
b	5 cm	3 cm	
c	4 cm		12 cm^2
d		8 cm	20 cm^2

Extension **Work**

The right-angled triangle shown has an area of 24 cm^2.

Find other right-angled triangles, with different measurements, which also have an area of 24 cm^2.

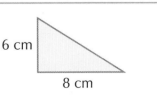

6 cm

8 cm

Area of a parallelogram

To find the area, A, of a parallelogram, you need to know the length of its base, b, and its height, h. The height of the parallelogram is sometimes known as its **perpendicular height**.

The diagrams show that the parallelogram has the same area as that of a rectangle with the same base and height. So, the area of a parallelogram is base × height. That is:

$$A = b \times h = bh$$

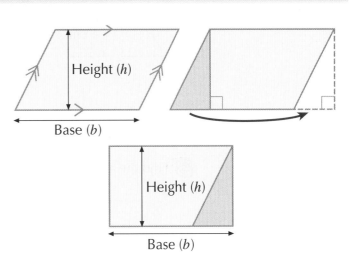

Example 6.4 ▷ Calculate the area of this parallelogram.

Here, $b = 10$ cm and $h = 6$ cm, which gives:
$$A = 6 \times 10 = 60 \text{ cm}^2$$

Example 6.5 ▷ Calculate the area of this parallelogram.

Here, $b = 3$ cm and $h = 5$ cm, which gives:
$$A = 3 \times 5 = 15 \text{ cm}^2$$

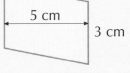

Exercise 6B

1 Use the formula $A = b \times h$ to find the area of each of these parallelograms.

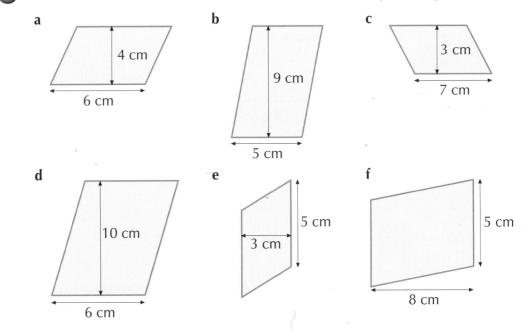

2 Find the area of each of the following parallelograms.

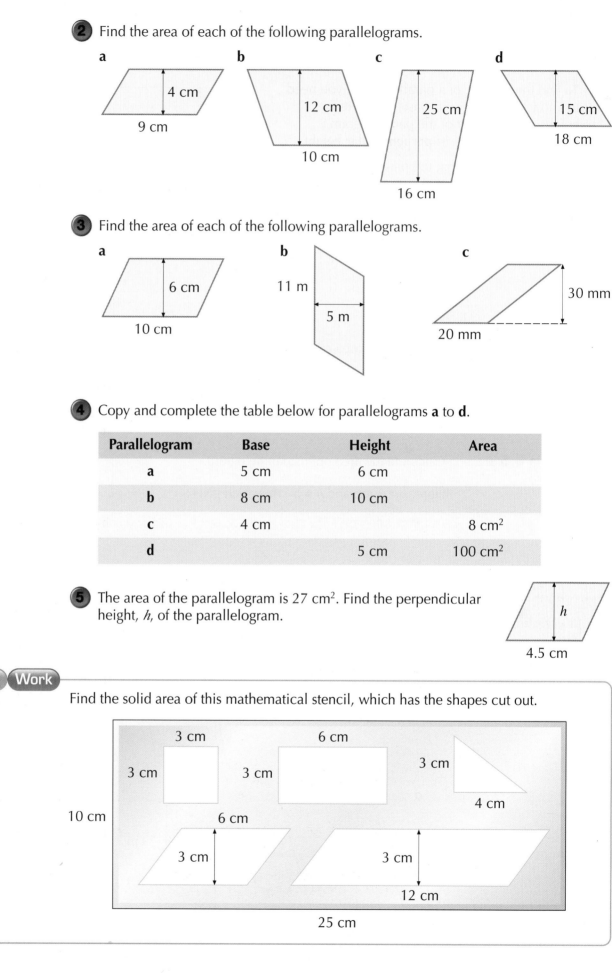

a
4 cm
9 cm

b
12 cm
10 cm

c
25 cm
16 cm

d
15 cm
18 cm

3 Find the area of each of the following parallelograms.

a
6 cm
10 cm

b
11 m
5 m

c
30 mm
20 mm

4 Copy and complete the table below for parallelograms **a** to **d**.

Parallelogram	Base	Height	Area
a	5 cm	6 cm	
b	8 cm	10 cm	
c	4 cm		8 cm²
d		5 cm	100 cm²

5 The area of the parallelogram is 27 cm². Find the perpendicular height, h, of the parallelogram.

h

4.5 cm

Extension Work

Find the solid area of this mathematical stencil, which has the shapes cut out.

3 cm

6 cm

3 cm

3 cm

3 cm

3 cm

4 cm

10 cm

6 cm

3 cm

6 cm

3 cm

12 cm

25 cm

86

Volume of a cuboid

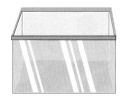

Volume is the amount of space inside a three-dimensional (3-D) shape.

The diagram shows a cuboid which measures 4 cm by 3 cm by 2 cm. The cuboid is made up of cubes of edge length 1 cm. The top layer consists of 12 cubes and, since there are two layers, the cuboid has altogether 24 cubes.

The volume of the cuboid is therefore found by calculating:

$$4 \text{ cm} \times 3 \text{ cm} \times 2 \text{ cm} = 24 \text{ cm}^3$$

Hence, the volume of a cuboid is found by multiplying its length by its width by its height:

Volume of cuboid = length × width × height

$$V = l \times w \times h = lwh$$

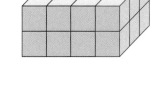

The metric units of volume in common use are:

- Cubic millimetre (mm^3)
- Cubic centimetre (cm^3)
- Cubic metre (m^3)

The capacity of a 3-D shape is the volume of liquid or gas it can hold. The metric unit of capacity is the litre (l), where:

$$1 \text{ litre} = 1000 \text{ cm}^3$$

Example 6.6 ▷ Find the volume of the cuboid shown on the right.

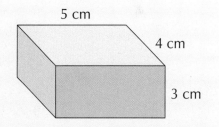

The volume of the cuboid is given by:

$$V = lwh$$

Putting in the values for l, w and h gives:

$$V = 5 \times 4 \times 3$$
$$= 60 \text{ cm}^3$$

Example 6.7 ▷ Calculate the volume of the tank shown. Then work out the capacity of the tank in litres.

$$V = lwh$$

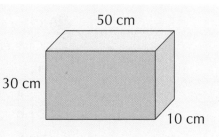

Putting in the values for l, w and h gives:

$$V = 50 \times 30 \times 10 = 15\,000 \text{ cm}^3$$

Since $1000 \text{ cm}^3 = 1$ litre, the capacity of the tank $= 15\,000 \div 1000 = 15$ litres

1 Which of the units below can be used for volume?

m^2 mm cm^2 m^3 cm^3 m km^2 mm^3

2 For each cuboid below, write the length (l), the width (w) and the height (h) as a number of cubes. Use your answers to work out the volume of the cuboid.

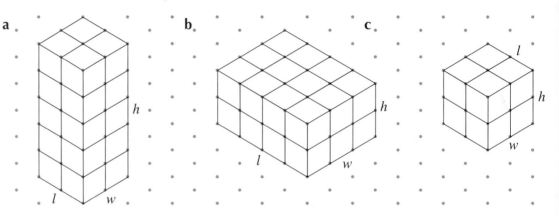

3 Use the formula $V = l \times w \times h$ to work out the volume of each of these cuboids.

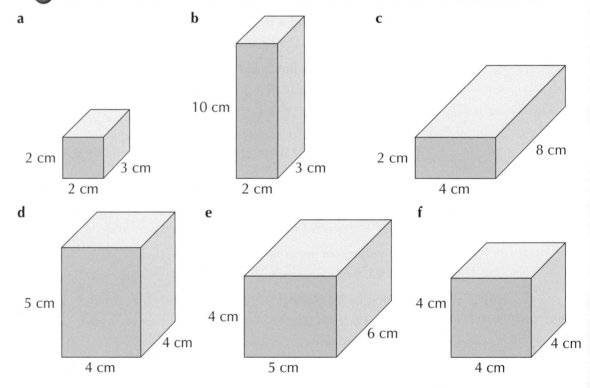

4 Copy and complete this table for cuboids **a** to **e**.
Give each answer with the correct unit.

	l	w	h	V
a	3 m	5 m	4 m	
b	12 mm	6 mm	5 mm	
c	30 cm	40 cm	10 cm	
d	1 m	5 m	4 m	
e	15 cm	20 cm	5 cm	

5 Find the volume for each of the cubes with the following edge lengths.

    a 2 cm   **b** 5 cm   **c** 10 cm

6 Find the volume of a hall that is 30 m long, 15 m wide and 8 m high.

FM **7** The diagram shows the dimensions of a rectangular carton of orange juice.

    a Find the volume of the carton, giving your answer in cubic centimetres.

    b How many litres of orange juice does the carton hold?

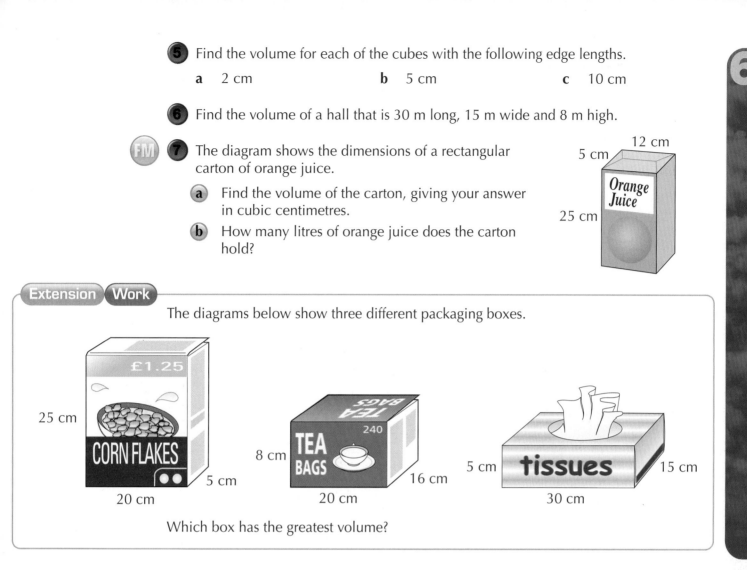

Extension Work

The diagrams below show three different packaging boxes.

Which box has the greatest volume?

Imperial units

In Britain, there is a gradual switch to the metric system of units. But many people still prefer to use the imperial system of units, as the examples on the left show.

The following imperial units are still commonly used, so you should be familiar with them.

Imperial units of length	Imperial units of mass	Imperial units of capacity
12 inches (in) = 1 foot (ft)	16 ounces (oz) = 1 pound (lb)	8 pints (pt) = 1 gallon (gal)
3 feet = 1 yard (yd)	14 pounds = 1 stone (st)	
1760 yards = 1 mile	2240 pounds = 1 ton	

Example 6.8 Change 3 ft 6 in into inches.

1 ft = 12 in, so 3 ft = $3 \times 12 = 36$ in

Hence, 3 ft 6 in = $36 + 6 = 42$ in

Example 6.9 Change 32 lb into stones and pounds.

1 st = 14 lb, so divide 32 lb by 14, which gives 2 stones with 4 pounds left over.

Hence, 32 lb = 2 st 4 lb

(Note that if you use a calculator, the answer will be given as a decimal number.)

Rough metric equivalents of imperial units

As Britain changes to the metric system, you need to be able to convert from imperial units to metric units by using suitable approximations. It is useful to know the following rough metric equivalents of imperial units. If accuracy is required, the exact conversion factor should be used. The symbol ≈ means 'is approximately equal to'.

Units of length	Units of mass	Units of capacity
1 in ≈ 2.5 cm	1 oz ≈ 30 g	$1\frac{3}{4}$ pints ≈ 1 litre
1 yard ≈ 1 m	1 lb ≈ 500 g	1 gallon ≈ 4.5 litre
5 miles ≈ 8 km		

Example 6.10 Approximately how many kilometres are in 20 miles?

5 miles ≈ 8 km

So, 20 miles ≈ $4 \times 8 \approx 32$ km

Example 6.11 Approximately how many gallons are in 18 litres?

1 gallon ≈ 4.5 litres

So, divide 18 litres by 4.5, which gives 4 gallons.

Exercise 6D

1 Change each of the following into the unit given in brackets.

    a 4 ft (in)   **b** 2 ft 8 in (in)   **c** 4 yd (ft)   **d** 10 yd (ft)

    e 2 miles (yd)   **f** 2 lb (oz)   **g** 1 lb 4 oz (oz)   **h** 5 st (lb)

    i 2 st 10 lb (lb)   **j** 5 gallons (pints)   **k** $3\frac{1}{2}$ gallons (pints)

2 Change each of the following into the units given in brackets.

    a 24 in (ft)   **b** 40 in (ft and in)   **c** 15 ft (yd)

    d 20 ft (yd and ft)   **e** 48 oz (lb)   **f** 8 oz (lb)

    g 35 oz (lb and oz)   **h** 56 lb (st)   **i** 40 lb (st and lb)

    j 16 pints (gallons)   **k** 25 pints (gallons and pints)

③ Each picture shows an imperial measure. Which metric amount is approximately the same as the imperial amount?

a

1 pound

| 100 g | 200 g | 500 g | 1 kg |

b

1 in
(inch)

| 1 cm | 2.5 cm | 5 cm | 7.5 cm |

c

1 gallon

| 1 litre | 2 litres | 4.5 litres | 10 litres |

d

LONDON
5 miles

| 2 km | 4 km | 6 km | 8 km |

e

1 yard

| 1 m | 1.5 m | 2 m | 5 m |

④ **a** Copy and complete the table to show the conversions between miles and kilometres.

b About how many kilometres is 12.5 miles?

miles	km
5	8
10	
15	
20	
50	
100	

⑤ **a** Copy and complete the table to show the conversions between pints and litres.

b About how many litres is 35 pints?

pints	litres
1.75	1
3.5	
3	
4	
5	
17.5	

FM **6** Here is a recipe for flapjacks. The recipe gives the amounts of ingredients in ounces (oz).

Re-write the recipe, giving the amounts in grams (g). Remember that 1 oz is about 30 g.

Flapjacks	
Butter	4 oz
Sugar	2 oz
Oats	5 oz
Flour	1 oz
Syrup	2 tablespoons

FM **7** Change each of the following imperial quantities into the approximate metric quantity given in brackets.

a) 3 in (cm) b) 12 in (cm) c) 12 ft (m) d) 30 ft (m)
e) 10 miles (km) f) 25 miles (km) g) 2 oz (g) h) 5 oz (g)
i) 2 lb (g) j) 7 pints (l) k) 10 gallons (litre)

FM **8** Pierre is on holiday in England and he sees this sign near to his hotel. Approximately how many metres is it from his hotel to the beach?

To the beach → 500 yards

FM **9** Mike is travelling on a German autobahn and he sees this road sign. He knows that it means that the speed limit is 120 km/hr. What is the approximate speed limit in miles per hour?

120

FM **10** Steve needs 6 gallons of petrol to fill the tank of his car. The pump dispenses petrol only in litres. Approximately how many litres of petrol does he need?

Extension Work

1 Working in pairs or groups, draw a table to show each person's height and weight in imperial and in metric units.

2 a Calculate the number of inches in a mile.

   b Calculate the number of ounces in a ton.

Finding the mid-point of a line segment

The next example will remind you how to plot points in all four quadrants using x- and y- coordinates.

It will also show you how to find the coordinates of the mid-point of a line which joins two points.

Example 6.12 ▷ The coordinates of the points of A, B, C and D on the grid are A(4, 4), B(–2, 4), C(2, 1) and D(2, –3).

The mid-point of the line segment which joins A to B is X. (X is usually referred to as the mid-point of AB.) From the diagram, the coordinates of X are (1, 4). Notice that the *y*-coordinates are the same for all three points on the line.

The mid-point of CD is Y. From the diagram, the coordinates of Y are (2, –1). Notice that the *x*-coordinates are the same for all three points on the line.

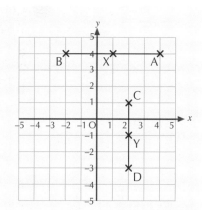

Exercise 6E

1 Copy the grid on the right on to centimetre-square paper. Then plot the points A, B, C, D, E and F.

    a Write down the coordinates of the points A, B, C, D, E and F.

    b Using the grid to help you, write down the coordinates of the mid-point of each of the following line segments.

        i AB   **ii** AC   **iii** BD
        iv CE   **v** DF

2 Copy the grid on the right on to centimetre-square paper and plot the points J, K, L and M.

    a Write down the coordinates of the points J, K, L and M.

    b Join the points to form the trapezium JKLM. Using the grid to help you, write down the coordinates of the mid-point of each of the following line segments.

        i JK   **ii** JM   **iii** LM   **iv** KL

3 Copy the grid on the right and plot the points A, B, C, D, E and F.

    a Write down the coordinates of the points A, B, C, D, E and F.

    b Using the grid to help, write down the coordinates of the mid-point of each of the following line segments.

        i AB   **ii** CD   **iii** BE   **iv** EF

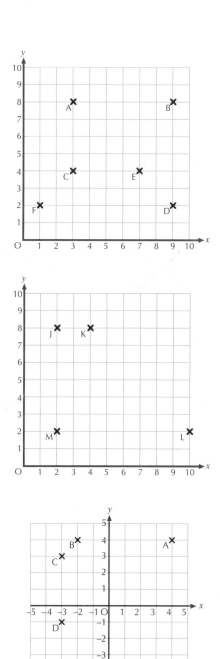

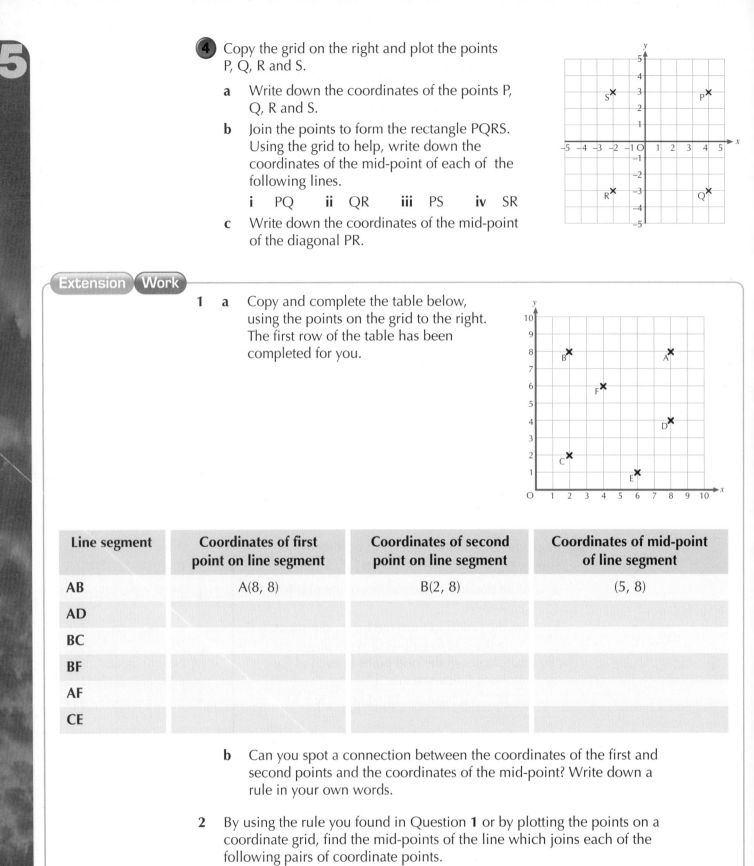

4 Copy the grid on the right and plot the points P, Q, R and S.

   a Write down the coordinates of the points P, Q, R and S.

   b Join the points to form the rectangle PQRS. Using the grid to help, write down the coordinates of the mid-point of each of the following lines.

      i PQ   **ii** QR   **iii** PS   **iv** SR

   c Write down the coordinates of the mid-point of the diagonal PR.

Extension Work

1 **a** Copy and complete the table below, using the points on the grid to the right. The first row of the table has been completed for you.

Line segment	Coordinates of first point on line segment	Coordinates of second point on line segment	Coordinates of mid-point of line segment
AB	A(8, 8)	B(2, 8)	(5, 8)
AD			
BC			
BF			
AF			
CE			

   b Can you spot a connection between the coordinates of the first and second points and the coordinates of the mid-point? Write down a rule in your own words.

2 By using the rule you found in Question **1** or by plotting the points on a coordinate grid, find the mid-points of the line which joins each of the following pairs of coordinate points.

   a A(3, 2) and B(3, 6)   **b** C(4, 6) and D(6, 10)

   c E(3, 2) and F(5, 4)   **d** G(8, 6) and H(2, 3)

   e I(5, 6) and J(−3 , −2)

5

4   I can plot and use coordinates in the first quadrant.

5   I can change imperial units into metric units using rough equivalents.

I can plot and use coordinates in all four quadrants.

I can find the area of a right-angled triangle.

I can find the volume of a cuboid by counting cubes.

6   I can find the area of any triangle, using the formula $A = \dfrac{b \times h}{2}$.

I can find the area of a parallelogram, using the formula $A = b \times h$.

I can find the volume of a cuboid using the formula $V = l \times w \times h$.

National Test questions

1   *2000 Paper 2*

How many kilometres are there in 5 miles?

Copy and complete the missing part of the sign.

Footpath to Hightown
5 miles or ..... kilometres

2   *2002 Paper 1*

A scale measures in grams and in ounces.

Use the scale to answer these questions.

a   About how many ounces is 400 grams?

b   About how many grams is 8 ounces?

c   About how many ounces is 1 kilogram?
Explain your answer.

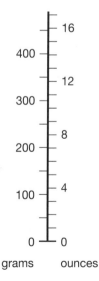

3 *2006 4–6 Paper 1*

a P is the **midpoint** of line AB.

What are the coordinates of point **P**?

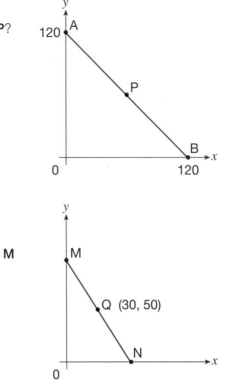

b Q is the **midpoint** of line MN.

The coordinates of Q are (30, 50).

What are the coordinates of points **M** and **N**?

4 *2003 5–7 Paper 2*

An adult needs about **1.8 litres** of water each day to stay healthy.

How many glasses is that?

225 ml

5 *2004 4–6 Paper 2*

The triangle and the rectangle shown have the **same area**.

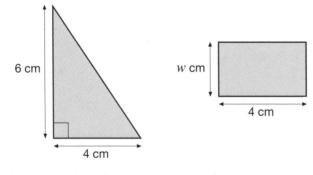

6 cm

4 cm

w cm

4 cm

Work out the value of *w*.

Show your working.

6 *2007 4–6 Paper 2*

The diagram shows a shaded parallelogram drawn inside a rectangle.

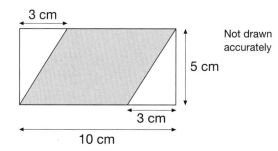

Not drawn accurately

What is the **area** of the shaded parallelogram?

You **must** give the correct unit with your answer.

7 *2002 4–6 Paper 2*

The drawing shows 2 cuboids that have the **same volume**.

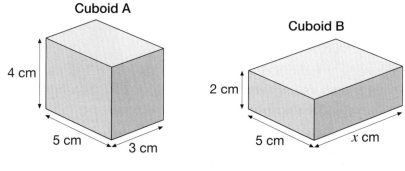

a What is the volume of cuboid A?

Remember to state your units.

b Work out the value of the length marked x.

FM Athletics stadium

An athletics stadium is having a 'face-lift'.

1 The high jump zone is going to be resurfaced.
The zone can be divided into four identical triangles as shown.

   a What is the area of one of the triangles?

   b What is the total area of the high jump zone?

   c Resurfacing costs £60 per square metre.
     What is the cost to resurface the high jump zone?

15 m

15 m

2 A warm-up zone for the athletes is also going to be resurfaced.

The zone is in the shape of a parallelogram as shown.

   a What is the total area of the warm-up zone?

   b Resurfacing costs £48 per square metre.
     What is the cost to resurface the warm-up zone?

40 m

20 m

3 The shot-put, hammer and javelin zones are all going to have new turf.

Each zone is in the shape of a triangle as shown.

Work out the area of each zone.

Shot-put

23 m

17 m

Hammer

75 m

55 m

Javelin

92 m

48 m

4 A new winners' podium is going to be built.

This sketch shows the dimensions.

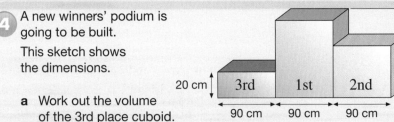

3rd   1st   2nd

20 cm

60 cm

40 cm

80 cm

90 cm   90 cm   90 cm

   a Work out the volume of the 3rd place cuboid.

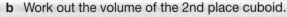

   b Work out the volume of the 2nd place cuboid.

   c Work out the volume of the 1st place cuboid.

   d What is the total volume of the podium?

5 This sketch shows the dimensions of the sandpit for the long jump.

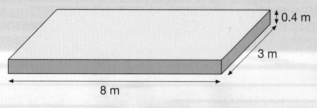

0.4 m

3 m

8 m

a How many cubic metres of sand does the sandpit hold when full?

b 0.6 m³ of sand weighs 1 tonne. How many tonnes of sand are needed to fill the sandpit?

6 A ramp for wheelchair access into the stadium is going to be built.

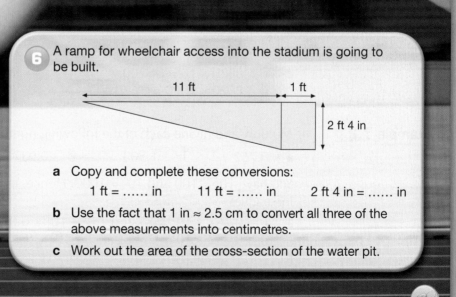

11 ft   1 ft

2 ft 4 in

a Copy and complete these conversions:

1 ft = ... in   11 ft = ... in   2 ft 4 in = ... in

b Use the fact that 1 in ≈ 2.5 cm to convert all three of the above measurements into centimetres.

c Work out the area of the cross-section of the water pit.

<table>
<tr><td colspan="2">

This chapter is going to show you

- How to extend your ability to work with powers of 10
- How to round numbers and use rounded numbers to estimate the results of calculations
- How to write recurring decimals
- How to multiply and divide decimals
- How to use your calculator efficiently
</td><td>

What you should already know

- How to multiply and divide by 10 and 100
- Basic column methods for addition, subtraction, multiplication and division
</td></tr>
</table>

Powers of 10

You have met powers of 10 before. This section will give you more practice at multiplying and dividing by powers of 10. The table shows you some powers of 10.

Power	10^0	10^1	10^2	10^3	10^4
Value	1	10	100	1000	10 000

Example 7.1

Multiply and divide each of the following numbers by: **i** 10 **ii** 1000

a 250 **b** 74 000 **c** 8620

a i $250 \times 10 = 2500$ $250 \div 10 = 25$
ii $250 \times 1000 = 250\,000$ $250 \div 1000 = 0.25$

b i $74\,000 \times 10 = 740\,000$ $74\,000 \div 10 = 7400$
ii $74\,000 \times 1000 = 74\,000\,000$ $74\,000 \div 1000 = 74$

c i $8620 \times 10 = 86\,200$ $8620 \div 10 = 862$
ii $8620 \times 1000 = 8\,620\,000$ $8620 \div 1000 = 8.62$

Example 7.2

Multiply and divide each of the following numbers by: **i** 10^2 **ii** 10^3

a 0.752 **b** 1.508 **c** 0.0371

You have $10^2 = 100$ and $10^3 = 1000$. Hence, multiplying and dividing by each of them gives:

a i $0.752 \times 10^2 = 75.2$; $0.752 \div 10^2 = 0.007\,52$
ii $0.752 \times 10^3 = 752$; $0.752 \div 10^3 = 0.000\,752$

b i $1.508 \times 10^2 = 150.8$; $1.508 \div 10^2 = 0.015\,08$
ii $1.508 \times 10^3 = 1508$; $1.508 \div 10^3 = 0.001\,508$

c i $0.0371 \times 10^2 = 3.71$; $0.0371 \div 10^2 = 0.000\,371$
ii $0.0371 \times 10^3 = 37.1$; $0.0371 \div 10^3 = 0.000\,0371$

Exercise 7A

1 Multiply each of the following numbers by: **i** 10 **ii** 100
   a 9   **b** 73   **c** 124   **d** 810   **e** 3700

2 Divide each of the following numbers by: **i** 10 **ii** 10
   a 9000   **b** 730 000   **c** 1 244 000
   d 34 000   **e** 37 000 000

3 Multiply each of the following numbers by: **i** 10 **ii** 100 **iii** 1000
   a 8.7   **b** 0.32   **c** 103.5   **d** 0.09   **e** 23.06

4 Divide each of the following numbers by: **i** 10 **ii** 100 **iii** 1000
   a 8.7   **b** 0.32   **c** 103.5   **d** 0.09   **e** 23.06

5 Multiply each of the following numbers by: **i** 10 **ii** 10^2
   a 2.7   **b** 0.45   **c** 207   **d** 0.08   **e** 41.7

6 Divide each of the following numbers by: **i** 10 **ii** 10^2
   a 2.7   **b** 0.45   **c** 207   **d** 0.08   **e** 41.7

7 Calculate each of these.
   a 6.34×100 **b** $47.3 \div 100$ **c** 66×1000
   d $2.7 \div 1000$ **e** $3076 \times 10\,000$ **f** $7193 \div 10\,000$
   g 3.76×100 **h** $2.3 \div 100$ **i** 0.09×100
   j $3.09 \div 10$ **k** 2.35×10 **l** $0.01 \div 100$

Extension Work

Multiplying by 0.1 is the same as dividing by 10, and dividing by 0.1 is the same as multiplying by 10.

1 What is multiplying by 0.01 the same as?

2 What is dividing by 0.01 the same as?

3 Now work out each of the following.
   a 39×10^2 **b** $48 \div 10^2$ **c** 5.8×10^3
   d $3.4 \div 10^2$ **e** 5.61×10^3 **f** $0.48 \div 10^2$
   g 0.328×10^3 **h** $0.032 \div 10^2$ **i** $467 \div 10^2$
   j 32.08×10^2 **k** $234 \div 10^3$ **l** 0.009×10^3
   m 9.2×0.1 **n** $0.64 \div 0.1$ **o** 0.84×0.01
   p $8.71 \div 0.01$

Rounding

There are two main uses of rounding. One is to give sensible answers and the other is to help when estimating the answer to a problem.

Example 7.3 ▷ Round each of these numbers to: **i** one decimal place. **ii** two decimal places.

    a   7.822   **b**   8.565   **c**   9.018

    a **i**   7.8 to one decimal place   **ii**   7.82 to two decimal places

    b **i**   8.6 to one decimal place   **ii**   8.57 to two decimal places

    c **i**   9.0 to one decimal place   **ii**   9.02 to two decimal places

Example 7.4 ▷ Estimate the answer to each of the following.

    a   8.9 + 7.3   **b**   6.1 × 3.8

The method is to round each of the numbers to the nearest whole number.

    a   8.9 + 7.3 is approximately 9 + 7 = 16

    b   6.1 × 3.8 is approximately 6 × 4 = 24

Example 7.5 ▷ Estimate the answer to each of the following.

    a   77.1 − 19.9   **b**   89 ÷ 31   **c**   71 × 58

The method is to round each of the numbers to the nearest ten.

    a   77.1 − 19.9 is approximately 80 − 20 = 60

    b   89 ÷ 31 is approximately 90 ÷ 30 = 3

    c   71 × 58 is approximately 70 × 60 = 7 × 6 × 100 = 4200

Exercise 7B

1 Round these numbers to one decimal place.

    a   2.34   **b**   4.57   **c**   3.68   **d**   7.89   **e**   2.09

    f   3.12   **g**   4.58   **h**   3.24   **i**   4.71   **j**   4.55

2 Round these numbers to two decimal places.

    a   2.364   **b**   4.348   **c**   3.231   **d**   7.812

    e   2.092   **f**   3.222   **g**   8.436   **h**   5.678

3 Round each of the following numbers to:

    i   one decimal place.   **ii**   two decimal places.

    a   2.367   **b**   13.0813   **c**   8.907   **d**   20.029

    e   0.999   **f**   4.0599   **g**   0.853   **h**   3.14159

4 Round each number to the nearest whole number and use these answers to estimate the value of each calculation.

a	3.9 + 8.2	**b**	8.3 + 1.7	**c**	7.1 − 1.8	**d**	6.9 − 3.1
e	6.1 × 7.6	**f**	9.2 × 8.9	**g**	7.8 ÷ 1.9	**h**	9.2 ÷ 3.1

5 Round each number to the nearest 10 and use these answers to estimate the value of each calculation.

a	39 + 82	**b**	83 + 17	**c**	71 − 18	**d**	69 − 31
e	61 × 76	**f**	92 × 89	**g**	78 ÷ 19	**h**	92 ÷ 31

Extension Work

Below are four calculations and four exact answers.

Use estimations to match up each calculation to its answer.

8.3 × 3.9	114 ÷ 15	9.3 × 6.1	84 ÷ 3.2
56.73	32.37	26.25	7.6

Multiplying decimals

This section will give you more practice in multiplying integers (whole numbers) and decimals.

Example 7.6 Write down the answer to each of the following, using the fact that 27 × 4 = 108

  a   27 × 0.4   **b**   2.7 × 4   **c**   2.7 × 0.4

  a   There is one decimal place in the multiplication 27 × 0.4, so there is one decimal place in the answer. Therefore you have:

$$27 \times 0.4 = 10.8$$

  b   There is one decimal place in the multiplication 2.7 × 4, so there is one decimal place in the answer. Therefore you have:

$$2.7 \times 4 = 10.8$$

  c   There are two decimal places in the multiplication 2.7 × 0.4, so there are two decimal places in the answer. Therefore you have:

$$2.7 \times 0.4 = 1.08$$

Example 7.7 Find each of the following.

  a   0.3 × 0.05   **b**   900 × 0.4   **c**   50 × 0.04

  a   There are three decimal places in the multiplication, so there are three in the answer. Therefore, you have:

$$0.3 \times 0.05 = 0.015$$

  b   Rewrite as an equivalent product. That is:

$$900 \times 0.4 = 90 \times 4 = 360$$

  c   As in part **b**, giving: 50 × 0.04 = 5 × 0.4 = 2

Example 7.8 ▷ Without using a calculator, work out 134 × 0.6.

There are several ways to do this. Three are shown (a column method and two box methods). Whichever method you use, you should first estimate the answer:

134 × 0.6 ≈ 100 × 0.6 = 60

Remember also that there is one decimal place in the product, so there will be one in the answer.

In the first two methods, the decimal points are ignored in the multiplication and then placed in the answer.

Column method
```
    134
  ×   6
    804
    ₂ ₂
```

Box method 1

	100	30	4	Total
6	600	180	24	804

Box method 2

	100	30	4	Total
0.6	60	18	2.4	80.4

By all three methods the answer is 80.4.

Exercise 7C

Do not use a calculator to answer any of these questions.

1 Write down the answers to each of the following, using the fact that 83 × 24 = 1992

   a 8.3 × 24   **b** 83 × 2.4   **c** 8.3 × 2.4   **d** 0.83 × 0.24

2 Write down the answers to each of the following, using the fact that 250 × 32 = 8000

   a 2.5 × 32   **b** 250 × 3.2   **c** 2.5 × 3.2   **d** 2.5 × 0.32

3 Work out each of the following.

   a 2.6 × 5   **b** 3.4 × 6   **c** 4.91 × 4   **d** 6.12 × 5

   e 31.5 × 7   **f** 22.4 × 8   **g** 14.6 × 6   **h** 19.1 × 4

4 Work out each of the following.

   a 10 × 0.5   **b** 0.7 × 10   **c** 0.3 × 100   **d** 0.6 × 10

   e 10 × 0.7   **f** 0.8 × 100   **g** 100 × 0.1   **h** 0.4 × 100

5 Work out each of the following.

   a 40 × 0.5   **b** 0.7 × 20   **c** 0.3 × 200   **d** 0.6 × 50

   e 40 × 0.7   **f** 0.8 × 300   **g** 400 × 0.1   **h** 0.4 × 500

6 Work out the answer to each of these.

   a 0.3 × 0.6   **b** 0.5 × 0.5   **c** 0.9 × 0.7   **d** 0.6 × 0.6

   e 0.9 × 0.8   **f** 0.7 × 0.6   **g** 0.5 × 0.8   **h** 0.4 × 0.4

   i 0.7 × 0.7   **j** 0.9 × 0.3   **k** 0.4 × 0.8   **l** 0.3 × 0.2

7 a Without using a calculator work out the answer to 123 × 4.

   b Use your answer to part **a** to write down the answers to the following.

      i 1.23 × 0.4   **ii** 12.3 × 0.04

1 Work out each of the following.

 a 0.7 × 0.7

 b 0.3 × 0.3

 c 0.7 × 0.7 − 0.3 × 0.3

 d 0.7 − 0.3

2 What do you notice about your answers to questions 1c and 1d?

3 Repeat using two other decimals which add up to 1 (for example 0.8 and 0.2, or 0.87 and 0.13)

 See if you can guess the answers.

Dividing decimals

This section will give you more practice in dividing integers (whole numbers) and decimals.

Example 7.9 Work out each of these.

 a 0.8 ÷ 2 b 0.12 ÷ 3 c 27.5 ÷ 5 d 17.4 ÷ 4

 a There is one decimal place in the division 0.8 ÷ 2, so there is one decimal place in the answer. Therefore you have:

 0.8 ÷ 2 = 0.4

 b There are two decimal places in the division 0.12 ÷ 3, so there are two decimal places in the answer. Therefore you have:

 0.12 ÷ 3 = 0.04

 c There is one decimal place in the division 27.5 ÷ 5, so there is one decimal place in the answer. Therefore you have:

 27.5 ÷ 5 = 5.5

 d To complete the calculation without a remainder you have to work out 17.40 ÷ 4 so there are two decimal places in the division 17.40 ÷ 4, so there are two decimal places in the answer. Therefore you have:

 17.40 ÷ 4 = 4.35

Exercise 7D **Do not use a calculator to answer any of these questions.**

1 Work out each of the following.

 a 0.6 ÷ 3 b 0.9 ÷ 3 c 2.4 ÷ 4 d 3.5 ÷ 5

 e 2.1 ÷ 7 f 4.8 ÷ 8 g 5.4 ÷ 9 h 6.4 ÷ 8

2 Work out each of the following.

 a 0.36 ÷ 2 b 0.45 ÷ 5 c 0.16 ÷ 4 d 0.45 ÷ 9

 e 0.24 ÷ 6 f 0.81 ÷ 9 g 0.63 ÷ 7 h 0.56 ÷ 8

3 Work out each of the following.

   a $2.42 \div 2$ **b** $3.25 \div 5$ **c** $6.44 \div 4$ **d** $8.55 \div 9$

   e $5.22 \div 6$ **f** $8.01 \div 9$ **g** $4.27 \div 7$ **h** $2.56 \div 8$

4 Work out each of the following.

   a $18.02 \div 2$ **b** $37.95 \div 5$ **c** $23.04 \div 4$ **d** $49.14 \div 9$

   e $18.36 \div 6$ **f** $99.18 \div 9$ **g** $16.52 \div 7$ **h** $10.24 \div 8$

5 The perimeter of a square is 4.32 cm. Work out the length of one side.

6 Eight cakes cost £3.76.

   How much does one cake cost?

Extension **Work**

1 Given that $548 \div 8 = 68.5$, work out each of these.

   a $548 \div 80$ **b** $5480 \div 8$ **c** $54.8 \div 8$

2 Given that $1380 \div 3 = 460$, work out each of these.

   a $138 \div 3$ **b** $13.8 \div 3$ **c** $1380 \div 30$

Efficient use of calculators

It is important that you know how to use your calculator. You should be able to use the basic functions ($\times$, $\div$, $+$, $-$) and the square, square root and brackets keys. You have also met the memory and sign-change keys. This exercise introduces the fraction and power keys.

Example 7.10

Use a calculator to work out:

a $4.7 \div (7.5 + 2.3)$ **b** $\dfrac{2.1 + 3.2}{0.2}$ **c** $\frac{1}{2} + \frac{2}{5}$ **d** $\sqrt{2.16 + 0.09}$

a Key in the calculation as it is written: $4 . 7 \div (7 . 5 + 2 . 3) =$

    The display will either show the fraction $\frac{47}{98}$ or the decimal 0.4795918367.

b There are two ways to key in this calculation:

    using the brackets keys in the calculation: $(2 . 1 + 3 . 2) \div 0 . 2$

    … or, using the fraction button: ▪⬚⁄⬚ / ▪⁄⬚

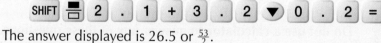

    The answer displayed is 26.5 or $\frac{53}{2}$.

c Key in the following:

    SHIFT ⬚⁄⬚ 1 ▼ 2 ▶ + ⬚⁄⬚ 2 ▼ 5 =

    The answer displayed is $\frac{9}{10}$.

d Key in the following:

    √▪ (2 . 1 6 + 0 . 0 9) =

    The answer displayed is 1.5.

Exercise 7E — Use your calculator to work out each of these questions.

1 Use a calculator to work these out.

a $(3.6 + 8.1) \div 1.5$ b $6.4 - (4.1 \times 2.5)$ c $(2.1 + 9.6) - (3.4 + 4.7)$

d $5.75 \div (4.6 - 2.1)$ e $3.4 + \sqrt{144}$ f $\sqrt{121} - 11$

g $(3.5 + 2.3)^2$ h $(19.8 - 3.46)^2$

2 Use a calculator to work these out.

a $\dfrac{2.6 + 3.6}{0.2}$ b $\dfrac{20.3 - 5.7}{0.1}$ c $\dfrac{6.9 + 1.5}{0.5 + 0.6}$

d $\dfrac{5.6}{0.8} + 2.5$ e $19.7 - \dfrac{64}{0.4}$

3 Use a calculator to work these out.

a $\frac{1}{2} + \frac{1}{3}$ b $\frac{2}{7} + \frac{4}{5}$ c $\frac{5}{8} - \frac{4}{13}$ d $5.6 + \frac{17}{20}$

4 Use a calculator to work these out.

a $\sqrt{1024}$ b 25^2 c $84^2 + \sqrt{6889}$

d $\sqrt{1522756} - 35^2$ e $\sqrt{9876} + 1149$ f $\sqrt{874} - 145$

g $\sqrt{7^2 + 24^2}$ h $\sqrt{61^2 - 60^2}$

Extension Work

Find the calculator button with ○'''. This can be used for calculations with time.

To put 2 hours 15 minutes into your calculator, key in:

[2] [○'''] [1] [5] [○'''] [=]

Now try to work out the following.

a Add 3 hours and 15 minutes to 2 hours and 50 minutes.

b Subtract 1 hour and 55 minutes from 3 hours and 25 minutes.

c Multiply 1 hour and 20 minutes by 4.

Solving problems

Example 7.11 ▷ Which jar of jam offers the better value?

The larger jar is four times bigger than the smaller jar.

So four small jars would cost 4 × 89p = £3.56

One large jar costs £3.59.

So the smaller jar is better value.

Example 7.12 ▶ A box contains 12 identical toy cars:

Each toy has 4 lights.
Each toy weighs 200 g.
The box weighs 150 g.

a How many lights are there altogether?

b If 3 cars are removed, what is the total weight of the box and its contents?

a 12 cars with 4 lights each = 12 × 4 = 48 lights.

b If 3 cars are removed, there are 9 left.
The cars weigh 9 × 200 g = 1800 g
The box weighs 150 g
So the total weight = 1800 + 150 = 1950 g

Exercise 7F

1 Find two odd numbers that add up to 48.

2 The product of 2 and 3 is 6, because 2 × 3 = 6. Work out the product of 6 and 7.

FM 3 A cupboard space is 70 cm high. Tins are 15 cm high. How many layers of tins will fit in the cupboard?

4 Here is a rule for the number grids.
Use the rule to fill in the missing numbers.

This number is the difference of the numbers on the bottom line. ⟶

	2	
8		6

a

	......	
22		17

b

	......	
2		−3

c

	8	
15		......

d

	15	
......		......

FM 5 Yogurts are sold individually for 35p. They are also sold in multipacks of 6 for £1.99. Which is cheaper?

6 The total age of two brothers is 110 years. The difference in their ages is 4 years. How old is the younger brother?

7 There are 5 blue, 3 red and 2 white counters in a bag.
The counters are numbered from 1 to 10. Each counter weighs 6 g.
Match each statement to the correct calculation:

The weight of the odd numbered counters		10 × 6
The total weight of the counters		(5 + 3) × 6
The weight of the counters that are blue or red		5 × 6

FM **8** A photocopying company charges 5p per sheet. How many sheets can be photocopied for £3?

9 Olivia is twice as old as Jack. The sum of their ages is 36 years. How old are they?

FM **10** There are 600 people in a building. Half of them are men and one third of them are women. What fraction are children?

Extension **Work**

Here is a magic square.
All the rows and columns add up to 34.
Complete the magic square

There are lots of ways of making 34 in this magic square using patterns of 4 numbers.
For example, 9 + 7 + 4 + 14 = 34 or 3 + 8 + 9 + 14 = 34.

How many ways can you find to make 34?

	2	3	
5			
9	7	6	12
4	14		1

LEVEL BOOSTER

4
I can add and subtract decimals with up to two decimal places.
I can round numbers to the nearest 10, 100 and 1000.

5
I can multiply and divide by simple powers of 10.
I can round numbers to one decimal place.
I can use the brackets, square and square root keys on my calculator.

6
I can round numbers to two or more decimal places.
I can use the power and roots buttons on my calculator.

1 *2007 3–5 Paper 2*

Here is some information about some bags of marbles:

Altogether, there are 10 bags

Each bag contains 12 marbles

Each marble weighs 7 grams

Use the information to match each question below with the correct calculation.
The first one is done for you.

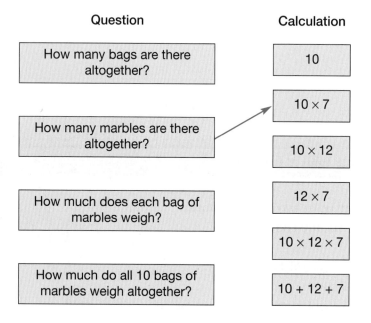

Question
How many bags are there altogether?
How many marbles are there altogether?
How much does each bag of marbles weigh?
How much do all 10 bags of marbles weigh altogether?

Calculation

10

10 × 7

10 × 12

12 × 7

10 × 12 × 7

10 + 12 + 7

2 *2001 4–6 Paper 1*

The table shows the approximate populations of five different places:

Place	Approximate population
London	7 000 000
Sheffield	700 000
Harrogate	70 000
Ash Vale	7000
Binbrook	700

a Which of these places has a population of about **seventy thousand**?

b Use the table to complete these sentences:

The population of **Harrogate** is about **10 times** as big as the population of ......

The population of ...... is about **100** times as big as the population of **Harrogate**.

The population of **Sheffield** is about ...... times as big as the population of **Ash Vale**.

3 *2002 Paper 1*

a Peter's height is 0.9 m. Lucy is 0.3 m taller than Peter. What is Lucy's height?

b Lee's height is 1.45 m. Misha is 0.3 m shorter than Lee. What is Misha's height?

c Zita's height is 1.7 m. What is Zita's height in centimetres?

FM **4** *2002 Paper 2*

Some people use yards to measure length.

The diagram shows one way to change yards to metres.

Number of yards — × 36 — × 2.54 — ÷ 100 — Number of metres

a Change 100 yards to metres.

b Change 100 metres to yards.

Show your working.

5 *2006 5–7 Paper 1*

a Show that **9 × 28 is 252**.

b What is **27 × 28**?

You can use part **a** to help you.

FM **6** *2006 5–7 Paper 2*

A shop sells toilet rolls.

You can buy them in packs of 9 or packs of 6.

Which pack gives you better value for money?

You **must** show your working.

Pack of 9 toilet rolls
£3.90

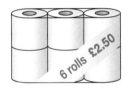

Pack of 6 toilet rolls
£2.50

9 rolls £3.90

6 rolls £2.50

7 *2007 5–7 Paper 2*

The value of π correct to 7 decimal places is **3.1415927**.

a Write the value of π correct to **4 decimal places**.

b Which value below is closest to the value of π?

$$\frac{179}{57} \qquad 3\frac{1}{7} \qquad \left(\frac{16}{9}\right)^2 \qquad \frac{355}{113}$$

8 *2006 5–7 Paper 1*

a Put these values in order of size with the **smallest first**:

$5^2 \qquad 3^2 \qquad 3^3 \qquad 2^2$

b Look at this information:

5^5 is 3125

What is 5^7?

FM Paper

Paper sizes

Standard paper sizes are called A0, A1, A2 and so on.
A0 is approximately 1188 mm by 840 mm.
The next size A1 is found by cutting A0 in half.

Here is a diagram of a piece of paper of size A0.

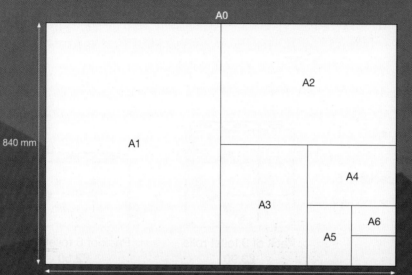

Paper for sale

1 ream = 500 sheets

Reams of Paper – Special offer

Grade of paper	Prices		
	1 ream	5–9 reams	10+ reams
Standard	£2.10	SAVE $\frac{1}{3}$ per ream	EXTRA 10% discount
Special	£1.80		
Quality	£3.00		
Photo	£3.60		

Example for Standard paper:

1 ream costs £2.10
5 reams at full price = 5 × £2.10 = £10.50
Saving = $\frac{1}{3}$ of £10.50 = £3.50
Cost of 5 reams = £7.00
10 reams with $\frac{1}{3}$ off = 2 × £7.00 = £14.00
Extra 10% discount = £1.40
Cost of 10 reams = £12.60

Buy 5 reams
You save
£3.50

Buy 10 reams
You save
£8.40

1 How many sheets of paper are there in 5 reams of paper?

2 The thickness of a piece of paper is 0.1 mm.
How high would 2 reams (1000 sheets) of this paper be?
Give your answer in centimetres.

3 Here is a table of paper sizes.

Paper size	A0	A1	A2	A3	A4	A5
Length (mm)	1188	840	.594			
Width (mm)	840	594				

Copy and complete the table.
Check your result for A4 paper by measuring.

4 How many pieces of A4 paper would be needed to make a piece of A1 paper?

5 Look at the special offers and work out the cost of:
a 3 reams of Special grade paper.
b 5 reams of Quality grade paper.
c 10 reams of Photo grade paper.

6 Work out the saving if you buy 20 reams of Quality grade paper using the offers.

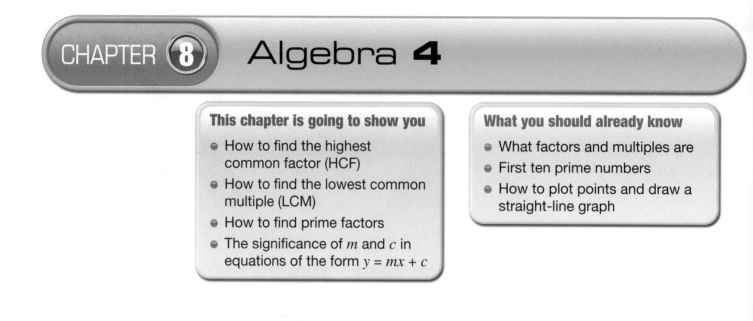

This chapter is going to show you

- How to find the highest common factor (HCF)
- How to find the lowest common multiple (LCM)
- How to find prime factors
- The significance of m and c in equations of the form $y = mx + c$

What you should already know

- What factors and multiples are
- First ten prime numbers
- How to plot points and draw a straight-line graph

LCM and HCF

Look at these diagrams.

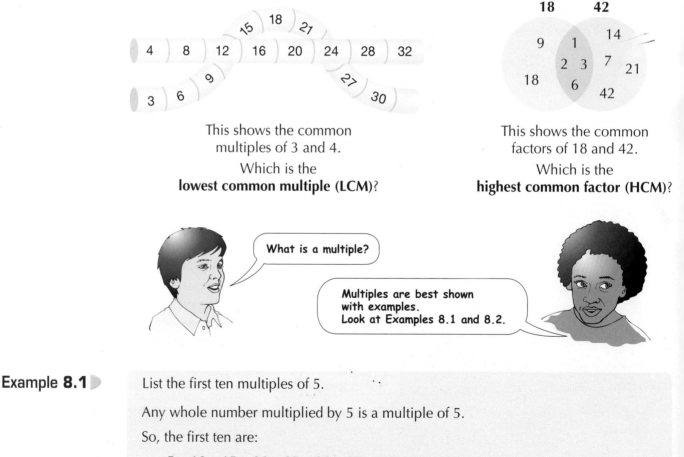

| | | 18 | 42 |

This shows the common multiples of 3 and 4.

Which is the **lowest common multiple (LCM)**?

This shows the common factors of 18 and 42.

Which is the **highest common factor (HCM)**?

What is a multiple?

Multiples are best shown with examples.
Look at Examples 8.1 and 8.2.

Example 8.1 ▷ List the first ten multiples of 5.

Any whole number multiplied by 5 is a multiple of 5.

So, the first ten are:

5   10   15   20   25   30   35   40   45   50

Example 8.2 ▷ Is 105 a multiple of 3?

If 105 can be divided by 3 exactly, it must be a multiple of 3.

Now, 105 ÷ 3 = 35. Hence, 105 is a multiple of 3.

Lowest common multiple (LCM)

Any pair of numbers has many common multiples. The lowest of these is called the LCM. This can be found by listing the first few multiples of both numbers until you see the first common number.

Example 8.3 ▷ Find the LCM of 6 and 8.

Write out the first few multiples of each number:

6 12 18 **24** 30 36 42 **48** 54 …

8 16 **24** 32 40 **48** 56 …

You can see which are the common multiples, the lowest of which is 24.

So, **24** is the LCM of 6 and 8.

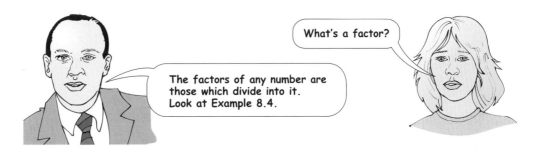

What's a factor?

The factors of any number are those which divide into it. Look at Example 8.4.

Example 8.4 ▷ Write down the factors of 24.

The factors are best found in pairs, for example:

1 × 24 2 × 12 3 × 8 4 × 6

Putting these into numerical order gives:

1 2 3 4 6 8 12 24

Highest common factor (HCF)

The highest common factor of two numbers is found by following these three steps.

- List the factors of each number.
- Look for and list the common factors.
- Look for the highest common factor in this list.

Example 8.5 ▷ Find the HCF of 18 and 42.

List the factors of each number:

1 **2** **3** **6** 9 18

1 **2** **3** **6** 7 14 21 42

You can see that the HCF of 18 and 42 is **6**.

Exercise 8A

1 Write down the numbers in the list below which are multiples of the following.

   a 2   **b** 3   **c** 5   **d** 9

         12   6   21   20   63   88   9   55   27   4   65

2 Write down the first 10 multiples of the following numbers.

   a 3   **b** 5   **c** 7   **d** 10   **e** 12

3 Write down all the factors of the following numbers.

   a 4   **b** 21   **c** 27   **d** 30   **e** 36

4 Use your answers to Question **2** to help you to find the LCM of the following pairs.

   a 3 and 5   **b** 5 and 10   **c** 7 and 10   **d** 10 and 12

5 Use your answers to Question **3** to help you to find the HCF of the following pairs.

   a 12 and 21   **b** 12 and 36   **c** 25 and 30   **d** 27 and 36

6 Find the LCM of the following pairs.

   a 3 and 7   **b** 6 and 12   **c** 4 and 7   **d** 8 and 12

   e 9 and 15   **f** 8 and 20   **g** 9 and 30   **h** 10 and 15

7 Find the HCF of the following pairs.

   a 16 and 20   **b** 8 and 30   **c** 10 and 15   **d** 20 and 24

   e 3 and 12   **f** 6 and 16   **g** 27 and 36   **h** 30 and 45

8 **a** What is the HCF and LCM of the pairs below?

     i 3, 5   **ii** 4, 7   **iii** 3, 8

   b Two numbers, x and y, have an HCF of 1. What is the LCM of x and y?

Extension Work

1 What is the HCF and LCM of the pairs below?

   a 4, 8   **b** 5, 10   **c** 6, 12

   d 8, 16   **e** 7, 14

2 In Question 1, the second number in each pair is twice the first number.
What is the HCF and LCM of x and $2x$?

3 What is the HCF and LCM of the pairs below?

   a 4, 6   **b** 8, 12   **c** 6, 9

   d 10, 15   **e** 12, 18   **f** 14, 21

4 In Question 3, the second number in each pair is one and a half times
the first number.
What is the HCF and LCM of x and $\frac{3}{2}x$?

Powers and roots

Square numbers

The area of a square whose sides have a le[ngth] which is written as x^2. This is why x^2 is called 'x [squared]' or the 'square of x'. Hence, when any number is multiplied by [itself, the] answer is called the **square of the number** or the **number s[quared]**.

As with x^2, the short way to write the square of any number is, for example:

6 squared $= (6 \times 6) = 6^2$

13 squared $= (13 \times 13) = 13^2$

Square roots

Taking the **square root** is the inverse (opposite) of squaring. Hence, the square root of any given number is a number which, when multiplied by itself, produces the given number.

A square root is shown by the sign $\sqrt{\ }$. For example, $\sqrt{9} = 3$

square

5 ⟶ 25

square root

Example 8.6

Since $5^2 = 25$, then $\sqrt{25} = 5$

$9^2 = 81$, then $\sqrt{81} = 9$

$11^2 = 121$, then $\sqrt{121} = 11$

Cubed numbers

The volume of a cube whose sides have a length of x is $x \times x \times x$, which is written as x^3. This is why x^3 is called 'x cubed' or the cube of x. Hence, when any number is multiplied by itself, and again by itself, the answer is called the **cube of the number** or the **number cubed**.

Volume x^3

Cube roots

Taking the **cube root** is the inverse (opposite) of cubing. Hence the cube root of any given number is a number which, when multiplied by itself twice, produces the given number.

A cube root is shown by the sign $\sqrt[3]{\ }$. For example, $\sqrt[3]{27} = 3$

cube

4 ⟶ 64

cube root

Example 8.7

Since $2^3 = 8$, then $\sqrt[3]{8} = 2$

$5^3 = 125$, then $\sqrt[3]{125} = 5$

Example 8.8

Work out each of these: **a** 7^2 **b** 5^3

a $7^2 = 7 \times 7 = 49$

b $5^3 = 5 \times 5 \times 5 = 125$

... by itself, makes 100. It is 10.

... the following:

... = 8 $3 \times 3 \times 3 = 27$ $4 \times 4 \times 4 = 64$

Area x^2

... 7 show a square and a cube, both with a side length of x.
... table.

	1 cm	2 cm	3 cm	4 cm	5 cm	6 cm	7 cm	8 cm	9 cm	10 cm
	1 cm²									
...ube	1 cm³									

... table in Question **1** to work out each of the following.

                b $\sqrt{4}$ **c** $\sqrt{9}$ **d** $\sqrt{36}$ **e** $\sqrt{49}$

f $\sqrt[3]{1}$ **g** $\sqrt[3]{27}$ **h** $\sqrt[3]{216}$ **i** $\sqrt[3]{8}$ **j** $\sqrt[3]{343}$

3 Find the positive value of x that makes each of the following equations true.

  a $x^2 = 25$ **b** $x^2 = 49$ **c** $x^2 = 81$ **d** $x^2 = 1$

  e $x^2 = 121$ **f** $x^2 = 64$ **g** $x^2 = 100$ **h** $x^2 = 1\,000\,000$

4 Find the value of each of the following.

  a $11^2 + 11^3$ **b** $12^2 + 12^3$ **c** $13^2 + 13^3$

5 For each number in the circle, match it with its square root in the rectangle.
Pair them up and write down as for example, $\sqrt{100} = 10$.

19	18	13	14
15	21	20	17
22	16	12	

400 196
324 256
225 361
289

6 **a** Explain how you can tell that $\sqrt{12}$ is between 3 and 4.
  b Explain how you can tell that $\sqrt{40}$ is between 6 and 7.
  c What two consecutive whole numbers is $\sqrt{60}$ between?
  d What two consecutive whole numbers is $\sqrt{90}$ between?

7 **a** Explain how you can tell that $\sqrt[3]{5}$ is between 1 and 2.
  b Explain how you can tell that $\sqrt[3]{19}$ is between 2 and 3.
  c What two consecutive whole numbers is $\sqrt[3]{100}$ between?
  d What two consecutive whole numbers is $\sqrt[3]{50}$ between?

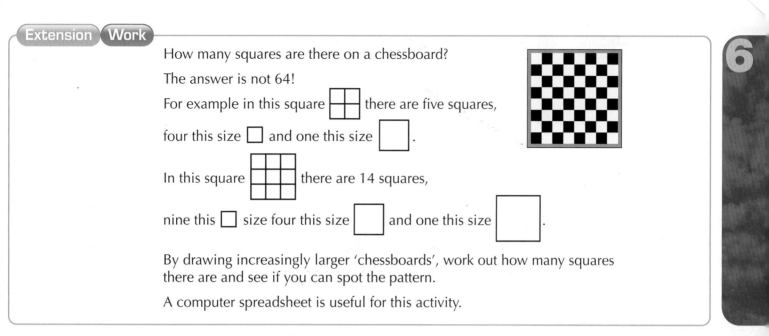

How many squares are there on a chessboard?

The answer is not 64!

For example in this square there are five squares,

four this size and one this size .

In this square there are 14 squares,

nine this size four this size and one this size .

By drawing increasingly larger 'chessboards', work out how many squares there are and see if you can spot the pattern.

A computer spreadsheet is useful for this activity.

Prime factors

A prime number can only be divided exactly by itself and one. The first 10 prime numbers are: 2, 3, 5, 7, 11, 13, 17, 19, 23, 29. You need to know these.

The prime factors of a number are the prime numbers which, when multiplied together, give that number.

There are two ways to find prime factors.

Example 8.10

Find the prime factors of 12.

Using a prime factor tree, split 12 into 3×4.

Since 4 can be split into 2×2, this gives:
$$12 = 3 \times 2 \times 2$$

Use powers to simplify the answer:
$$12 = 3 \times 2^2$$

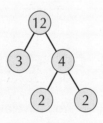

Example 8.11

Find the prime factors of 40.

Use the divide method. That is, dividing by the smallest prime number:

$$
\begin{array}{c|c}
2 & 40 \\
2 & 20 \\
2 & 10 \\
5 & 5 \\
\hline
 & 1
\end{array}
$$

So, $40 = 2 \times 2 \times 2 \times 5$ which gives $2^3 \times 5$ (again using powers to simplify the answer)

1 These are the prime factors of different numbers. What are the numbers?

a $2 \times 2 \times 5$ b $2 \times 3 \times 3$ c $3 \times 3 \times 5$ d $2 \times 3 \times 5$

e $2 \times 2 \times 2 \times 5$ f $2 \times 3 \times 3 \times 5$ g $2 \times 2 \times 5 \times 5$ h $2 \times 3 \times 5 \times 5$

2 What numbers are represented by each of the following sets of prime factors?

a $2^3 \times 7$ b $2^2 \times 3^2$ c $2 \times 3^2 \times 5$ d 3×5^2

3 Use a prime factor tree to find the prime factors of each of the following numbers.

a 15   b 20   c 24   d 32   e 35
f 18   g 21   h 28   i 36   j 45

4 Use the division method to find the prime factors of each of the following numbers.

a 160   b 144   c 90   d 150   e 196
f 180   g 216   h 108   i 126   j 450

Extension Work

The prime numbers less than 100 are 2, 3, 5, 7, 11, 13, 17, 19, 23, 29, 31, 37, 41, 43, 47, 53, 61, 67, 71, 73, 79, 83, 89, 91 and 97.

1   How many prime numbers less than 100 are one more than a multiple of 6 (for example, 13)?

2   How many prime numbers less than 100 are one less than a multiple of 6 (for example, 11)?

3   How many prime numbers less than 100 are neither one less nor one more than a multiple of 6?

4   What do the answers to parts **1**, **2** and **3** suggest about prime numbers greater than 3?

Graphs of equations of the form $y = mx + c$

You have already met graphs plotted from functions with the form $y = mx + c$, where m and c are any numbers (see pages 44–46). These are always straight-line graphs.

Example 8.12

Draw a graph of the equation $y = 3x + 1$.

First, construct a table of easy values for x as shown below.

x	0	1	2	3
$y = 3x + 1$	1	4	7	10

Next, draw the axes on graph paper. Mark the values for x on the horizontal axis, and those for y on the vertical axis.

Then plot the points given in the table, and join them with a straight line.

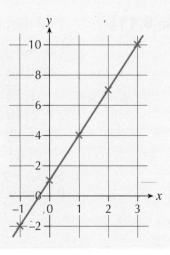

Exercise 8D

Each question in this exercise is a short investigation into the positions of the graphs of equations written in the form $y = mx + c$. After completing the investigations, you should find something very important and useful about the values of m and c, which will help you to see where the straight-line graph lies for each equation.

1 **a** Copy and complete the table for the equations shown.

b Draw a grid with its x-axis from 0 to 3 and its y-axis from 0 to 7.

c Draw the graph for each equation in the table.

d What do you notice about each graph?

x	0	1	2	3
$y = x + 1$	1			
$y = x + 2$		3		
$y = x + 3$			5	
$y = x + 4$				7

e Use what you have noticed to draw the graphs of these equations.
  i $y = x + 5$ **ii** $y = x + 0.5$

2 **a** Copy and complete the table for the equations shown.

b Draw a grid with its x-axis from 0 to 3 and its y-axis from 0 to 10.

c Draw the graph for each equation in the table.

d What do you notice about each graph?

x	0	1	2	3
$y = 2x + 1$	1	3		7
$y = 2x + 2$		4		
$y = 2x + 3$			7	
$y = 2x + 4$				10

e If you draw a graph of $y = mx + c$, where m and c are any numbers, what does the value of c tell you about the straight-line graph?

f Use what you have noticed to draw the graphs of these equations.
  i $y = 2x + 5$ **ii** $y = 2x + 0.5$

3 **a** Copy and complete the table for the equations shown.

b Draw a grid with its x-axis from 0 to 3 and its y-axis from 0 to 12.

c Draw the graph for each equation in the table.

d What do you notice about each graph?

x	0	1	2	3
$y = x$	0	1		
$y = 2x$		2		
$y = 3x$			6	
$y = 4x$				12

e Use what you have noticed to draw the graphs of these equations.
  i $y = 5x$ **ii** $y = 0.5x$

4 **a** Copy and complete the table for the equations shown.

b Draw a grid with its x-axis from 0 to 3 and its y-axis from 0 to 16.

c Draw the graph for each equation in the table.

d What do you notice about each graph?

x	0	1	2	3
$y = x + 4$	4			
$y = 2x + 4$		6		
$y = 3x + 4$			10	
$y = 4x + 4$				16

e If you draw a graph of $y = mx + c$, where m and c are any numbers, what does the value of m tell you about the straight-line graph?

f Use what you have noticed to draw the graphs of these equations.
  i $y = 5x + 4$ **ii** $y = 0.5x + 4$

Extension Work

The line $x + y = 6$ passes through points (0, 6), (1, 5), (2, 4), (3, 3), (4, 2), (5, 1), (6, 0).

Draw axes with x and y from 0 to 10.

Plot the points above and join them up.

Now find six points that the line $x + y = 5$ passes through
Hint: Start with (0, 5)) and plot these on the same graph.

You should now be able to draw, without plotting any points, the lines
$x + y = 10$ and $x + y = 3$.

LEVEL BOOSTER

4
I can write down the multiples of any whole number.
I can work out the factors of numbers under 100.

5
I can write down and recognise the sequence of square numbers.
I know the squares of all numbers up to 15^2 and the corresponding square roots.
I know the cubes of 1, 2, 3, 4, 5 and 10 and the corresponding cube roots.
I can use a calculator to work out powers of numbers.
I know that the square roots of positive numbers can have two values, one positive and one negative, for example $\sqrt{36} = +6$ or -6.
I can write down the highest common factor of a pair of numbers such as 6 and 8.

6
I can find the lowest common multiple (LCM) for pairs of numbers; for example, the LCM of 24 and 30 is 120.
I can find the highest common factor (HCF) for pairs of numbers; for example, the HCF of 24 and 30 is 6.
I can write a number as the product of its prime factors; for example, $24 = 2 \times 2 \times 2 \times 3 = 2^3 \times 3$.

1 *2002 Paper 1*

There are four different ways to put 6 students into equal-size groups.

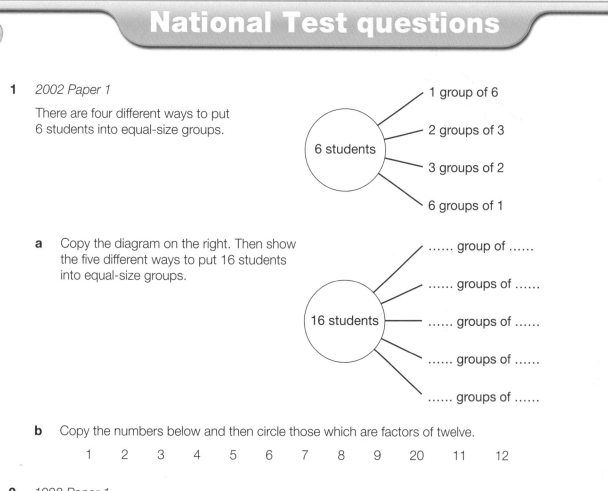

6 students

1 group of 6

2 groups of 3

3 groups of 2

6 groups of 1

a Copy the diagram on the right. Then show the five different ways to put 16 students into equal-size groups.

16 students

...... group of ......

...... groups of ......

...... groups of ......

...... groups of ......

...... groups of ......

b Copy the numbers below and then circle those which are factors of twelve.

1   2   3   4   5   6   7   8   9   20   11   12

2 *1998 Paper 1*

A jigsaw has three different sorts of piece.

Corner pieces,
with 2 straight sides

Edge pieces,
with 1 straight side

Middle pieces,
with 0 straight sides

a This jigsaw has 24 pieces altogether, in 4 rows of 6. Copy and complete the table below to show how many of each sort of piece this jigsaw has.

Corner pieces:	......
Edge pieces:	......
Middle pieces:	......
	Total: 24

b Another jigsaw has 42 pieces altogether, in 6 rows of 7. Copy and complete the table below to show how many of each sort of piece this jigsaw has.

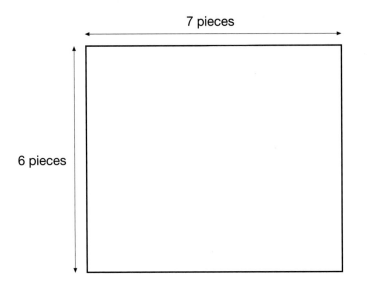

7 pieces

6 pieces

Corner pieces:	
Edge pieces:	
Middle pieces:	
Total: 42	

c A square jigsaw has 64 middle pieces.

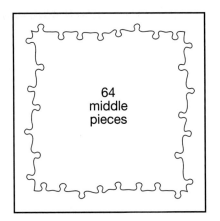

64 middle pieces

Corner pieces:	
Edge pieces:	
Middle pieces: 64	
Total:	

Copy and complete the table above to show how many of each sort of piece the square jigsaw has, and the total number of pieces.

Remember that the total must be a square number.

3 *2006 3–5 Paper 1*

a I am thinking of a number.
My number is a **multiple of 4**.

Which of the statements below is true?
- My number must be even
- My number must be odd
- My number could be odd or even

Explain how you know.

b I am thinking of a **different** number.
My number is a **factor of 20**.

Which of the statements below is true?
- My number must be even
- My number must be odd
- My number could be odd or even

Explain how you know.

FM Packages

Maximum package dimensions

The Post Office will only accept packages that follow the following rules.

Regular cuboidal packages

The length (greatest dimension) cannot be longer than 1.5 m.

The girth is the distance around the package (2 × width + 2 × height).

The girth and the length put together must not exceed 3 m in total.

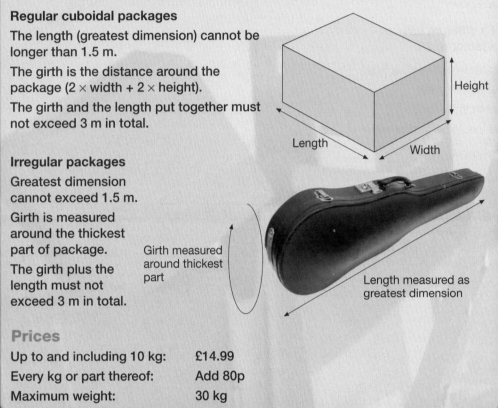

Irregular packages

Greatest dimension cannot exceed 1.5 m.

Girth is measured around the thickest part of package.

The girth plus the length must not exceed 3 m in total.

Girth measured around thickest part

Length measured as greatest dimension

Prices

Up to and including 10 kg:	£14.99
Every kg or part thereof:	Add 80p
Maximum weight:	30 kg

Use the information above to answer these questions.

1 For each of the following cuboidal packages:
   i write down the length.   **ii** work out the girth.   **iii** work out length plus girth.

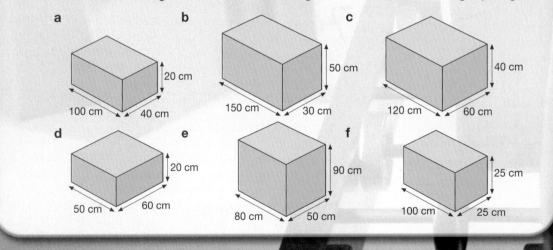

a 20 cm, 100 cm, 40 cm

b 50 cm, 150 cm, 30 cm

c 40 cm, 120 cm, 60 cm

d 20 cm, 50 cm, 60 cm

e 90 cm, 80 cm, 50 cm

f 25 cm, 100 cm, 25 cm

2 Which of the packages in Question 1 would not be acceptable to the Post Office?

3 Cubes have the same length, width and height.
Work out the value of length plus girth for cubes with sides of:

  a 20 cm   **b** 25 cm   **c** 30 cm

  d 40 cm   **e** 50 cm   **f** 60 cm

d cm
d cm   *d* cm

4 For each of the cuboidal packages in the following table say whether it is acceptable to the Post Office.
If it is not, give a reason why.

Package	Weight	Length	Width	Height
A	15 kg	1.2 m	70 cm	20 cm
B	22 kg	160 cm	30 cm	20 cm
C	10 kg	110 cm	80 cm	10 cm
D	40 kg	90 cm	50 cm	20 cm
E	16 kg	80 cm	60 cm	30 cm
F	20 kg	90 cm	70 cm	40 cm
G	32 kg	1 m	60 cm	60 cm
H	3000 g	1.8 m	20 cm	20 cm
I	4 kg	50 cm	50 cm	50 cm
J	18 kg	140 cm	50 cm	30 cm

5 For each of the acceptable packages in Question 1, work out the cost of postage.

6 Each of the following cuboidal packages is at the limit of acceptability.
Work out the missing dimension.

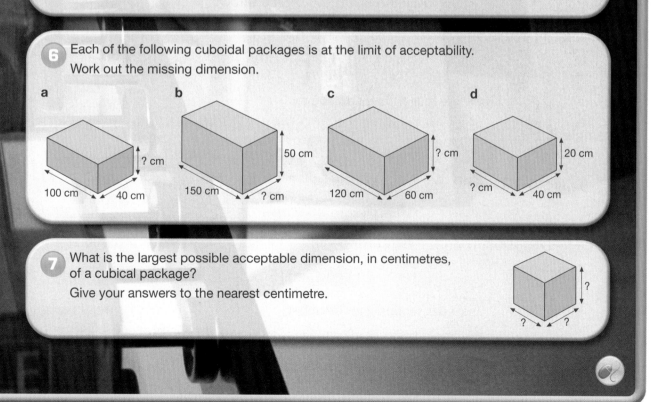

a

100 cm   40 cm   ? cm

b

150 cm   ? cm   50 cm

c

120 cm   60 cm   ? cm

d

? cm   40 cm   20 cm

7 What is the largest possible acceptable dimension, in centimetres, of a cubical package?
Give your answers to the nearest centimetre.

?   ?   ?

This chapter is going to show you

- How to record mutually exclusive outcomes
- How to solve probability problems involving mutually exclusive outcomes
- How to use a two-way table or sample space diagram to calculate probabilities
- How to work out probabilities in different situations
- How to obtain estimates of probability

What you should already know

- Some basic ideas about chance and probability
- How to use a probability scale
- How to calculate probabilities for single events

Combinations

Toss a coin twice and then make a list of all possible combinations (also called outcomes).

First throw	Second throw
Head	Head
Head	Tail
Tail	Head
Tail	Tail

There are four different outcomes.

Example 9.1

Joel goes shopping for breakfast.

He brings back bread, sausage, eggs, beans and mushrooms.

He can only cook three things for breakfast at a time.

Write down the different combinations of three of these items.

Example 9.1
continued

If we write these down logically and orderly, we are more likely not to miss any out. Notice the way we write down the possible combinations.

Note that the order of the three items does not matter in this instance.

Bread	Sausage	Egg	Beans	Mushrooms
●	●	●		
●	●		●	
●	●			●
●		●	●	
●		●		●
●			●	●
	●	●	●	
	●	●		●
	●		●	●
		●	●	●

Creating a table to complete and completing it in an orderly, logical way shows us there are 10 different combinations Joel could choose.

Exercise 9A

 1 Here is a simple set menu in a café.

Write down all the different ways of choosing one main meal with one sweet.

Main course
Roast chicken
Pizza
Lasagne
Quiche

Sweets
Ice cream
Cheesecake
Apple pie

2 Three children Amy, Joe and Milly, have to travel in a car. Two have to sit in the back. Write down all the different outcomes if two of these children sit in the back.

3 A football team have five substitutes: Steve, Mark, Chris, Deon and Marcus.

Only three substitutes can be chosen during the game.

Write down the different outcomes of which three could be chosen as substitutes.

4 I have three coins. I throw them all in the air and see how they land. There are four different combinations for the way the coins can land on Heads or Tails. Write down all four different combinations (the order written down doesn't matter).

5 I flip a coin three times in a row. There are eight different combinations of Heads and Tails this time. Write down all eight different outcomes.

6 Here is a set menu in a café.

Write down all the different ways of choosing one starter, one main meal and one sweet.

Starter	Main course	Sweets
Soup	Roast chicken	Ice cream
Garlic bread	Pizza	Cheesecake
Chicken wings	Lasagne	Apple pie
Quiche		

Extension Work

Imagine a Formula 1 race between two racing cars (called A and B). They could finish the race in two different ways, AB or BA.

Now look at a three-car race. How many ways can they finish the race?

Extend this problem to four cars, and so on. Put your results into a table. See if you can work out a pattern to predict how many different ways a 10-car race could finish.

When you have finished this, you can explore what the factorial (!) button does on a calculator. (This may help you to solve the racing car problem.)

Calculating probabilities

Look at the spinners. Which one is most likely to land on red? Remember, the answer is not how many times a colour appears, but the probability that it will appear.

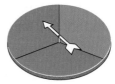

$$\text{Probability of event} = \frac{\text{Number of successes}}{\text{Total number of outcomes}}$$

Sometimes you have to look at more than one event. To do this you can use diagrams, called **sample spaces**, to record the possible outcomes. Look at the sample space for two coins.

	Head	Tail
Head	H,H	H,T
Tail	T,H	T,T

You can now work out the probability of throwing two Heads.

The diagram shows that there is only one way of getting two Heads. It also shows that there are four possible outcomes altogether.

So, the probability is $\frac{1}{4}$.

Example 9.2

A coin is tossed and a dice is rolled.

a Use a sample space diagram to show all the possible outcomes.

b What is the probability of tossing a Head and rolling a 6?

a

	1	2	3	4	5	6
Head	H, 1	H, 2	H, 3	H, 4	H, 5	H, 6
Tail	T, 1	T, 2	T, 3	T, 4	T, 5	T, 6

b Head and 6 is one of the 12 spaces on the diagram, so the probability is $\frac{1}{12}$.

Example 9.3 ▷ An ice-cream man sells vanilla, chocolate and strawberry flavours. A girl buys an ice-cream, saying to the man: 'You can choose the flavours.'

a What is the probability that the girl gets her favourite flavour if she buys a single scoop?

b She asks for two scoops, each scoop a different flavour. Make a list of the different combinations she could buy.

a She has only one favourite flavour, so the probability that she gets that one out of three flavours = $\frac{1}{3}$.

b Vanilla and chocolate
Vanilla and strawberry
Chocolate and strawberry

You could also list them in reverse order, as well. This would imply that the scoops are the opposite way round.

Exercise 9B

 A set of cards are numbered 1 to 20. One card is picked at random. Give the probability for each of the following cases.

a Even
b Has only one digit
c Has 1 on it
d Has 2 on it
e Is less than 5
f Is greater than 8
g Is a multiple of 3 (3, 6, 9, …)

2 These two spinners are spun. The scores on the spinners are added together to get the total score.

a Copy and complete the sample space diagram for the total scores.

	1	2	3
1	2		
2			
3			

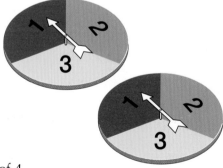

b Write down the probability of a total score of 4.
c Write down the probability of a total greater than 30.

 A bag contains two red, two blue and two black pens. Two pens are chosen at random.
a List the possible outcomes.
b Write down the probability of choosing red and black pens.

4 Tom, Nicola and Matt each buy a drink. They either choose cola or lemonade.

a Copy and complete the table.

b What is the probability that Nicola and Matt choose different drinks?

Tom	Nicola	Matt
Cola	Cola	Lemonade

5 Two dice are rolled and the scores are added together. Copy and complete the sample space of scores.

	1	2	3	4	5	6
1	2	3				
2	3					

a What is the most likely total?

b What is the probability that the total is the following?

    i 2   **ii** 5   **iii** 1   **iv** 12

    v Even   **vi** Odd   **vii** 10, 11 or 12

    viii 6 or 8   **ix** Less than 4   **x** Less than or equal to 4

Extension **Work**

The scores on these two spinners are added to get a total score.

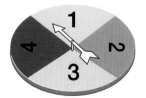 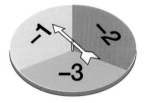

a Complete a sample space to show the total scores.

b What is the most likely total?

c What is the probability for each of the following totals?

    i 1   **ii** 3   **iii** 5   **iv** −2

    v −3   **vi** 0   **vii** Greater than 0   **viii** 2 or −2

Estimates of probability

 In an experiment to test whether a dice is biased, the dice was rolled 120 times. These are the results.

Number on dice	1	2	3	4	5	6
Frequency	18	25	20	22	14	21

Do you think that the dice is biased?

Number 2 was rolled 25 times out of 120. So, an **estimate of the probability** of rolling number 2 is given by:

$$\frac{25}{120} = 0.208$$

The fraction $\frac{25}{120}$ is called the **estimate of the probability** or the **relative frequency**.

Relative frequency is an estimate of probability based on experimental data. The relative frequency may be the only way of estimating probability when events are not equally likely.

$$\text{Relative frequency} = \frac{\text{Number of successful trials}}{\text{Total number of trials}}$$

Example 9.4

Look again at the test results given opposite.

A dice is rolled 120 times. Here are the results.

Number on dice	1	2	3	4	5	6
Frequency	18	25	20	22	14	21

a Write down the relative frequency of a score of 6.

b How could you obtain a more accurate estimate than the relative frequency?

a Number 6 was rolled 21 times so the relative frequency is $\frac{21}{120}$.

b A more accurate estimate could be obtained by carrying out more trials.

Exercise 9C

1 A four-sided spinner was spun 100 times. Here are the results.

Number on spinner	1	2	3	4
Frequency	20	25	23	32

a What is the estimated probability of a score of 4?

b What is the estimated probability of an even score?

c Do you think from these results that the spinner is biased? Give a reason for your answer.

5

2 A drawing pin was thrown and the number of times that it landed point up was recorded at regular intervals. The results are shown in the table.

  a Copy and complete the table for the estimated probabilities.

Number of throws					10	20	30	40	50
Number of times pin lands point up					6	13	20	24	32
Estimate of probability of landing point up					$\frac{3}{5}$				

  b What is the best estimate of the probability of the pin landing point up?

3 A bag contains yellow and blue cubes. Cubes are picked from the bag, the colour recorded and the cubes replaced.

  a Copy and complete the table for the relative frequencies for the number of times a blue cube is chosen.

Number of trials			10	25	50	100
Number of times blue cube chosen			3	8	15	28
Relative frequency			0.3			

  b What is the best estimate of the probability of picking a blue cube from the bag?

Extension Work

In an experiment to test whether a dice is biased, the dice is rolled 120 times. These are the results.

Number on dice	1	2	3	4	5	6
Frequency	18	25	20	22	14	21

Number 2 was rolled 25 times out of 120. So, for example, you would expect it to be rolled 50 times out of 240. The expected number of successes can be calculated from the formula:

  Expected number of successes = Relative frequency × Number of trials

Hence, in this case, the expected number of times number 2 is rolled is given by:

$$\frac{25}{120} \times 240 = 50$$

1 A four sided spinner was spun 100 times. Here are the results.

Number on spinner	1	2	3	4
Frequency	20	25	23	32

If the spinner was spun 500 times, how many times would you expect to get a score of 4?

2 A drawing pin was thrown and the number of times it landed point up was recorded at regular intervals. The results are shown in the table.

Number of throws	10	20	30	40	50
Number of times pin lands point up	6	13	20	24	32
Relative frequency of landing point up	0.6				

How many times would you expect the pin to land point up in 200 throws?

3 A bag contains yellow and blue cubes. Cubes are picked from the bag, and the cubes replaced. The results are shown in the table.

Number of trials	10	25	50	100
Number of times blue cube chosen	3	8	15	28
Relative frequency	0.3			

You are told that altogether there are 75 cubes in the bag. What is the best estimate of the number of blue cubes in the bag?

LEVEL BOOSTER

4
I can extract information from tables and lists.
I can interpret a frequency diagram.

5
I can understand and am able to use the probability scale from 0 to 1.
I can find and justify probabilities from equally likely events.
I can find probabilities based on experimental evidence.

1 *2003 Paper 1*

A teacher has five number cards. She says:

'I am going to take a card at random.

Each card shows a different positive whole number.

It is certain that the card will show a number less than 10.

It is impossible that the card will show an even number.'

What numbers are on the cards?

2 *2006 3–5 Paper 1*

Make three copies of the diagram of a spinner below:

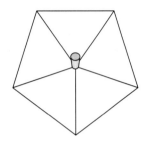

On each spinner, write **five numbers** to make the following statements correct:

a It is **certain** that you will get a number **less than 6**.

b It is **more likely** that you will get an **even** number than an **odd** number.

c It is **impossible** that you will get a **multiple of 3**.

3 *2006 3–5 Paper 2*

I buy **12 packets** of cat food in a box.

The table shows the different varieties in the box.

Variety	Number of packets
Cod	3
Salmon	3
Trout	3
Tuna	3

a I am going to take out a packet at random from the box.

What is the **probability** that it will be **cod**?

b My cat eats **all** the packets of cod.
I am going to take out a packet at random from the ones left in the box.

What is the **probability** that it will be **salmon**?

c A different type of cat food has **10 packets** in a box.
The probability that the variety is chicken is **0.7**.

What is the **probability** that the variety is **not** chicken?

4 *2007 3–5 Paper 1*

Fred has a bag of sweets.

He is going to take a sweet from the bag at random.

a What is the **probability** that Fred will get a **black** sweet?

b Write down the missing **colour** from the sentence below:

The probability that Fred will get a ...... sweet is $\frac{1}{4}$.

Contents

3 yellow sweets
5 green sweets
7 red sweets
4 purple sweets
1 black sweet

FM Class test

A Year 9 class sat some practice tests before their SATs. The following are their test results.

Name	Gender	English	Maths	Science
John Addy	M	17	45	32
Sean Allsop	M	43	37	41
Sally Emerson	F	65	54	48
Gerry Evans	M	28	65	55
Kay Gilbert	F	76	84	78
Zoe Ginn	F	49	46	57
Zahir Greer	M	87	24	43
Isabell Harding	F	93	75	68
Muhanad Hatamleh	M	72	56	51
Liah Huxter	F	69	74	78
Sahid Jallya	M	25	62	65
Molly Kenward	F	51	37	42
Brian Keys	M	48	53	49
Daniel Mann	M	55	85	73
John O'Dubhchair	M	62	39	35
Godwin Osakwe	M	38	41	27
Krishna Pallin	M	78	56	67
Joy Peacock	F	69	76	65
William Qui	M	87	92	89
Alan Runciman	M	92	34	45
Billie Speed	M	64	74	76
Robert Spooner	M	44	67	61
Joyce Tapman	F	53	43	39
Vi Thomas	F	37	57	64
Cliff Tompkins	M	48	43	51
Lesley Wallace	F	68	58	52
Madge Webb	F	74	42	44
John Wilkins	M	35	41	47
Jenny Wong	F	69	58	43
Jo Zunde	F	94	98	96

Use the given information to answer these questions.

1 How many pupils are in the class?

2 How many more boys are there than girls?

3 **a** Look at the results and write down your estimated guess of the mean test score for each subject.
   b Calculate the mean test results for each subject.
   c Comment on the accuracy of your guesses.

4 Draw a scatter diagram for the results in the following subjects.
   a English and maths
   b English and science
   c Maths and science

5 Comment on the correlation shown in the three scatter diagrams you have drawn.

6 On your scatter diagrams, use colours to highlight the males and the females and comment on any gender differences now apparent from these results.

7 Draw a stem and leaf diagram for each set of results.

8 From your stem and leaf diagrams, state the median score of each and comment on your results.

9 Create a grouped frequency table for each set of results using the boundaries 1–20, 21–40, 41–60, 61–80 and 81–100.

10 Use the grouped frequency tables to draw a bar chart for each set of results.

11 Comment on which test appears to be the easiest and which the hardest.

Geometry and Measures **3**

Enlargements

The three transformations you have met so far (reflections, rotations and translations) do not change the size of the object. You are now going to look at a transformation that does change the size of an object. It is called **enlargement**. The illustration shows a picture which has been enlarged.

The diagram shows △ABC enlarged to give △A′B′C′.

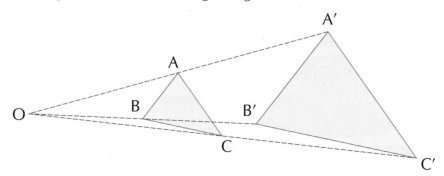

Each side of ΔA'B'C' is twice as long as the corresponding side of ΔABC. Notice also that OA' = 2 × OA, OB' = 2 × OB and OC' = 2 × OC. That is, ΔABC is enlarged by a **scale factor** of two about the **centre of enlargement**, O, to give the **image** ΔA'B'C'. The dashed lines are called the **guidelines** or **rays** for the enlargement.

To enlarge a shape, a **centre of enlargement** and a **scale factor** are needed.

Example 10.1

Enlarge the triangle XYZ by a scale factor of two about the centre of enlargement, O.

Draw rays OX, OY and OZ. Measure the length of each ray. Multiply each length by two. Then extend each ray to its new length measured from O and plot the points X', Y' and Z'. Join X', Y' and Z'. ΔX'Y'Z' is the enlargement of ΔXYZ by a scale factor of two about the centre of enlargement, O.

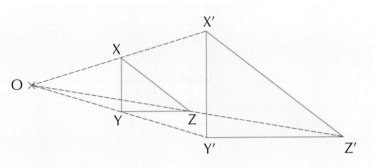

Example 10.2

The **object** rectangle ABCD on the coordinate grid shown has been enlarged by a scale factor of 3 about the origin, O, to give the **image** rectangle A'B'C'D'.

The coordinates of the object are: A(0, 2), B(3, 2), C(3, 1) and D(0, 1). The coordinates of the image are: A'(0, 6), B'(9, 6), C'(9, 3) and D'(0, 3).

Notice that when a shape is enlarged by a scale factor about the origin of a coordinate grid, the coordinates of the enlarged shape can be found by multiplying the coordinates of the original shape by the scale factor.

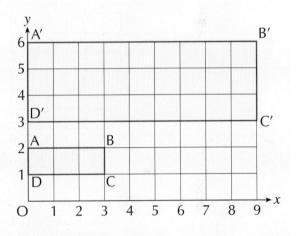

Exercise 10A

1. Draw copies of (or trace) the shapes below. Then enlarge each one by the given scale factor about the centre of enlargement O.

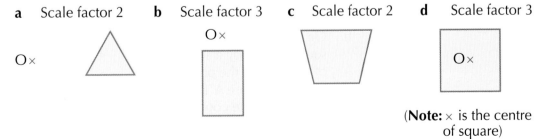

a Scale factor 2 b Scale factor 3 c Scale factor 2 d Scale factor 3

(**Note:** × is the centre of square)

2 Copy each diagram below on to centimetre-square paper. Then enlarge each one by the given scale factor about the origin O.

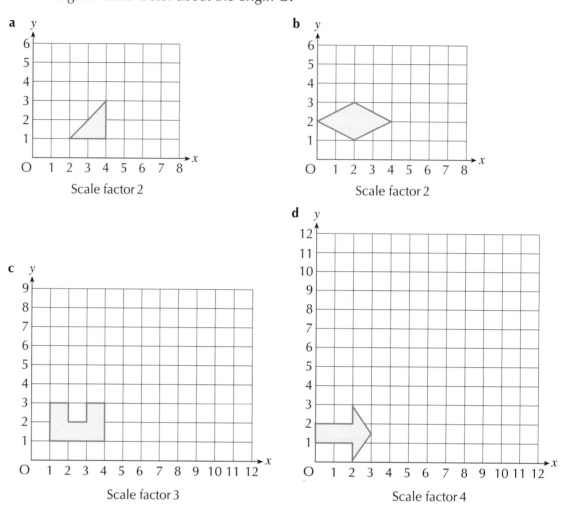

a

Scale factor 2

b

Scale factor 2

c

Scale factor 3

d

Scale factor 4

3 Draw axes for x and y from 0 to 10 on centimetre-square paper. Plot the points A(4, 6), B(5, 4), C(4, 1) and D(3, 4) and join them together to form the kite ABCD. Enlarge the kite by a scale factor of 2 about the point (1, 2).

4 Copy the diagram shown on to centimetre-square paper.

    a Enlarge the square ABCD by a scale factor of two about the point (5, 5). Label the square A′B′C′D′. Write down the coordinates of A′, B′, C′ and D′.

    b On the same grid, enlarge the square ABCD by a scale factor of three about the point (5, 5). Label the square A″B″C″D″. Write down the coordinates of A″, B″, C″ and D″.

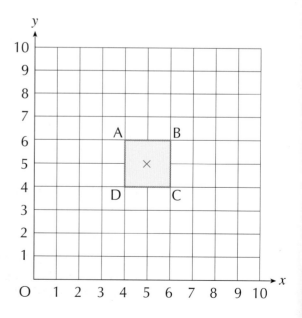

c On the same grid, enlarge the square ABCD by a scale factor of four about the point (5, 5). Label the square A‴B‴C‴D‴. Write down the coordinates of A‴, B‴, C‴ and D‴.

d What do you notice about the coordinate points that you have written down?

⑤ Copy the diagram shown on to centimetre-square paper.

a What is the scale factor of the enlargement?

b By adding suitable rays to your diagram, find the coordinates of the centre of enlargement.

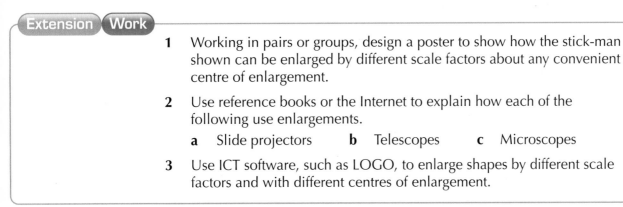

Extension Work

1 Working in pairs or groups, design a poster to show how the stick-man shown can be enlarged by different scale factors about any convenient centre of enlargement.

2 Use reference books or the Internet to explain how each of the following use enlargements.

a Slide projectors **b** Telescopes **c** Microscopes

3 Use ICT software, such as LOGO, to enlarge shapes by different scale factors and with different centres of enlargement.

Circumference of a circle

How can you measure exactly the **circumference** of a circle?

Is there a relation between the length of the diameter and the circumference?

Exercise 10B will show you.

Exercise 10B

You will need compasses, a 30 cm ruler and a piece of fine, high-quality string at least 40 cm long.

Copy the following table and draw circles with the given radii.

Measure the circumference of each circle by tracing the string round the circumference as shown. Mark the length on the string with a pencil. Measure this length with a ruler and complete the table. Calculate the last column to one decimal place.

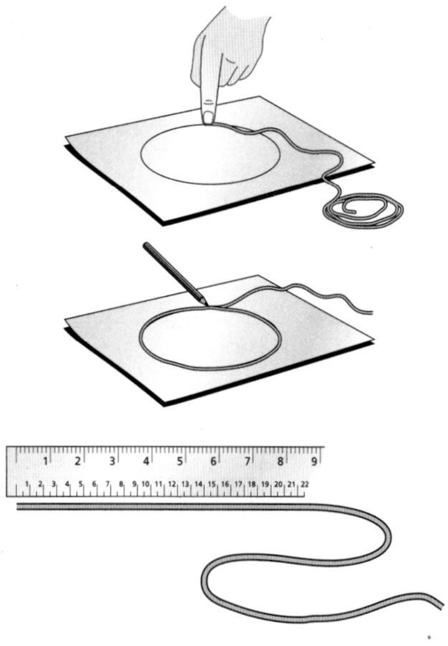

5

Radius r (cm)	Diameter d (cm)	Circumference C (cm)	$C \div d$
1			
1.5			
2			
2.5			
3			
3.5			
4			
4.5			
5			
5.5			
6			

What do you notice about the last column?

Can you say how the circumference is related to the diameter?

Write down in your book what you have found out.

6

Extension Work

Draw a circle on paper and cut it out. Draw a narrow sector on the circle and cut it out. Make a cone with the remaining, larger sector.

What happens as you increase the size of the removed sector?

Using scale drawings

A **scale drawing** is a smaller (or sometimes larger) drawing of an actual object. The scale must always be clearly given by the side of or beneath the scale drawing.

Here you are going to be shown how to draw a shape to its full size from a scale drawing.

Example 10.3

The rectangle on the right has been drawn to scale.

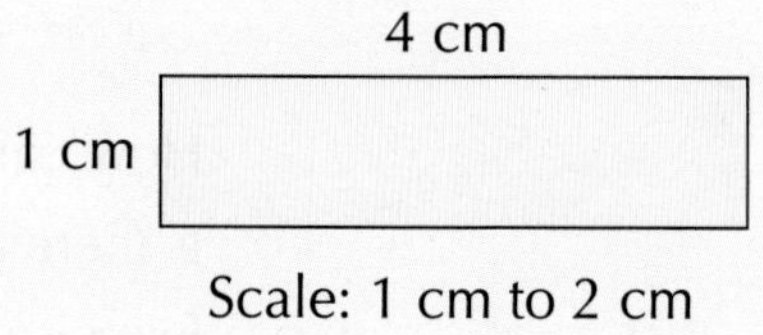

The scale shows that each centimetre on the diagram represents 2 cm on the full-sized rectangle.

4 cm, 1 cm

Scale: 1 cm to 2 cm

So, the length of the full-sized rectangle is 4×2 cm = 8 cm

The width of the full-sized rectangle is 1×2 cm = 2 cm

The rectangle can now be drawn with its actual measurements, as shown on the right.

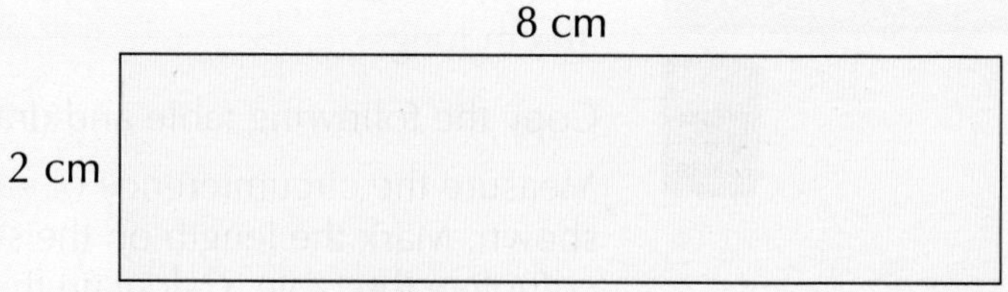

8 cm, 2 cm

1. The following rectangles are drawn to scale. Measure each of the sides. Then draw each rectangle to its full size.

a

Scale: 1 cm to 3 cm

b

Scale: 1 cm to 2 cm

c

Scale: 1 cm to 2 cm

d

Scale: 1 cm to 3 cm

2. The following shapes are drawn to scale. Measure each of the sides. Then draw each shape to its full size.

a

Scale: 1 cm to 3 cm

b

Scale: 1 cm to 2 cm

c

Scale: 1 cm to 2 cm

3. The following right-angled triangles are drawn to scale. Measure the vertical and horizontal sides of each of them. Then draw each triangle to its full size. Measure the length of the sloping side.

a

Scale: 1 cm to 2 cm

b

Scale: 1 cm to 3 cm

c

Scale: 1 cm to 4 cm

4. The shape below is drawn to scale.

Measure the vertical and horizontal sides and draw the shape to its full size.

Measure the length of the sloping side.

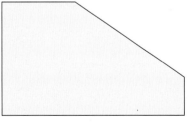

Scale: 1 cm to $1\frac{1}{2}$ cm

Extension **Work**

FM

Scales written as ratios

Sometimes, particularly on plans and maps, a scale is written with mixed units. For example: 1 cm to 2 m, 5 cm to 1 km, 1 cm to 20 km.

These scales can also be given as ratios. This involves giving both parts of the ratio in the same unit. So, for example, the scale 1 cm to 2 m is first changed into centimetres, giving 1 cm to 200 cm. This can be expressed as the ratio 1 : 200. Notice that the ratio has no units.

Similarly, the scale 5 cm to 1 km can be changed into centimetres as 5 cm to 100 000 cm. This can be written as the ratio 5 : 100 000, which can be simplified to 1 : 20 000.

Write each of the following scales as a ratio.

1 1 cm to 1 m   **2** 1 cm to 5 m

3 4 cm to 1 m   **4** 2 cm to 5 m

5 1 cm to 1 km   **6** 4 cm to 1 km

LEVEL BOOSTER

4 I can plot coordinates in the first quadrant.

5 I can use scale drawings.

6 I can enlarge shapes by a scale factor.

1 *2002 Paper 2*

Janet joins three points on a grid to make a triangle.
The coordinates of the points are:

(0, 0) (1, 1) (2, 0)

The area of Janet's triangle is 1cm².

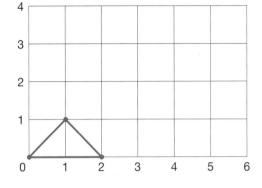

Dylan multiplies each of Janet's coordinates by 2.

Janet's coordinates	× 2	Dylan's coordinates
(0, 0)	—	(0, 0)
(1, 1)	—	(2, 2)
(2, 0)	—	(4, 0)

a What is the area of Dylan's triangle?

b Copy Janet's coordinates and multiply each of them by 3.

Janet's coordinates	× 3	New coordinates
(0, 0)	—	(...,...)
(1, 1)	—	(...,...)
(2, 0)	—	(...,...)

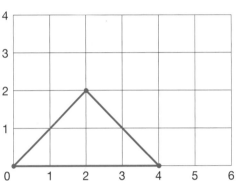

Plot the three points with the new coordinates on a copy of the grid.
Join them up to make a triangle.

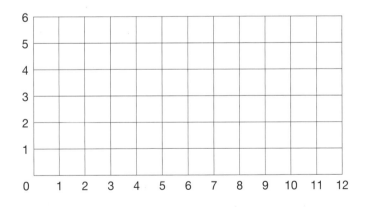

c What is the area of your triangle?

Nazir multiplies each of Janet's coordinates by another number.
He plots two of the points, (0, 0) and (10, 0), and joins them up.

d Plot Nazir's third point on a copy of the grid.

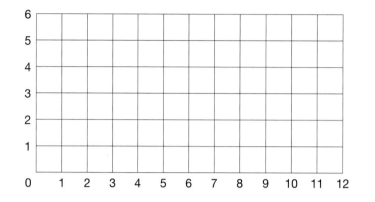

e By what number did Nazir multiply Janet's coordinates?

2 *1999 Paper 2*

This cuboid is made from four small cubes.

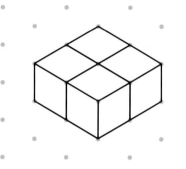

a On a copy of the isometric grid below, draw a cuboid which is twice as high, twice as long and twice as wide.

b Graham made this cuboid from three small cubes.

Mohinder wants to make a cuboid which is twice as high, twice as long and twice as wide as Graham's cuboid. How many small cubes will Mohinder need altogether?

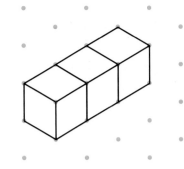

3 *2005 4–6 Paper 2*

Draw an **enlargement** of this rectangle with **scale factor 2**.

Use **point A** as the **centre** of enlargement.

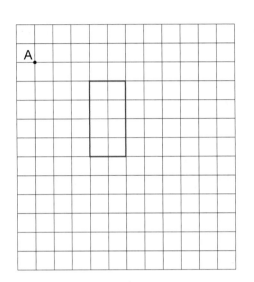

FM Map reading

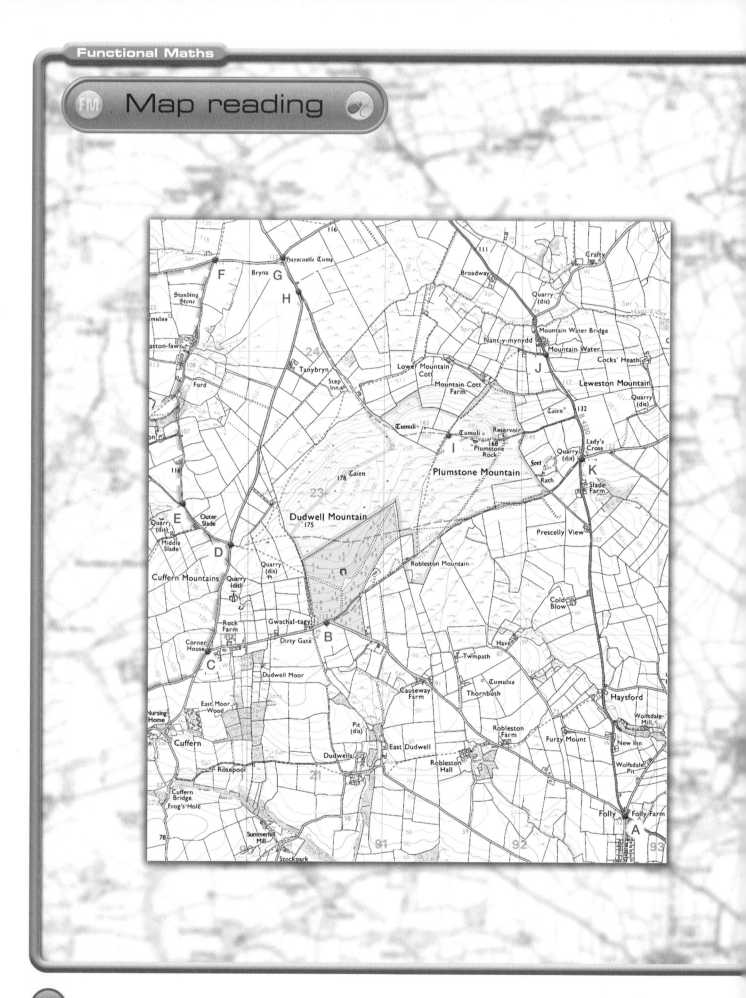

Katie and Richard go for a walk. The route they take is shown on the map. The map has a scale of 1 : 25000. They park their car at the point marked A. They walk from A to B, then B to C and so on until they arrive back at A.

Every 1 cm on the map is worth 0.25 km on the ground.

To work out the distances that Katie and Richard walk, measure the distance on the map in centimetres, then multiply this number by 0.25.

From A to B is 9.6 cm on the map, so 9.6 × 0.25 = 2.4 km on the ground.

Use the map to answer the questions below.

1 Copy and complete this table showing the distances that they walk.

From	To	Road or footpath	Distance on map	Distance on ground
A	B	Road	9.6 cm	2.4 km
B	C			
C	D			
D	E			
E	F			
F	G			
G	H			
H	I			
I	J			
J	K			
K	A			

2 What is the total distance that they walk on roads?

3 What is the total distance that they walk on footpaths?

4 How far do they walk altogether?

5 They leave their car at 10.00 am. They stop for a 1-hour lunch and a 30-minute rest. They walk for a total of $3\frac{1}{2}$ hours.

At what time do they get back to their car?

6 On a map, symbols are used to represent different things.

Represents a campsite   Represents a picnic site

a Draw an enlargement of the campsite symbol using a scale factor of 2.

b Draw an enlargement of the picnic site symbol using a scale factor of 3.

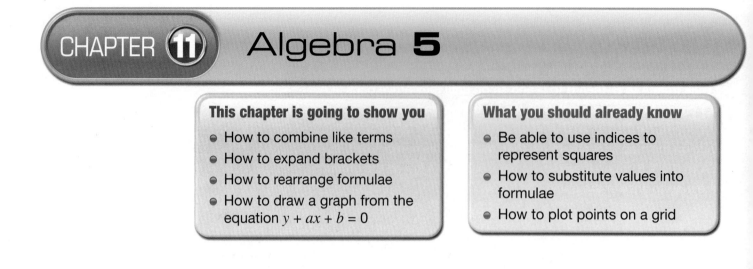

This chapter is going to show you

- How to combine like terms
- How to expand brackets
- How to rearrange formulae
- How to draw a graph from the equation $y + ax + b = 0$

What you should already know

- Be able to use indices to represent squares
- How to substitute values into formulae
- How to plot points on a grid

Like terms

Like terms are multiples of the same letter, or of the same combination of letters. Also, they can be the same power of the same letter or the same powers of the same combination of letters. For example:

x, $4x$, $\frac{1}{2}x$, $-3x$ Like terms which are multiples of x

$5ab$, $8ab$, $\frac{1}{2}ab$, $-2ab$ Like terms which are multiples of ab

y^2, $3y^2$, $\frac{1}{4}y^2$, $-4y^2$ Like terms which are multiples of y^2

The multiples are called **coefficients**. So, in the above examples, 1, 4, $\frac{1}{2}$, -3, 5, 8, $\frac{1}{2}$, -2, 3, $\frac{1}{4}$ and -4 are coefficients.

Only like terms can be added or subtracted to simplify an expression. For example:

$3ab + 2ab$ simplifies to $5ab$

$8x^2 - 5x^2$ simplifies to $3x^2$

Unlike terms cannot be simplified by addition or subtraction. For example:

$9a + 5a + 10b - 4b = 14a + 6b$

The expression $14a + 6b$ cannot be simplified because $14a$ and $6b$ are unlike terms.

Simplifying an expression means making it shorter by combining its terms where possible. This usually involves two steps:

- Collect the like terms into groups of the same sort.
- Combine each group of like terms, and simplify.

Example 11.1 ▷

Simplify $7x + 3y + 4x + 5t + 6y + 8$

First step is to collect the like terms together:

$7x + 4x + 3y + 6y + 5t + 8$

Second step is to combine the like terms:

$11x + 9y + 5t + 8$

This is the original expression's simplest form.

Example 11.2 Simplify $5a^2 + d^2 + 3a^2 - 4d^2 + 5e - 7$

First step is to collect the like terms together:

$5a^2 + 3a^2 + d^2 - 4d^2 + 5e - 7$

Second step is to combine the like terms:

$8a^2 - 3d^2 + 5e - 7$

This is the original expression's simplest form.

Example 11.3 Simplify $5a^2 + 4d - 3a^2 - 9d$

Collecting together its like terms gives:

$5a^2 - 3a^2 + 4d - 9d$

Combining them gives:

$2a^2 - 5d$ which is the original expression's simplest form.

Exercise 11A

1 Simplify each of these.

a	$3x + 4x$	**b**	$4a + 3a$	**c**	$7t + t$	**d**	$4y + y + 3y$
e	$8m - 2m$	**f**	$7k - 4k$	**g**	$5n - n$	**h**	$3p - 7p$

2 Simplify each of these.

a	$6m + m + 3m$	**b**	$2y + 4y + y$	**c**	$6t + 2t + t$	**d**	$5p + 2p + 4p$
e	$6n + 2n + 5n$	**f**	$5p + 3p + p$	**g**	$4t - t + 3t$	**h**	$4e - 2e + 5e$
i	$7k + 2k - 3k$	**j**	$6h + h - 2h$	**k**	$9m - 3m - m$	**l**	$5t + 3t - 2t$

3 Write down the perimeter, P, of each of the following shapes.

a

2t
3t
t
2t

b

2n
3n
3n

c

5m
2m
3m
4m

d

5k
3k
3k
2k

e

7w
3w
8w

f

2n
n
2n
n
4n
3n

4 Simplify each of the following expressions.

a	$4b + 3 + b$	**b**	$5x + 6 + 2x$	**c**	$q + 3 + 5q$	**d**	$5k + 2k + 7$
e	$4x + 5 - 2x$	**f**	$7k + 3 - k$	**g**	$5p + 1 - 3p$	**h**	$8d + 2 - 5d$
i	$6m - 2 - 4m$	**j**	$5t - 3 - 3t$	**k**	$5w - 7 - 2w$	**l**	$6g - 5 - 2g$
m	$2t + k + 5t$	**n**	$4x + 3y + 5x$	**o**	$3k + 2g + 4k$	**p**	$5h + w + 3w$
q	$7t + 3p - 4t$	**r**	$8n + 3t - 6n$	**s**	$p + 5q - 4q$	**t**	$4n + p - 2n$

5 Simplify each of the following expressions.

a	$3t + 4g + 6t + 3g$	**b**	$5x + y + 3x + 4y$	**c**	$3m + k + 4m + 3k$
d	$6x + 4y - 3x + 2y$	**e**	$7m + p - 3m + 2p$	**f**	$4n + 3t - n + 2t$
g	$7k + 4g - 3k - g$	**h**	$6d + 5b - 3d - 2b$	**i**	$5q + 4p - 3q - p$
j	$5g - k + 3g + 4k$	**k**	$6x - 2y + x + 3y$	**l**	$5d - 2e - 8d + e$

The prime numbers up to 20 are 2, 3, 5, 7, 11, 13, 17 and 19.

1 Joe said: 'Two prime numbers can never add together to make another prime number.' Is Joe correct? Explain your answer.

2 Can you make any prime numbers as the sum of three prime numbers? Explain your answer.

Expanding brackets

When a number or a letter is next to brackets everything in the brackets has to be multiplied by that number or letter if the brackets are to be removed.

This process is called **expanding the brackets** or **multiplying out**.

Example 11.4

Expand $3(4h + 5)$

Multiply each term by 3:

$3 \times 4h + 3 \times 5$

which gives: $12h + 15$

Example 11.5

Expand $-2(6m - 5p - 4)$

Multiply each term by -2:

$-2 \times 6m - 2 \times -5p - 2 \times -4$

which gives: $-12m + 10p + 8$

Move the negative term to obtain: $10p - 12m + 8$

Example 11.6

Expand $m(4p + 2)$

Multiply each term by m:

$m \times 4p + m \times 2$

which gives: $4mp + 2m$

Example 11.7

Expand $t(5t - 3)$

Multiply each term by t:

$t \times 5t - t \times 3$

which gives: $5t^2 - 3t$

① Multiply out each of the following brackets.

a $2(m + 3)$	**b** $3(k - 4)$	**c** $3(a + 2)$	**d** $5(3 - p)$
e $2(3x + 4)$	**f** $5(2x + 3)$	**g** $4(2t - 1)$	**h** $5(4m + 7)$
i $3(2x + 1)$	**j** $4(3k - 2)$	**k** $2(5b + 3)$	**l** $7(2 - 4m)$
m $8(3 + p)$	**n** $5(4 - t)$	**o** $6(w - g)$	**p** $8(p + t)$
q $9(2k - 6)$	**r** $5(2m + w)$	**s** $3(3t - 2d)$	**t** $2(3x - 4y)$

② Write down an expression for the area, A, of each of the following rectangles.

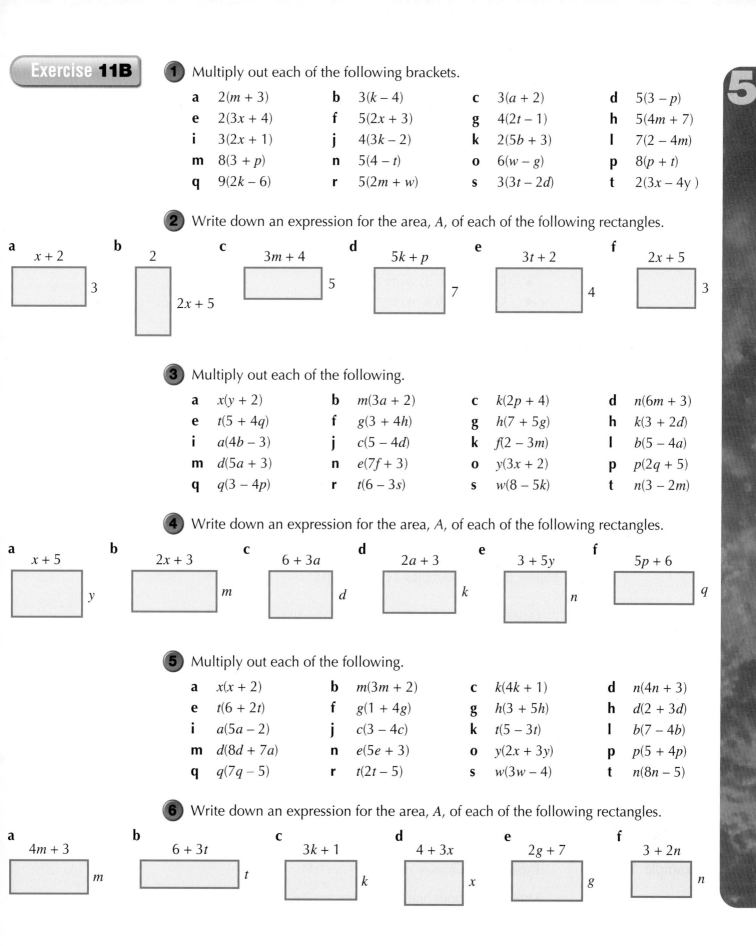

a $x + 2$ 3

b 2 $2x + 5$

c $3m + 4$ 5

d $5k + p$ 7

e $3t + 2$ 4

f $2x + 5$ 3

③ Multiply out each of the following.

a $x(y + 2)$	**b** $m(3a + 2)$	**c** $k(2p + 4)$	**d** $n(6m + 3)$
e $t(5 + 4q)$	**f** $g(3 + 4h)$	**g** $h(7 + 5g)$	**h** $k(3 + 2d)$
i $a(4b - 3)$	**j** $c(5 - 4d)$	**k** $f(2 - 3m)$	**l** $b(5 - 4a)$
m $d(5a + 3)$	**n** $e(7f + 3)$	**o** $y(3x + 2)$	**p** $p(2q + 5)$
q $q(3 - 4p)$	**r** $t(6 - 3s)$	**s** $w(8 - 5k)$	**t** $n(3 - 2m)$

④ Write down an expression for the area, A, of each of the following rectangles.

a $x + 5$ y

b $2x + 3$ m

c $6 + 3a$ d

d $2a + 3$ k

e $3 + 5y$ n

f $5p + 6$ q

⑤ Multiply out each of the following.

a $x(x + 2)$	**b** $m(3m + 2)$	**c** $k(4k + 1)$	**d** $n(4n + 3)$
e $t(6 + 2t)$	**f** $g(1 + 4g)$	**g** $h(3 + 5h)$	**h** $d(2 + 3d)$
i $a(5a - 2)$	**j** $c(3 - 4c)$	**k** $t(5 - 3t)$	**l** $b(7 - 4b)$
m $d(8d + 7a)$	**n** $e(5e + 3)$	**o** $y(2x + 3y)$	**p** $p(5 + 4p)$
q $q(7q - 5)$	**r** $t(2t - 5)$	**s** $w(3w - 4)$	**t** $n(8n - 5)$

⑥ Write down an expression for the area, A, of each of the following rectangles.

a $4m + 3$ m

b $6 + 3t$ t

c $3k + 1$ k

d $4 + 3x$ x

e $2g + 7$ g

f $3 + 2n$ n

a   Write down any three-digit number whose first and last digits have a difference of more than one (for example, 472 or 513).

b   Reverse the order of the digits (for the examples above, 274 and 315).

c   Subtract the smaller number from the larger number.

d   Reverse the digits of the answer to part **c** and add this number to the answer to part **c**.

e   Multiply the answer by one million.

f   Subtract 733 361 573.
   ● Then, under each 2 in your answer, write the letter P.
   ● Under each 3, write the letter L.
   ● Under each 4, write the letter R.
   ● Under each 5, write the letter O.
   ● Under each 6, write the letter F.
   ● Under each 7, write the letter A.
   ● Under each 8, write the letter I.

g   Now read your letters backwards.

Expanding and simplifying

Sometimes, two brackets have to be expanded and the results added together.

You have met both of these processes before. Now you are going to put them together. Follow through examples 11.8 to 11.10.

Example 11.8

Expand and simplify $4(5 + 2y) + 2(5y - 6)$

Multiply out both brackets, to obtain: $20 + 8y + 10y - 12$

Bring like terms together, which gives: $8y + 10y + 20 - 12$

Simplify to obtain: $18y + 8$

Example 11.9

Expand and simplify $4(2u + 3i) - 2(u - 2i)$

Multiply out both brackets, to obtain: $8u + 12i - 2u + 4i$

Bring like terms together, which gives: $8u - 2u + 12i + 4i$

Simplify to obtain: $6u + 16i$

Example 11.10

Expand and simplify $x(3x + 4) - x(x - 5)$

Multiply out both brackets, to obtain: $3x^2 + 4x - x^2 + 5x$

Bring like terms together, which gives: $3x^2 - x^2 + 4x + 5x$

Simplify to obtain: $2x^2 + 9x$

Exercise 11C

1 Expand and simplify each of the following expressions.

   a $2(3x + 4) + 3(x + 2)$ **b** $4(2k + 3) + 3(4k + 7)$

   c $5(2t + 3) + 2(3t + 4)$ **d** $4(3q + 2) + 3(2q + 1)$

   e $6(3h + 2) + 4(2h - 1)$ **f** $5(6 + 3f) + 2(2 - 3f)$

   g $4(3 - 2y) + 3(2 + 3y)$ **h** $6(2t - 5) + 3(5t - 2)$

2 Expand and simplify each of the following expressions.

   a $3(2x + 5) - 2(x + 3)$ **b** $5(2k + 4) - 2(4k + 1)$

   c $6(3t + 4) - 3(2t + 5)$ **d** $7(2q + 3) - 4(3q + 4)$

   e $8(2h + 5) - 3(4h - 2)$ **f** $7(w + 4) - 3(2w - 3)$

   g $5(4x - 3) - 3(3x - 2)$ **h** $9(2t - 3) - 2(6t - 3)$

3 Expand and simplify each of the following expressions.

   a $x(2x + 5) + x(4x + 3)$ **b** $p(3p + 4) + p(2p + 1)$

   c $k(5k + 3) + k(2k + 4)$ **d** $d(3d + 5) + d(2d + 3)$

   e $n(5n + 6) + n(3n - 5)$ **f** $f(5f + 3) + f(3f - 2)$

   g $p(p - 5) + p(2p - 4)$ **h** $y(5y - 2) + y(4y - 3)$

4 Expand and simplify each of the following expressions.

   a $x(8x + 5) - x(4x + 1)$ **b** $p(5p + 4) - p(2p + 1)$

   c $k(4k + 4) - k(2k + 3)$ **d** $d(3d + 7) - d(2d + 4)$

   e $n(7n + 5) - n(3n - 2)$ **f** $f(6f + 5) - f(3f - 4)$

   g $p(3p - 1) - p(p - 5)$ **h** $y(4y - 3) - y(2y - 7)$

Extension Work

   a Write down any three different, whole numbers smaller than ten. For example: 2, 5 and 8.

   b Add up these three numbers. Call this total x.

   c Make all the six possible two-digit numbers using these three different numbers. For example: 25, 28, 52, 58, 82 and 85.

   d Add up all six numbers. Call this total y.

   e Divide y by x and write down the answer.

   f Repeat this for other sets of three different whole numbers smaller than ten. What do you notice?

Graphs from functions

There are different ways to write functions down. For example, the function:

$$x \rightarrow 4x + 3$$

can also be written as:

$$y = 4x + 3$$

with the inputs as x and the outputs as y.

This latter way of writing functions is simpler when it comes to drawing graphs.

Every function has a graph associated with it, which we find by finding ordered pairs, or coordinates, from the function, and plotting them. Every graph of a linear function is a straight line.

Example 11.11 ▷ Draw a graph of the function:

$$y = 3x + 1$$

First, we draw up a table of simple values for x:

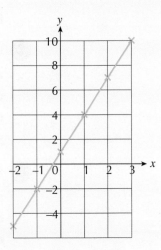

x		−2	−1	0	1	2	3
$y = 3x + 1$		−5	−2	1	4	7	10

Then we plot each point on a grid, and join up all the points.

Notice that the line we have drawn is actually hundreds of other coordinates too – *all* of these obey the same rule of the function, that is $y = 3x + 1$. Choose any points on the line that have not been plotted and show that this is true.

Exercise 11D

1 a Complete the table below for the function $y = x + 3$.

x	−2	−1	0	1	2	3
$y = x + 3$			3			

b Draw a grid with its x-axis from −2 to 3 and y-axis from −1 to 7.

c Use the table to help draw, on the grid, the graph of the function $y = x + 3$.

2 a Complete the table below for the function $y = x - 2$.

x	−2	−1	0	1	2	3
$y = x - 2$			−2			

b Draw a grid with its x-axis from −2 to 3 and y-axis from −4 to 2.

c Use the table to help draw, on the grid, the graph of the function $y = x - 2$.

3 a Complete the table below for the function $y = 4x + 1$.

x	−2	−1	0	1	2	3
$y = 4x + 1$			1			

b Draw a grid with its x-axis from −2 to 3 and y-axis from −7 to 13.

c Use the table to help draw, on the grid, the graph of the function $y = 4x + 1$.

4 a Complete the table below for the function $y = 4x - 1$.

x	–2	–1	0	1	2	3
$y = 4x - 1$			–1			

b Draw a grid with its x-axis from –2 to 3 and y-axis from –9 to 11.

c Use the table to help draw, on the grid, the graph of the function $y = 4x - 1$.

5 a Complete the table below for the functions shown.

x	–2	–1	0	1	2	3
$y = 2x + 5$	1					11
$y = 2x + 3$		1			7	
$y = 2x + 1$			1	3		
$y = 2x - 1$			–1	1		
$y = 2x - 3$		–5			1	

b Draw a grid with its x-axis from –2 to 3 and y-axis from –7 to 11.

c Draw the graph for each function in the table above.

d What two properties do you notice about each line?

e Use the properties you have noticed to draw the graphs of these functions.

   i $y = 2x + 2.5$ **ii** $y = 2x - 1.5$

6 a Complete the table below for the functions shown.

x	–2	–1	0	1	2	3
$y = 3x + 4$	–2					13
$y = 3x + 2$		–1			8	
$y = 3x$			0	3		
$y = 3x - 2$			–2	1		
$y = 3x - 4$	–7				2	

b Draw a grid with its x-axis from –2 to 3 and y-axis from –10 to 13.

c Draw the graph for each function in the table above.

d What two properties do you notice about each line?

e Use the properties you have noticed to draw the graphs of these functions.

   i $y = 3x + 2.5$ **ii** $y = 3x - 2.5$

Extension Work

1 Draw the graphs of:

   $y = 0.5x - 2$ and $y = 0.5x + 2$

2 Now draw, without any further calculations, the graphs of:

   $y = 0.5x - 1$ and $y = 0.5x + 3$

LEVEL BOOSTER

4 I can simplify expressions such as $3x + 2y - x + 5y$ by collecting like terms.

5 I can expand brackets such as $3(2x - 3)$.

6 I can expand and simplify expressions such as $2(3x + 1) - 3(2x - 4)$.
I can draw graphs of the form $y = 4x + 1$, for example, by plotting points.

National Test questions

1 *2007 3–5 Paper 2*

   a Here is an expression:

      $2a + 3 + 2a$

    Which expression below shows it written as simply as possible?

      $7a$ $7 + a$ $2a + 5$ $4a + 3$ $4(a + 3)$

   b Here is a different expression:

      $3b + 3 + 5b - 1$

    Write this expression as simply as possible.

2 *2000 Paper 1*

   Write each expression in its simplest form.

   a $7 + 2t + 3t$

   b $b + 7 + 2b + 10$

   c $(3d + 5) + (d - 2)$

   d $3m - (-m)$

3 *Adapted from 2002 Paper 1*

   a Simplify $(6n + 8) - (2n + 3)$.

   b What expression should be in the bracket if $2(?) = 6n + 8$?

4 *2000 Paper 1*

   a Two of the expressions below are equivalent. Write them down.

      $5(2y + 4)$ $5(2y + 20)$ $7(y + 9)$ $10(y + 9)$ $2(5y + 10)$

b   One of the expressions below is not a correct factorisation of $12y + 24$. Which one is it? Write down your answer.

$12(y + 2)$ $3(4y + 8)$ $2(6y + 12)$ $12(y + 24)$ $6(2y + 4)$

c   Factorise this expression: $7y + 14$.

d   Factorise this expression as fully as possible: $6y^3 - 2y^2$.

FM Trip to Rome

Tom and his wife Geri live in Silkstone. Their friends Stan and his wife Olive live in Barlborough. They both want to take a 7-day holiday in Rome. There are two airports in Rome, Ciampino (CIA) and Fiumicino (FCO).

The diagram shows the local airports, the costs of flights on the days they want to fly and the cost of parking a car for 7 days. Prices for flights are per person and include all taxes and fees.

The diagram also shows the main roads from their homes to the airports.

Motorways and dual carriageways are shown solid and minor roads are shown dotted.

Junctions are marked with arrows and the distances between arrows are shown in miles.

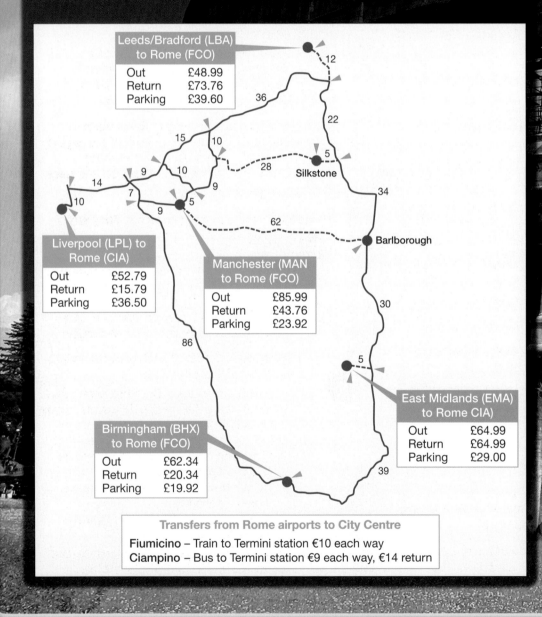

Leeds/Bradford (LBA) to Rome (FCO)

Out	£48.99
Return	£73.76
Parking	£39.60

Liverpool (LPL) to Rome (CIA)

Out	£52.79
Return	£15.79
Parking	£36.50

Manchester (MAN to Rome (FCO)

Out	£85.99
Return	£43.76
Parking	£23.92

East Midlands (EMA) to Rome CIA)

Out	£64.99
Return	£64.99
Parking	£29.00

Birmingham (BHX) to Rome (FCO)

Out	£62.34
Return	£20.34
Parking	£19.92

Transfers from Rome airports to City Centre

Fiumicino – Train to Termini station €10 each way
Ciampino – Bus to Termini station €9 each way, €14 return

Use the information to answer these questions.

1 What does the flight to Rome cost from East Midlands airport?

2 Which airport has the cheapest flight to Rome?

3 Which airport has the cheapest parking?

4 What is the total cost for two people to fly to Rome and back from Leeds/Bradford airport?

5 Which is the cheapest of the five airports for two people to fly to Rome and back and park their car for seven days?

6 **a** How far is it from Silkstone to Leeds/Bradford airport?

   b How much of this distance is on minor roads?

To calculate the driving time to the airports the following rules are used.

- On motorways assume an average speed of 60 miles per hour.
- On minor roads assume an average speed of 30 miles per hour.
- Allow 15 minutes to park the car and get to the terminal.

7 Using the rule above, how long will it take to drive 86 miles on a motorway?

8 Using the rule above, how long will it take to drive 28 miles on minor roads?

Tom is comparing the flights from Leeds/Bradford and Manchester.

9 How long will it take Tom to drive from Silkstone to Leeds/Bradford airport?

10 How long will it take Tom to drive from Silkstone to Manchester airport?

11 Which of the two airports would be the cheapest for Tom and Geri to fly to Rome and back and park their car?
Show all your calculations.

12 Tom knows that the running cost of his car is 80p per mile.

   a How much will it cost to drive from Silkstone to Leeds/Bradford airport?

   b How much will it cost to drive from Silkstone to Manchester airport?

13 When the cost of driving to the airports is added to the other costs, which of the airports is cheaper? Remember that the driving distance is from home to the airport and back.
Show all your calculations.

The friends decide to travel together. They work out two possible arrangements.

Plan 1: Stan and Olive will pick up Tom and Geri and the four will fly from Leeds/Bradford. Stan's car has a running cost of 90p per mile.

Plan 2: Tom and Geri will pick up Stan and Olive and the four will fly from East Midlands.

14 **a** Work out the cost of each plan taking into account all possible costs.

   b The flight from Leeds/Bradford leaves at 09.00. The flight from East Midlands leaves at 06.30. Allow 10 minutes to pick up friends at their house and remember that they need to arrive at the airport 2 hours before the flight leaves.

   i What time would Stan need to leave home for Plan 1?

   ii What time would Tom need to leave home for Plan 2?

   c Which plan would you advise the friends to go for? Give reasons for your choice.

CHAPTER 12 Solving Problems and Revision

This chapter is going to give you practice in National Test questions about

- Fractions, percentages and decimals
- The four rules, ratios and directed numbers
- Algebra – the basic rules and solving linear equations
- Algebra – graphs
- Geometry and measures
- Statistics

Number 1 – Fractions, decimals and percentages

Exercise 12A

Do not use a calculator for the first eight questions.

1. How much of each shape is shaded? Tick the correct box.

a

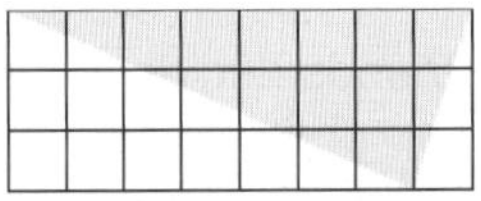

More than half ☐

Half ☐

Less than half ☐

b

More than a third ☐

A third ☐

Less than a third ☐

c

More than a quarter ☐

A quarter ☐

Less than a quarter ☐

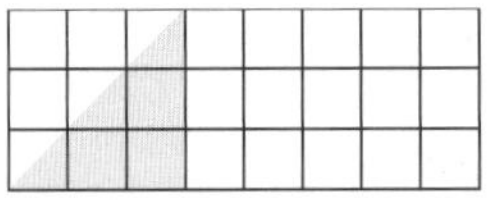

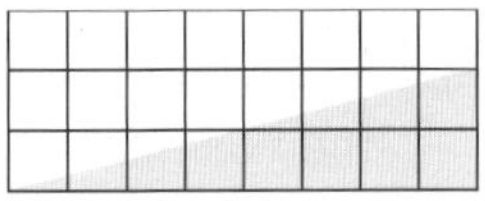

2. **a** Add 356 to half of 422.

   b Take a quarter of 156 from 200.

FM

3. **a** A Scots pine tree is 4.35 m tall. A larch pine is 84 cm taller. How tall is the larch pine?

   b From Barnsley to Sheffield via the motorway is 26.45 km. If you go via the ordinary roads it is 3.8 km shorter. How far is it from Barnsley to Sheffield via the ordinary roads?

4. If $\frac{5}{12}$ of the members of a youth club are girls, what fraction are boys?

5 This is the sign at an airport's long-stay car park.

How much would it cost to park at the airport for 9 days?

FLYPARK

£6.50 per day or
£42.50 for a full week.

6 The following method can be used to work out 12% of 320:

10% of 320 = 32
1% of 320 = 3.2
1% of 320 = 3.2
―――――――――――――
12% of 320 = 38.4

Use a similar method or a method of your own to work out 28% of 480.

 7 a About 33% of this rectangle is dotted.

About what **percentage** is: **i** striped?   **ii** plain?

b About $\frac{1}{8}$ of this rectangle is red.

About what **percentage** is: **i** blue?   **ii** white?

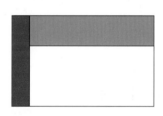

 8 Some bathroom scales measure in stones and pounds, whilst others measure in kilograms. One way to change from stones and pounds to kilograms is shown below.

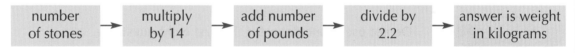

| number of stones | → | multiply by 14 | → | add number of pounds | → | divide by 2.2 | → | answer is weight in kilograms |

Convert 11 stone 10 pounds to kilograms.

You may use a calculator for the rest of the exercise.

9 The train fare for an adult from Sheffield to London is £97. A child's fare is 35% less than this. How much is a child's fare?

10 Identify which four of the following numbers are equivalent.

0.06   60%   0.60 $\frac{6}{100}$ $\frac{3}{5}$ 6% $\frac{6}{10}$

11 Calculate the following, giving your answers as fractions.

a $\frac{3}{5} + \frac{1}{3}$ **b** $\frac{5}{9} - \frac{1}{6}$ **c** $2\frac{3}{4} + 1\frac{2}{5}$

6

FM **12** Jack's Jackets is having a sale.

Calculate the sale price of a jacket that is normally priced at £42.60.

FM **13** This table shows the populations (in **thousands**) of the eight largest towns in the UK in 1991 and in 2001. It also shows the percentage change in the populations of the towns over that 10-year period.

Town	London	Birmingham	Leeds	Glasgow	Sheffield	Liverpool	Manchester	Bristol
1991	6 800	1 007	717	660	529	481	439	407
2001	7 200	1 017	731	692	531	456		423
% change	5.9%	1%	2.0%	4.8%	0.3%	−5.2%	−3.2%	

a How many more people lived in Leeds than Sheffield in 2001?

b Calculate the population of Manchester in 2001.

c Calculate the percentage change in the population of Bristol over the 10 years.

Number 2 – The four rules, ratios and directed numbers

4

Exercise 12B

Do not use a calculator for the first eight questions.

1 a Add together 143 and 328.   b Subtract 183 from 562.

c Multiply 66 by 4.   d Divide 132 by 6.

2 a Fill in the missing numbers on the number lines below.

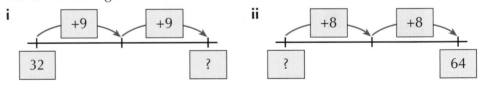

i   +9   +9   32   ?

ii   +8   +8   ?   64

b On this number line, both steps are the same size. How big is each step?

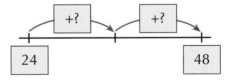

+?   +?   24   48

3 Copy and fill in the missing numbers.

a $783 - ? = 348$ b $? - 234 = 621$ c $34 \times ? = 918$

d $4629 = ? + 68$ e $? \div 33 = 19$ f $568 = 879 - ?$

1 **a** Brenda buys fish, chips and mushy peas.
  i How much does she pay?
  ii How much change does she get from a £10 note?
b Abdul has £2.15. He wants a burger and a chip butty.
  Does he have enough money?

PRICE LIST	
Fish	£1.65
Chips	£0.80
Mushy Peas	£0.45
Burger	£1.25
Bread Bun	£0.30

5 Use +, −, × or ÷ to make each calculation correct.

For example, for 3 … 7 = 2 … 5, you could insert '+' and '×' to give 3 + 7 = 2 × 5.

a 9 … 6 = 20 … 5   **b** 15 … 3 = 4 … 3
c 5 … 2 = 15 … 5   **d** 8 … 4 = 4 … 2

6 A teacher has 32 pupils in her class. She decides to buy each pupil a pen for Christmas, costing 98p. How much will it cost her altogether?

7 **a** Copy each number sequence below and put in the correct sign, '<', '=' or '>', to make each one true.
  i −6 … −2   **ii** 8 − 6 … − 2   **iii** 7 − 7 … 5 − 8

b Here is a list of numbers.

  −8 −6 −4 −2 0 1 3 5

  i Choose two numbers from the list that have a total of −1.
  ii What is the total of all the numbers in the list?
  iii Choose two different numbers from the list to make the lowest possible value when put in these boxes.

  □ − □ = ……

8 Write a number at the end of each equation to make it correct.

  a 27 + 53 = 17 + …   **b** 76 − 28 = 66 − …
  c 50 × 17 = 5 × …   **d** 400 ÷ 10 = 4000 ÷ …

You may use a calculator for the rest of the exercise.

9 Give the missing number for each of these number chains.

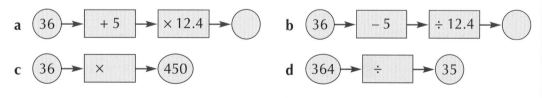

a (36) → [+ 5] → [× 12.4] → ( )   **b** (36) → [− 5] → [÷ 12.4] → ( )

c (36) → [×] → (450)   **d** (364) → [÷] → (35)

 10 Litter bins cost £29 each. A school has a budget of £500 to spend on bins. How many bins can the school afford?

11 Alf and Bert are paid £48 for doing a job. They decide to share the money in the ratio 3 : 5. How much does Alf get?

FM **12** A car company wants to move 700 cars by rail. Each train can carry 48 cars.

   a How many trains will be needed to move the 700 cars?

   b Each train costs £3745. What is the total cost of the trains?

   c What is the **cost per car** of transporting them by train?

FM **13** **a** A bus travels 234 miles in 4 hours and 30 minutes. What is the average speed of the bus?

   b A car travels 280 miles at an average speed of 60 miles per hour. How long was the car travelling for? Give your answer in hours and minutes.

Algebra 1 – Basic rules and solving linear equations

Exercise 12C   **Do not use a calculator for this exercise.**

FM **1** This advertisement shows how much a plumber charges.

   a How much would Ivor charge for a job that lasted 2 hours?

   b If Ivor charged £110 for a job, how long did it last?

> **Ivor Wrench**
> **Emergency plumber**
> £30 callout charge
> plus £20 per hour

2 Solve the following equations.

   a $x + 5 = 7$ **b** $3x = 12$ **c** $x - 6 = 10$

3 A box of pencils contains x pencils and costs £y.

   a How many pencils are there in 6 boxes?

   b How much do 5 boxes cost?

   c Which expression represents the cost of x boxes of pencils?

      i £$(x + y)$ **ii** £xy

4 **a** What is the next coordinate in the list below?

      (2, 1),   (4, 3),   (6, 5),   (8, 7),   …

   b Explain why the coordinate (29, 28) could not be part of this sequence.

5 **a** Phil has a bag of beads.

     We can't see how many beads are in the bag. Call the number of beads which Phil starts with in his bag x.

Phil puts 4 more beads into the bag.

Write an expression to show the total number of beads in Phil's bag now.

b   Keri has a bag of marbles.

Call the number of marbles which Keri starts with in her bag y.

Keri drops two of the marbles out of her bag and loses them.

Write an expression to show the total number of marbles in Keri's bag now.

c   Rhani has 4 bags of beads.

Each bag has n beads inside.

Rhani takes some beads out.

Now the total number of beads in Rhani's 4 bags is $4n - 8$.

Which of the following statements below could be true?

    A   Rhani took 2 beads out of every bag.
    B   Rhani took 2 beads out of only 2 bags.
    C   Rhani took 4 beads out of every bag
    D   Rhani took 4 beads out of just two bags
    E   Rhani took 8 beads out of one bag and only 1 out of another.
    F   Rhani took 12 beads out of one bag.

6 a, b and c represent the weights in kilograms of three children, Ali, Billie and Charlie.

a   Match each of the following algebraic expressions with one of the statements below.

$$a = 30 \qquad b = 2a$$
$$b + c = 75 \qquad \frac{a + b + c}{3} = 35$$

Statement 1: Billie weighs twice as much as Ali.
Statement 2: The mean weight of all three children is 35 kg.
Statement 3: Ali weighs 30 kgs.
Statement 4: Billie and Charlie weigh 75 kg together.

b   Use the information to work out Billie's weight and Charlie's weight.

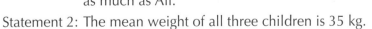

7 The diagram shows a square with sides of length $(n + 4)$ cm.

The square has been split into four smaller rectangles. The area of one rectangle is shown.

a Fill in the three missing areas with a number or an algebraic expression.

b Write down an expression for the total area of the square.

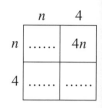

8 Expand the brackets and simplify the following expressions if possible.

a $4(x - 5)$ **b** $3(2x + 1) + 5x$ **c** $3(x - 2) + 2(x + 4)$

d $5(3x + 4) + 2(x - 2)$ **e** $4(2x + 1) - 3(x - 6)$

9 **a** When $x = 4$ and $y = 6$ work out the value of each of the three expressions below.

i $3x + 9$ **ii** $4x - y$ **iii** $2(3x + 2y + 1)$

b Solve the equations below to find the value of z in each case.

i $5z + 9 = 24$ **ii** $\dfrac{z - 8}{2} = 7$ **iii** $5z + 9 = 3z + 7$

10 Two friends, Selma and Khalid are revising algebra.

Selma says 'I am thinking of a number. If you multiply it by 6 and add 3 you get an answer of 12.'

Khalid says 'I am thinking of a number. If you multiply it by 3 and subtract 6 you get the same answer as adding the number to 7.'

a Call Selma's number x and form an equation. Then solve the equation.

b Call Khalid's number y and form an equation. Then solve the equation.

Algebra 2 - Graphs

Exercise 12D

Do not use a calculator for this exercise.

You will need graph paper or centimetre-squared paper.

For any graphs you are asked to draw, axes the size of the ones in the fourth question will be big enough.

1 Emma and Shehab are playing a game.

Emma has to make a line of four 'X's like this to win.

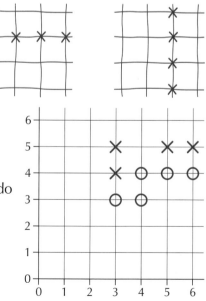

a Copy the grid below and place one more make a winning line for Emma.

b Write the coordinates of the 4 'X's in Emma's winning line.

c Look at the numbers in the coordinates. What do you notice?

2 **a** The point M is halfway between points A and C.
What are the coordinates of M?

b Shape ABCD is a square.
What are the coordinates of the point D?

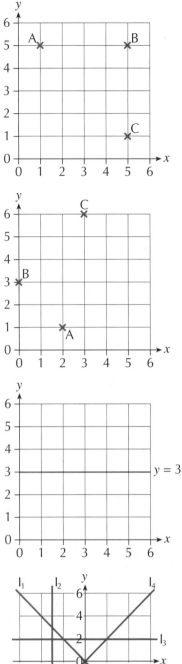

3 The graph shows points A, B and C.

a What are the coordinates of A and B?

b ABCD makes a rectangle. What are the coordinates of D?

4 The graph shows the line $y = 3$.

Copy the diagram and draw on it the graphs of the following.

a $y = 5$ **b** $x = 4$

5 Each of the lines labelled l_1, l_2, l_3 and l_4 has one of the equations in the list below. Match each line to its equation.

a $y = 2$ **b** $y = x$

c $x = -3$ **d** $y = -x$

 6 The distance–time graph shows the journey of a jogger on a 5-mile run. At one point she stopped to admire the view and at another point she ran up a steep hill.

a For how long did she stop to admire the view?

b What distance into her run was the start of the hill?

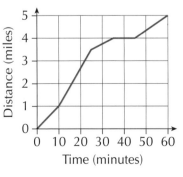

FM **7** In a house, the hot water tank automatically refills with cold water whenever hot water is taken out. The heating system then heats the water to a pre-set temperature.

Dad always has a shower in the morning. Mum always has a bath and the two children get up so late that all they do is wash their hands and faces.

The graph shows the temperature of the water in the hot water tank between 7 am and 9 am one morning.

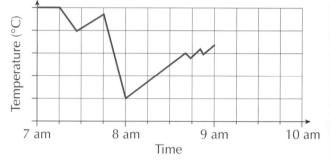

a At what time did Dad have his shower?

b At what time did Mum have her bath?

c At what time did the first child wash?

d Gran likes to have as hot a bath as possible, once everyone else has left the house at 9 am. Estimate at what time the water will be back to its maximum temperature.

8 Draw and label each of the following graphs.

a $y = 2x + 1$ **b** $y = \frac{1}{2}x - 1$ **c** $x + y = 3$

9 Does the point (20, 30) lie on the line $y = 2x - 10$? Explain your answer.

10 For every point on the graph of $x + y = 6$, the x- and y-coordinates add up to 6.

a Which of the following points lie on the line?

  i (3, −3)   **ii** (6, 0)   **iii** (−7, −1)   **iv** (−1, 7)

b On a grid draw the graph of $x + y = 6$.

Geometry and measures

Do not use a calculator for Questions 1 to 7.

You will find squared paper useful for Questions 5 and 12.

1 For each of the shapes below write down:

  i the number of lines of symmetry.

  ii the order of rotational symmetry.

    a   **b**   **c**

2 In parts **a** to **c** write down the name of the quadrilateral being described.

    a It has 4 right angles. It has 2 lines of symmetry.

    b It has 1 pair of equal angles. It has 2 pairs of equal sides.

    c It has no lines of symmetry. It has rotational symmetry of order 2.

    d Complete the following for a Rhombus.

        i It has ...... equal sides.

        ii It has ...... lines of symmetry.

        iii It has rotational symmetry of order ....

3 a What is the area of this rectangle?

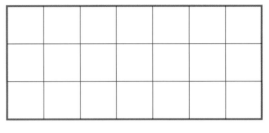

    b The rectangle is cut into four triangles as shown. What is the area of one of the larger triangles?

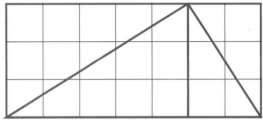

    c The four triangles are put together to form a kite. What is the area of the kite?

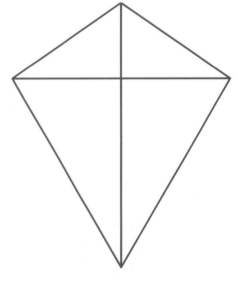

4 a Describe angles A–E in the diagram using the correct words chosen from this list.

        Acute   **Obtuse**

        Reflex   **Right-angled**

    b Is angle A bigger, smaller or the same size as angle C? Explain your answer.

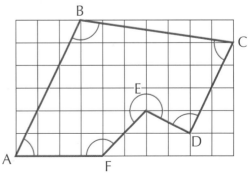

5 Copy each of the following diagrams and shade in more circles so that the dotted lines are lines of symmetry. You may find squared paper helpful.

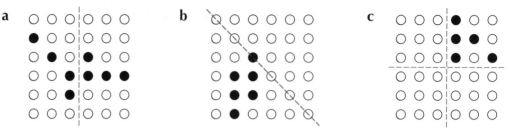

6 a Copy and complete the two-way table to show the symmetries of each of the shapes shown. Shape A has been done for you.

A   B   C   D   E   F   G

		Number of lines of symmetry				
		0	**1**	**2**	**3**	**4**
Order of rotational symmetry	**1**		A			
	2					
	3					
	4					

b Name a quadrilateral that has two lines of symmetry and rotational symmetry of order 2.

7 a Make an accurate construction of this triangle.
b Measure the angle at A.

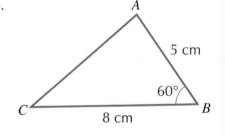

You may use a calculator for the rest of this exercise.

8 Find the values of angles *a*, *b* and *c* in this diagram. The lines marked with arrows are parallel.

9 This car speedometer shows speed in both miles per hour (mph) and kilometres per hour (kph). Use the speedometer to answer the following questions.

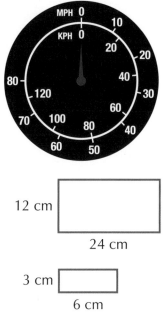

a How many kilometres are equivalent to 50 miles?

b Is someone travelling at 100 kph breaking the speed limit of 70 mph? Justify your answer.

c About how many miles is 150 km? Explain your answer.

10 a A rectangle measures 24 cm by 12 cm. What is its area?

b The rectangle is folded in half several times until it measures 6 cm by 3 cm. How many times was it folded?

c What is the ratio of the **areas** of the original rectangle and the smaller rectangle? Give your answer in its simplest form.

12 cm ⬚ 24 cm

3 cm ⬚ 6 cm

Statistics

Exercise 12F   **You do not need to use a calculator for this exercise.**

 1 This bar chart shows the favourite pets of 80 pupils.

a How many pupils chose a rabbit as their favourite pet?

b How many more pupils preferred a cat to a horse?

c What is the difference between the number of pupils who chose the most popular pet and those who chose the least popular?

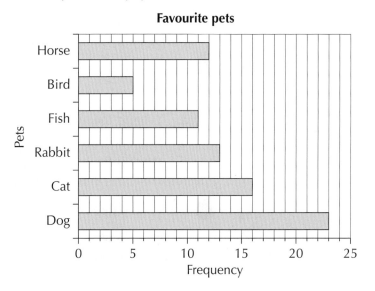

2 This table shows the types and colours of vehicles passing a school between 9 am and 10 am.

a How many white vans passed the school?

b How many lorries passed the school altogether?

c How many more blue vehicles than red vehicles passed the school?

	Red	Black	White	Blue
Lorries	2	6	0	3
Vans	3	1	7	2
Cars	6	5	9	8

FM **3** This is the calendar for the first two months of 2004.

JANUARY					
Mon		5	12	19	26
Tue		6	13	20	27
Wed		7	14	21	28
Thu	1	8	15	22	29
Fri	2	9	16	23	30
Sat	3	10	17	24	31
Sun	4	11	18	25	

FEBRUARY					
Mon		2	9	16	23
Tue		3	10	17	24
Wed		4	11	18	25
Thu		5	12	19	26
Fri		6	13	20	27
Sat		7	14	21	28
Sun	1	8	15	22	29

a The Disney marathon in Florida is on the second Sunday in January. What date is this?

b There are 5 days the same (Sundays) in February. This only happens every four years. Explain why.

c Mr Henry is going to Florida for a holiday. He arrives on the 22nd of January and leaves on the 11th of February. How many **nights** will he be in Florida?

4 a Zeenat rolls an ordinary six-sided dice. What is the probability that the dice shows an even number?

b Zeenat now rolls the dice and tosses a coin. One way that the dice and the coin could land is to show a head and a score of 1. This can be written as (H, 1).

Copy and complete the list below to show all the possible outcomes.

(H, 1), (H, 2), …

c Zeenat rolls the dice and it shows a score of 6. She rolls the dice again. What is the probability that the dice shows a score of 6 this time?

5 Hakim has 5 cards.

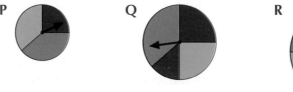

a What is the mode of the numbers on the cards?

b What is the median of the numbers on the cards?

c What is the mean of the numbers on the cards?

6 Look at the three different spinners, P, Q and R, below.

a Which spinner has the greatest chance of landing on red?

b Which spinner has an evens chance of landing on blue?

c Which two spinners have an equal chance of landing on green?

7 a At a leisure centre, people take part in one of five different sports.

The table shows the percentage of people who played badminton, five-a-side and squash on Saturday.

Copy the pie chart below and label the two sections for badminton and five-a-side.

Sport	Percentage
Badminton	20
Five-a-side	30
Squash	10
Swimming	
Running	

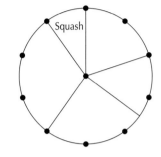

b On this Saturday, more people went swimming than went running.
Use the chart to estimate the percentage of people who:

i went swimming.　　**ii** went running.

c Altogether, 180 people played the different sports on Saturday.
Use the table below to find out how many played:

i five-a-side.　　**ii** badminton.

Sport	Percentage	Number of people
Badminton	20%	
Five-a-side	30%	
Squash	10%	18

d Altogether, 180 people played the different sports on Saturday and 280 people played the different sports on Sunday.

30% of the people played five-a-side on Saturday but only 20% of the people played five-a-side on Sunday.

Conrad said: '30% is more than 20%, so more people played five-a-side on Saturday.'

Explain why Conrad is wrong.

8 Two four-sided dice, each numbered 1, 2, 3, 4 are thrown.
The table shows all the possible total scores.

a When the two dice are thrown what is the probability that the total score is a square number?

b When the two dice are thrown what is the probability that the score is greater than 5?

c i Draw a table to show all the possible products if the numbers on each of the dice are multiplied together.

ii What is the probability that the product is a number less than 17?

Score on first dice

		1	2	3	4
Score on second dice	**1**	2	3	4	5
	2	3	4	5	6
	3	4	5	6	7
	4	5	6	7	8

5

6

9 A bag contains only red and blue marbles. A marble is to be taken from the bag at random.

It is twice as likely that the marble will be red as blue. Give a possible number of red and blue marbles in the bag.

10 Paul's marks for his last nine maths homeworks are:

9,   3,   5,   4,   4,   7,   5,   8,   6

a What is the range of his marks?

b What is the median mark?

c After checking the final homework, Paul realised that his teacher did not mark one of the questions. Once this had been marked, Paul's mark increased from 6 to 8.

Say whether each of the statements, **i**, **ii** and **iii** are true, false or if it is not possible to say. Explain your answers.

i The mode of the marks has increased.

ii The median mark has increased.

iii The mean mark has increased.

11 The probability that a ball taken at random from a bag is black is 0.7. What is the probability that a ball taken at random from the same bag is **not** black?

 More National Test practice provided in the Interactive Book.

Statistics **3** and Revision

<table>
<tr><td>

This chapter is going to show you

- Some of the statistical techniques you have met before
- How to make a hypothesis
- How to carry out a handling data investigation

</td><td>

What you should already know

- How to carry out a survey
- How to write a questionnaire
- How to collect data
- How to construct and interpret two-way tables
- How to construct and interpret frequency diagrams
- How to interpret scatter graphs
- How to calculate averages
- How to calculate a range
- How to construct and interpret a stem-and-leaf diagram

</td></tr>
</table>

Statistical techniques

This lesson will remind you of the statistical techniques that you have met before. You will be using these to carry out a handling data project.

The following tables show the vocabulary you should know before you start an investigation.

Statistics vocabulary

Collecting data

	Definition	Example
Questionnaire	A set of questions used to collect information from people	Here is an example of a poor question: How old are you? ☐ 0–10 ☐ 10–20 ☐ 20–30 ☐ over 30 It is poor because the categories overlap, so that both 10 and 20 are in two response sections.
Population	The set of people or objects being investigated	A school with 1000 pupils
Sample	Part of the whole population being used for analysis	50 pupils picked from the 1000 in a school
Survey	The collection of data from a sample of the population	Investigating the favourite colour of pupils in a school by asking 50 pupils
Census	The collection of data from an entire population	Investigating the favourite colour of pupils in a school by asking *every* pupil in the school

	Definition	Example
Data collection sheet or Observation sheet	A form for recording results	Favourite colours of 50 pupils: Blue ⎜⎜⎜⎜⎜ ⎜⎜⎜⎜⎜ Red ⎜⎜⎜⎜⎜ ⎜⎜⎜⎜⎜ ⎜⎜⎜⎜⎜ ⎜⎜⎜ Green ⎜⎜⎜⎜⎜ ⎜⎜⎜⎜⎜ ⎜⎜⎜⎜ Other ⎜⎜⎜⎜⎜ ⎜⎜⎜
Tally	A means of recording data quickly	
Raw data	Data which has not been sorted or analysed	Ages of 10 pupils: 12, 14, 13, 11, 12, 12, 15, 13, 11, 12
Primary data	Data that *you* have collected, usually by observation, surveys or experiments	Colours of cars on your street
Secondary data	Data collected by someone else and then used by you	Acceleration times of different cars

Two-way table — A table for combining two sets of data

	Ford	Vauxhall	Peugeot
Red	3	5	2
Blue	1	0	4
Green	2	0	1

Frequency table — A table showing the quantities of different items or values

Weight of parcels W (kg)	Number of parcels (frequency)
$0 < W \leq 1$	5
$1 < W \leq 2$	7
$W > 2$	3

Frequency diagram — A diagram showing the quantities of different items or values

BAR CHART

PIE CHART

LINE GRAPH

	Definition	Example
Stem-and-leaf diagram	A way of grouping data, in order	**Recorded speeds of 17 cars** 2 | 3 7 7 8 9 9 3 | 1 2 3 5 5 5 7 9 4 | 2 2 5 Key: 2 | 3 means 23 miles per hour
Population pyramid	A statistical diagram often used for comparing large sets of data	 **Age distribution in France (2000)**
Scatter graph or scatter diagram	A graph to compare two sets of data	

Processing data

	Definition	Example
Mode	The value that occurs *most* often	Find the mode, median, mean and range of this set of data 23, 17, 25, 19, 17, 23, 21, 23
Median	The *middle* value when the data is written in order (or the average of the middle two values)	Sorting the data into order, smallest first, gives: 17, 17, 19, 21, 23, 23, 23, 25 Mode = 23
Mean	The sum of all the values divided by the number of items of data	Median = $\dfrac{21 + 23}{2}$ = 22 Mean = $\dfrac{17 + 17 + 19 + 21 + 23 + 23 + 23 + 25}{8}$ = 21
Range	The difference between the largest and smallest values	Range = 25 − 17 = 8

Exercise 13A

1 Look at the population pyramid for France in the year 2000 on page 181.

 a Are there more males or females aged over 70? Explain your answer.

 b Which age group is the largest for males?

 c Which age group under 50 is the smallest for females?

2 Calculate the mode, the median and the mean for each set of data below.

 a 1, 1, 1, 4, 8, 17, 50

 b 2, 5, 11, 5, 8, 7, 6, 1, 4

 c £2.50, £4.50, £2, £3, £4.50, £2.50, £3, £4.50, £3.50, £4, £3.50

 d 18, 18, 19, 21, 24, 25

3 Criticise each of the following questions that were used in a questionnaire about travelling to school.

 a How do you travel to school?

 ☐ Walk   ☐ Bus   ☐ Car

 b How long does your journey take?

 ☐ 0–5 minutes   ☐ 5–10 minutes

 ☐ 10–15 minutes   ☐ 15–20 minutes

 c What time do you usually set off to school?

 ☐ Before 8.00 am   ☐ 8.00–8.15 am

 ☐ 8.15–8.30 am   ☐ Other

4 Below are the times taken (*T* seconds) by 20 pupils to run 100 m.

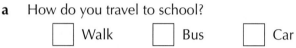

Boys	13.1	14.0	17.9	15.2	15.9	17.5	13.9	21.3	15.5	17.6
Girls	15.3	17.8	16.3	18.1	19.2	21.4	13.5	18.2	18.4	13.6

 a Copy and complete the two-way table to show the frequencies.

	Boys		Girls	
	Tally	Frequency	Tally	Frequency
$12 \leq T < 14$	||	2	||	2
$14 \leq T < 16$				
$16 \leq T < 18$				
$18 \leq T < 20$				
$20 \leq T < 22$				

 b Which is the modal class for the boys?

 c Which is the modal class for the girls?

5 19 pupils take a test. The total marks were shown on the stem-and-leaf diagram.

```
0 | 5 6 8 9
1 | 0 1 1 2 2 4 4 5 6 6 7 8 9 9
2 | 0
```

Key: 0 | 6 means 6

a Write down the lowest and highest scores.

b State the range of the marks.

c Work out the median mark.

d How many pupils scored 15 or more in the test?

6 A school quiz team is made up of pupils from four different classes. The table shows the number of pupils in the team from each class.

Class	Number of pupils
A	4
B	3
C	8
D	5

a Represent this information in a pie chart.

b Holly says, 'The percentage of pupils chosen from class C is double the percentage chosen from class A.' Explain why this might not be true.

Extension Work

FM

It was estimated that there were almost 59 million people living in the UK in 2001. This was an increase of 2.4% since 1991.

The graph shows the population (in thousands) of the UK between 1991 and 2001. Explain why it is misleading.

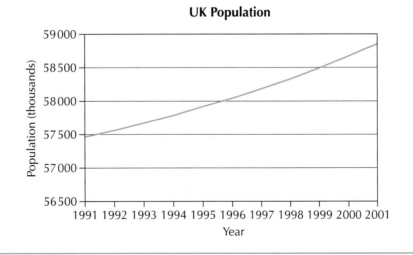

UK Population

A handling data project

In this section you are going to plan and write a handling data investigation. Look at the handling data cycle below. This shows the basic steps in an investigation.

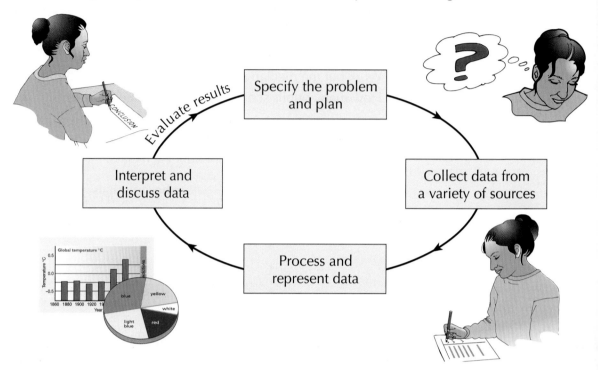

More detail is given about each step below. Follow this checklist when doing your investigation and writing your report.

- **Specify the problem and plan**
  - Statement of problem or topic to investigate
  - Hypothesis stating what you think the investigation will show
  - How you will choose your sample and sample size
  - Any practical problems you foresee
  - How you will obtain your data, possibly including how to avoid bias

- **Collect data from a variety of sources**
  - Follow initial plan and use a suitable data-collection sheet

- **Process and represent data**
  - Analysis of your results using appropriate statistical calculations and diagrams

- **Interpret and discuss data**
  - Comparison of results with your original hypothesis
  - List of any factors which might have affected your results and how you could overcome these in future
  - A final conclusion

Exercise 13B In pairs, investigate one of the following topics.

(FM) ① Compare the number of vehicles going in opposite directions on a road near you.

(FM) ② Compare the time taken to count down from 100 in different step sizes.

(FM) ③ Investigate the ability of people to estimate the lengths of straight lines.

(FM) ④ Compare the word lengths in two different newspapers.

(FM) ⑤ Choose your own investigation.

Extension Work

Choose one of the following tasks.

1 Working individually, write a report of your investigation using the checklist.

2 In your pairs, create a display which can be used as part of a presentation to show the other groups in your class how you carried out your investigation and what results you obtained.

3 If you have completed your report, then consider a different problem from the list in **Exercise 13B**. Write a plan of how you would investigate it, including how to overcome any problems encountered in your first project.

More National Test practice provided in the Interactive Book.

CHAPTER 14

Geometry and Measures **4** and Revision

<table>
<tr><td>

This chapter is going to show you

- Some of the methods already met when dealing with shapes
- How to carry out a shape and space investigation
- How to carry out a symmetry investigation

</td><td>

What you should already know

- How to find the area of 2-D shapes
- How to find the surface area and the volume of a cuboid
- How to use reflective and rotational symmetry

</td></tr>
</table>

Geometry revision

Before starting an investigation into geometry and measures, you must be familiar with all the formulae and terms which you have met so far.

This section provides a checklist before you start your investigation.

Perimeter and area

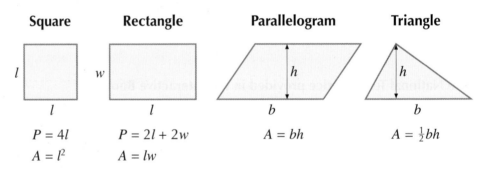

Square

$P = 4l$
$A = l^2$

Rectangle

$P = 2l + 2w$
$A = lw$

Parallelogram

$A = bh$

Triangle

$A = \frac{1}{2}bh$

Remember that the metric units for perimeter are the same as for length: millimetres (mm), centimetres (cm) and metres (m).

Remember that the metric units for area are: square millimetres (mm^2), square centimetres (cm^2) and square metres (m^2).

Volume and surface area

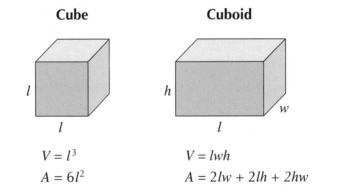

Cube

$V = l^3$
$A = 6l^2$

Cuboid

$V = lwh$
$A = 2lw + 2lh + 2hw$

Remember that the metric units for volume are:
cubic millimetres (mm^3)
cubic centimetres (cm^3)
cubic metres (m^3)

1 For each of the following rectangles, find: **i**   the perimeter.   **ii**   the area.

a
3 cm

3 cm

b
4 cm

5 cm

c
12 mm

10 mm

d
5 m

12 m

2 Find the area of each of the following triangles.

a
2 cm

4 cm

b
8 cm

5 cm

c
30 mm

20 mm

d
7 m

4 m

3 Find the area of each of the following parallelograms.

a
6 cm

11 cm

b
12 cm

8 cm

c
3 m

4 m

d
5 m

16 m

4 For each of the following cuboids, find: **i**   the surface area.   **ii**   the volume.

a
2 cm

5 cm   3 cm

b
5 cm

5 cm   5 cm

c
1 m

2 m

4 m

5 Calculate the area of the square drawn
on the centimetre grid.

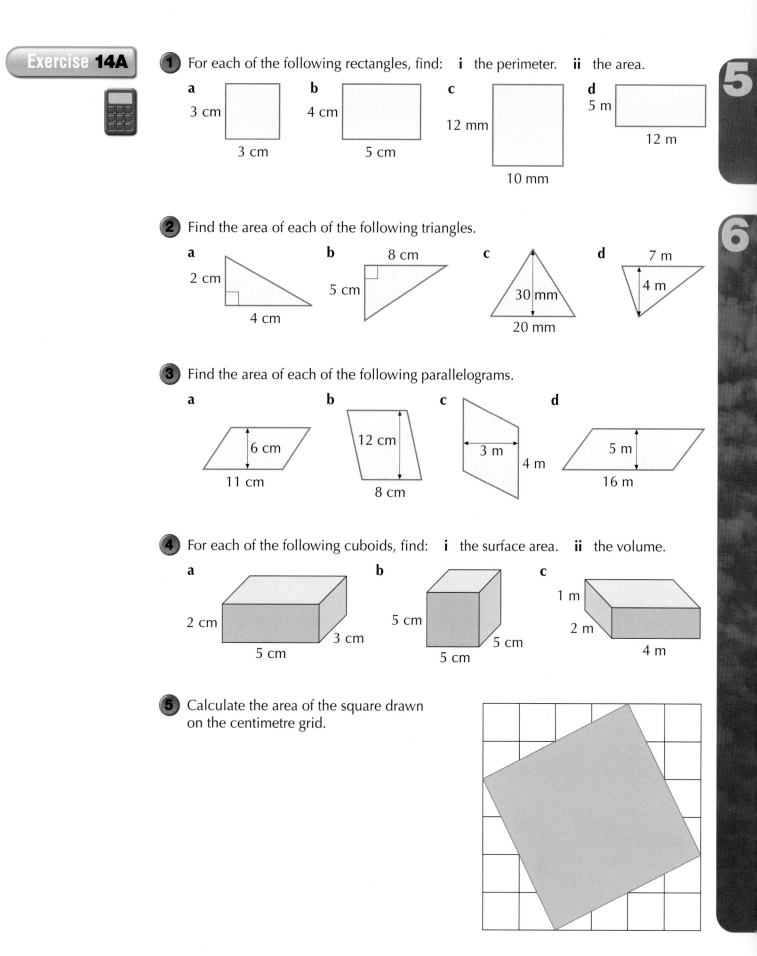

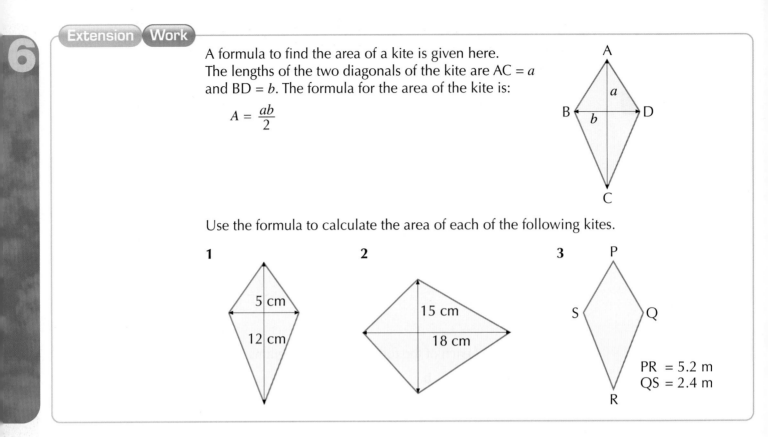

Extension Work

A formula to find the area of a kite is given here.
The lengths of the two diagonals of the kite are AC = *a*
and BD = *b*. The formula for the area of the kite is:

$$A = \frac{ab}{2}$$

Use the formula to calculate the area of each of the following kites.

1

5 cm

12 cm

2

15 cm

18 cm

3

P

S   Q

R

PR = 5.2 m
QS = 2.4 m

Geometry and measures investigations

When undertaking an investigation, you should carry out the following.

- Draw some easy examples first, making all diagrams clear with all measurements shown.

- Put your results in a table with suitable headings.

- Look for any patterns among the entries in the table.

- Describe and explain any patterns you spot.

- Try to find a rule or formula to explain each pattern.

- Try another example to see whether your rule or formula does work.

- Summarise your results with a conclusion.

- If possible, extend the investigation by introducing different questions.

Exercise 14B   Working in pairs or small groups, investigate one of the following.

 Investigate whether the perimeter and the area of a square can have the same value. Extend the problem by looking at rectangles.

188

2 For the growing squares on the grid below, investigate the ratio of the length of a side to the perimeter and the ratio of the length of a side to the area.

3 The shapes below are drawn on a 1 cm grid of dots.

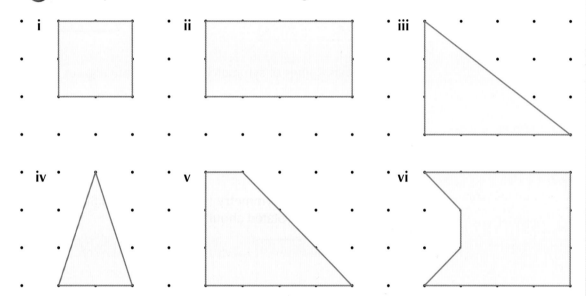

Shape	Number of dots on perimeter of shape	Number of dots inside shape	Area of shape (cm²)
i			
ii			
iii			
iv			
v			
vi			

a Copy and complete the table for each shape.

b Find a formula that connects the number of dots on the perimeter *P*, the number of dots inside *I* and the area *A* of each shape.

c Check your formula by drawing different shapes on a 1 cm grid of dots.

Symmetry revision

Before starting an investigation into symmetry, you must be familiar with the terms which you have met so far.

This section provides a checklist before you start your investigation.

There are two types of symmetry: **reflection symmetry** and **rotational symmetry**.

Some 2-D shapes have both types of symmetry, while some have only one type.

All 2-D shapes have rotational symmetry of order 1 or more.

Reflection symmetry

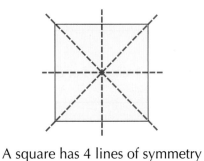

A square has 4 lines of symmetry   A parallelogram has no lines of symmetry

Remember that tracing paper or a mirror can be used to find the lines of symmetry of a shape.

Rotational symmetry

A 2-D shape has rotational symmetry when it can be rotated about a point to look exactly the same in its new position.

The **order of rotational symmetry** is the number of different positions in which the shape looks the same when rotated about the point.

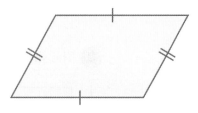

A square has rotational symmetry   This trapezium has rotational symmetry
of order 4   of order 1

Remember that tracing paper can be used to find the order of rotational symmetry of a shape.

Exercise 14C

5

1 Copy each of these shapes and draw its lines of symmetry. Write below each shape the number of lines of symmetry it has.

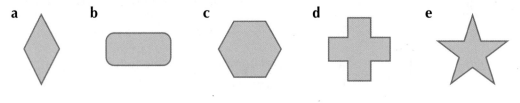

a   b   c   d   e

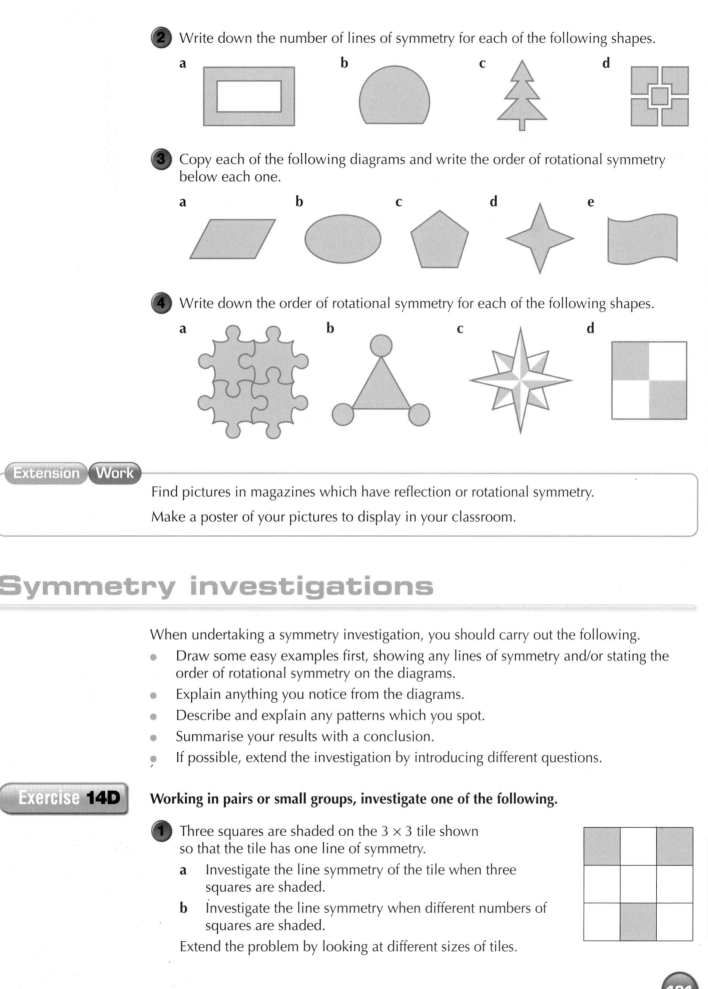

2 Write down the number of lines of symmetry for each of the following shapes.

a   b   c   d

3 Copy each of the following diagrams and write the order of rotational symmetry below each one.

a   b   c   d   e

4 Write down the order of rotational symmetry for each of the following shapes.

a   b   c   d

5

Extension   Work

Find pictures in magazines which have reflection or rotational symmetry.

Make a poster of your pictures to display in your classroom.

Symmetry investigations

When undertaking a symmetry investigation, you should carry out the following.

- Draw some easy examples first, showing any lines of symmetry and/or stating the order of rotational symmetry on the diagrams.
- Explain anything you notice from the diagrams.
- Describe and explain any patterns which you spot.
- Summarise your results with a conclusion.
- If possible, extend the investigation by introducing different questions.

Exercise 14D   **Working in pairs or small groups, investigate one of the following.**

1 Three squares are shaded on the 3 × 3 tile shown so that the tile has one line of symmetry.

   a   Investigate the line symmetry of the tile when three squares are shaded.

   b   Investigate the line symmetry when different numbers of squares are shaded.

Extend the problem by looking at different sizes of tiles.

6

2 Pentominoes are shapes made from five squares which touch edge to edge. Here are two examples.

Investigate line symmetry and rotational symmetry for different pentominoes.

Extend the problem by looking at hexominoes. These are shapes made from six squares which touch edge to edge.

3 In how many ways will the T-shape fit inside the 3 × 3 grid?

Investigate the number of ways the T-shape will fit inside a 1 cm square grid of any size.

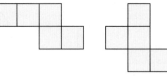

More National Test practice provided in the Interactive Book.

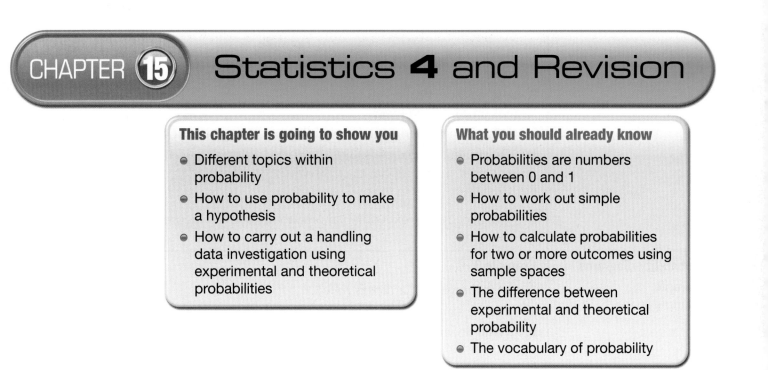

CHAPTER 15

Statistics **4** and Revision

<table>
<tr><td>This chapter is going to show you</td><td>What you should already know</td></tr>
<tr><td>

- Different topics within probability
- How to use probability to make a hypothesis
- How to carry out a handling data investigation using experimental and theoretical probabilities

</td><td>

- Probabilities are numbers between 0 and 1
- How to work out simple probabilities
- How to calculate probabilities for two or more outcomes using sample spaces
- The difference between experimental and theoretical probability
- The vocabulary of probability

</td></tr>
</table>

Revision of probability

Make sure that you are familiar with the vocabulary to do with probability which is listed in the table below.

Probability vocabulary

	Example
Probability scale Chance/likelihood Equally likely Certain Uncertain Very likely Unlikely Fifty–fifty chance/evens	0 0.5 1 Impossible Very unlikely Unlikely 50-50 Chance Likely Very likely Certain
Probability Event Outcome Random Experimental probability Theoretical probability Estimates of probability (relative frequency) Bias Fair	**Example 1** A fair spinner is numbered 1, 2, 3. **a** The spinner is spun twice. List all the outcomes. **b** How many possible outcomes are there if the spinner is spun 3 times? **a** 1, 1 1, 2 1, 3 2, 1 2, 2 2, 3 3, 1 3, 2 3, 3 **b** $3 \times 3 \times 3 = 27$

	Example
Probability (continued)	**Example 2** A six-sided dice is rolled 60 times. It lands on a 6 fifteen times. **a** What is the experimental probability of landing on a 6? **b** Do you think the dice is fair? **a** $\dfrac{15}{60} = \dfrac{1}{4}$ **b** No, because the experimental probability and the theoretical probability are different.
Probability diagrams Sample Sample space	**Example 3** A coin is thrown and a dice is rolled. **a** Draw a sample space diagram. **b** Write down the probability of getting a head and a 6. **a** <table><tr><td colspan="2"></td><td colspan="6" align="center">Dice</td></tr><tr><td colspan="2"></td><td>1</td><td>2</td><td>3</td><td>4</td><td>5</td><td>6</td></tr><tr><td rowspan="2">Coin</td><td>Head</td><td>H,1</td><td>H,2</td><td>H,3</td><td>H,4</td><td>H,5</td><td>H,6</td></tr><tr><td>Tail</td><td>T,1</td><td>T,2</td><td>T,3</td><td>T,4</td><td>T,5</td><td>T,6</td></tr></table> **b** $\dfrac{1}{12}$
Events Exhaustive Independent Mutually exclusive	**Example 4** In a raffle there are 100 tickets, coloured blue, green or yellow. The table shows the number of tickets of each colour.

Ticket colour	Number of tickets
Blue	50
Green	20
Yellow	30

a What is the probability of picking a blue ticket?
b What is the probability of picking a yellow ticket?
c What is the probability of picking a blue or green ticket?
d What is the probability of picking a ticket that is not green?

a $\dfrac{1}{2}$

b $\dfrac{3}{10}$

c $\dfrac{7}{10}$

d $1 - \dfrac{1}{5} = \dfrac{4}{5}$ |
| **Probability notation**
P(Event) | $P(\text{Green}) = \dfrac{1}{5}$ |

1 Ten cards are numbered 1 to 10. A card is picked at random. Work out the probability of picking:

a the number 5.

b an even number.

c a number greater than 8.

d a number less than or equal to 4.

2 Two coins are thrown.

a How many different outcomes are there?

b Work out the probability of getting no heads.

c Work out the probability of getting two heads.

d Work out the probability of getting exactly one head.

3 Matthew is either late, on time or early for school. The table shows his record over 10 days.

Late	On time	Early
1	3	6

Use the table to estimate the probability that on one day he is:

a late.

b on time.

c early.

d not late.

4 A group of 50 pupils are told to draw two straight lines on a piece of paper. Seven pupils draw parallel lines, twelve draw perpendicular lines and the rest draw lines which are neither parallel nor perpendicular.

Use these results to estimate the probability that a pupil chosen at random has:

a drawn parallel lines.

b drawn perpendicular lines.

c drawn lines that are neither parallel nor perpendicular.

5 A five-sided spinner is spun 50 times. Here are the results.

Number on spinner	1	2	3	4	5
Frequency	8	11	10	6	15

a Write down the experimental probability of the spinner landing on the number 4.

b Write down the theoretical probability of a fair, five-sided spinner landing on the number 4.

c Compare the experimental and theoretical probabilities and say whether you think the spinner is fair.

Extension Work

Using two dice, find the probability of rolling a double.

A probability investigation

Look again at the handling data cycle.

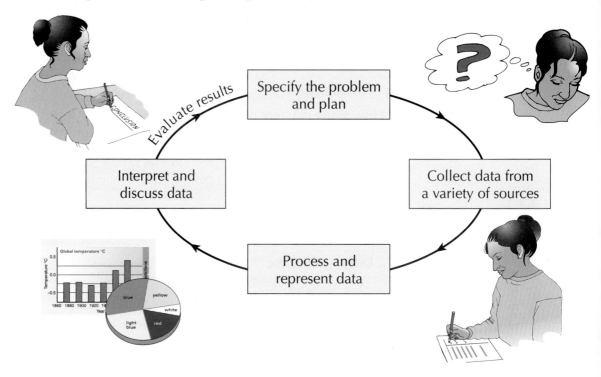

Use the handling data cycle to help you when completing your probability investigation. More detail is given about each step below.

- **Specify the problem and plan**
  - Statement of problem or topic to investigate
  - Hypothesis stating what you think the investigation will show
  - How you will choose your sample and sample size
  - Any practical problems you foresee
  - How you will obtain your data, possibly including how to avoid bias

- **Collect data from a variety of sources**
  - Follow initial plan and use a suitable data-collection sheet

- **Process and represent data**
  - Analysis of your results using appropriate statistical calculations and diagrams

- **Interpret and discuss data**
  - Comparison of results with your original hypothesis
  - List of any factors which might have affected your results and how you could overcome these in future
  - A final conclusion

Exercise 15B In small groups carry out an experiment to investigate one of the following.

1. Organise a class lottery. Get each person to choose 10 numbers, from 1 to 20. Have 10 separate draws and record who has a winning number each time (there may be more than one winner for each draw). Compare the theoretical and experimental probabilities of each player winning.

2. Investigate whether a drawing pin will land point up more often than point down. Use different-sized drawing pins to test whether the results are always the same.

3. Ask a member of your group to put ten coloured cubes in a bag, so that the rest of the group do not know what the colours are. Investigate how many times you need to pick a cube out and replace it in order to be able to predict accurately the contents of the bag.

4. Some people are luckier than others when rolling a dice.

5. A playing card usually lands face-up when dropped.

Extension Work

Choose one of the following tasks.

1 Working individually, write a report of your experiment using the checklist.

2 In small groups, create a display which can be used as part of a presentation to show the other groups in your class how you carried out your experiment and what results you obtained.

3 If you have completed your report, then consider a different problem from the list in **Exercise 15B**. Write a plan of how you would investigate it, including how to overcome any problems encountered in your first project.

 More National Test practice provided in the Interactive Book.

CHAPTER 16

GCSE Preparation

This chapter is going to

● Get you started on your GCSE course

BODMAS

You have already met BODMAS in Years 7 and 8. It gives the order in which mathematical operations are carried out in calculations.

Remember, that if a calculation is a string of additions and subtractions, or a string of multiplications and divisions, then the calculation is done from left to right.

B – Brackets
O – pOwers
DM – Division and Multiplication
AS – Addition and Subtraction

Example 16.1 ▷ Work out each of the following, using the order of operations given by BODMAS. Show each step of the calculation.

a $10 \div 2 + 3 \times 3$ **b** $10 \div (2 + 3) \times 3$

a Firstly, work out the division and multiplication, which gives $5 + 9$
Then work out the addition to give 14

b Firstly, work out the bracket, which gives $10 \div 5 \times 3$
There is a choice between division and multiplication, so decide on the order by working from left to right:
Work out the left-hand operation first, which gives 2×3
Then work out the remaining operation to give 6

Example 16.2 ▷ Work out: **a** $30 - 4 \times 2^2$ **b** $(30 - 4) \times 2^2$

Show each step of the calculation.

a Firstly, work out the power, which gives $30 - 4 \times 4$
Secondly, the multiplication, which gives $30 - 16$
Finally, the subtraction to give 14

b Firstly, work out the bracket, which gives 26×2^2
Secondly, the power, which gives 26×4
Finally, the multiplication to give 104

Do not use a calculator for this exercise.

1. Use BODMAS to work out each of the following.

   a $3 \times 6 + 7$
   b $8 \div 4 + 8$
   c $6 + 9 - 3$
   d $15 \div 3 + 7$
   e $4 \times 6 \div 2$
   f $3^2 \times 4 + 1$

2. Use BODMAS to work out each of the following. Remember to work out the brackets first.

   a $3 \times (3 + 7)$
   b $12 \div (3 + 1)$
   c $(9 + 4) - 4$
   d $4 \times (6 \div 2)$
   e $20 \div (2 + 3)$
   f $3 + (2 + 1)^2$

3. Write the operation that you do first in each of these calculations, and then work out each calculation.

   a $6 \times 2 - 3$
   b $4 + 3 \times 5$
   c $12 \div 2 - 3$
   d $15 - 5 \div 2$
   e $6 \times 2 \div 1$
   f $4 \times 6 - 3^2$

4. Use BODMAS to work out each of the following.

   a $16 - 4 \times 2$
   b $7 \times (4 + 3)$
   c $12 \div 4 + 8$
   d $(18 - 6) \div 4$
   e $15 \div (4 + 1)$
   f $12 + 4 \times 5$
   g $(24 \div 4) + 7$
   h $5 + 3^2 \times 2$
   i $5 \times 4 - 4^2$
   j $(3^2 + 1) \times 5$
   k $4^2 \times (4 - 1)$
   l $(6 - 1)^2 - 5$

5. Copy each of these calculations and then put in brackets to make each calculation true.

   a $4 \times 3 + 7 = 40$
   b $10 \div 2 + 3 = 2$
   c $18 \div 3 + 3 = 3$
   d $5 - 2 \times 4 = 12$
   e $20 - 5 \times 2 = 30$
   f $5 \times 12 - 8 = 20$
   g $10 - 2^2 \times 2 = 12$
   h $10 - 2^2 \times 2 = 128$
   i $24 \div 2^2 + 2 = 4$

6. Three dice are thrown. They give scores of 2, 4 and 5.

   A class makes the following sums with the numbers. Work them out.

   a $(2 + 4) \times 5 =$
   b $2 + 4 \times 5 =$
   c $4^2 + 5 =$
   d $4 \times (5 - 2) =$
   e $4 + 5 - 2 =$
   f $(4 + 5)^2 =$

7. Three dice give scores of 2, 3 and 6. Copy each of the calculations below, putting $\times$, $+$, $\div$, $-$ or () in each calculation to make it true.

   a $6 \dots 2 \dots 3 = 12$
   b $6 \dots 3 \dots 2 = 30$
   c $3 \dots 6 \dots 2 = 16$

Adding and subtracting negative numbers

Negative numbers are used to describe many situations. For example, temperatures, distances above and below ground or how much money you have or haven't got in your bank account.

Example 16.3 ▶ John is £42.56 overdrawn at the bank. He gets his wages of £189.50 paid in and takes out £30 in cash. How much has he got in the bank now?

An overdrawn amount is negative, so the calculation is:

−42.56 + 189.50 − 30

= 189.50 − 72.56

= £116.94

Example 16.4 ▶ Find the missing number to make each of these calculations true.

a   10 + ☐ = 7   **b**   −8 + ☐ = 12   **c**   − 9 − ☐ = 6

You should be able to work out the answers to these using your knowledge of number facts. If you find this difficult, try visualising a number line, or for more difficult questions, rearrange the equation to find the unknown.

a   ☐ = 7 − 10 = −3   **b**   ☐ = 12 + 8 = 20

c   −☐ = 6 + 9 = 15, so ☐ = −15

Exercise 16B

(FM) (1) The diagram shows a cliff, the sea and sea bed with various objects and places measured from sea level. Use the diagram to answer the questions below.

(a) How far above the sea bed are each of the following?
  i   The submarine
  ii The lighthouse
  iii The plane

(b) How far below the lighthouse are each of the following?
  i   The smugglers' cave
  ii The shark
  iii The submarine

(c) How far above (indicate with a +) or below (indicate with a −) the smugglers' cave are each of the following?
  i   The plane
  ii The shark
  iii The submarine

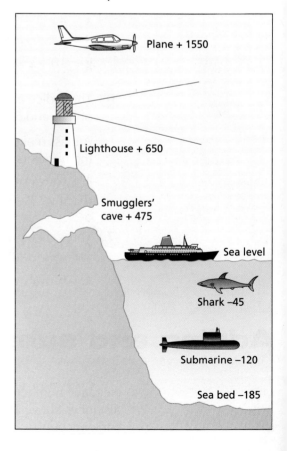

Plane + 1550

Lighthouse + 650

Smugglers' cave + 475

Sea level

Shark −45

Submarine −120

Sea bed −185

FM **2** Copy and complete the balance column in the statement table below.

Transaction	Amount paid in	Amount paid out	Balance
			£64.37
Standing order		£53.20	£11.17
Cheque	£32.00		
Direct debit		£65.50	
Cash	£20.00		
Wages	£124.80		
Loan		£169.38	

FM **3** Five temperatures are marked on the thermometer below.

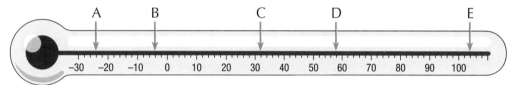

Calculate the difference between each of the following. Remember to give your answer in °C.

a A and B **b** A and D **c** A and E **d** C and E
e B and E **f** B and D **g** A and C **h** D and E

FM **4** Copy and complete each of the following.

a If +£9 means a profit of nine pounds, then … means a loss of nine pounds.

b If +45 m means 45 metres above sea level, then … means 45 metres below sea level.

c If –15 minutes means 15 minutes before midday, then … means 15 minutes after midday.

d If a train moving forwards at 5 mph is represented by +5, then –5 represents ….

5 Calculate each of the following.

a 7 – 5 + 6 **b** 6 – 8 – 3 **c** –4 – 3 – 6 **d** –1 + 3 + 6
e 2 – (–5) **f** –2 + (–3) **g** –2 + (–4) **h** +5 – (+7)
i –3 – –8 + 7 **j** +8 – +8 + –2 **k** –6 + –6 + +3 **l** –8 – –8 + –1
m –9 – +2 – –1 **n** –45 + 89 – 27 **o** +7 – –6 + –1 **p** –6 – +5 + –5

6 Copy these number lines, filling in the missing numbers on each.

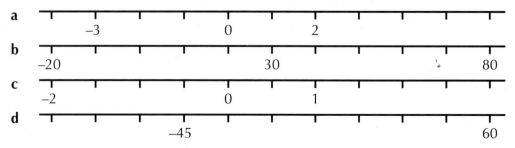

7 Work out the missing numbers from each of the boxes below in order to make each equation true.

a $3 + -5 = \boxed{}$ b $5 + \boxed{} = 9$ c $5 + \boxed{} = 2$

d $\boxed{} - -6 = 4$ e $-6 - \boxed{} = 3$ f $+ 7 - \boxed{} = 4$

g $-8 + -7 = \boxed{}$ h $\boxed{} - +4 = 0$ i $3 - 4 + \boxed{} = 6$

8 In a magic square, each row, column and diagonal adds up to the same 'magic number'. Copy and complete each of these magic squares and write down the 'magic number' for each one.

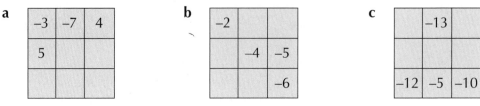

a
-3	-7	4
5		

b
-2		
	-4	-5
		-6

c
	-13	
-12	-5	-10

Multiples, factors and prime numbers

Example 16.5

Find the largest number less than 100 that is:
a a multiple of 3   b a multiple of 3 and 5

a This will be a number in the 3 times table that is close to 100:

$30 \times 3 = 90$
$31 \times 3 = 93$
$32 \times 3 = 96$
$33 \times 3 = 99$
$34 \times 3 = 102$

So, the largest multiple of 3 that is less that 100 is 99.

b Because 3 and 5 have no common factors, multiples common to 3 and 5 are multiples of 15:

15, 30, 45, 60, 75, 90, 105,...

So, the largest number under 100 that is a multiple of both 3 and 5 is 90.

Example 16.6

Find the factors of: a 35   b 180

a Find all the products that make 35:

$1 \times 35 = 35$ $5 \times 7 = 35$

So, the factors of 35 are {1, 5, 7, 35}.

b $1 \times 180 = 180$ $2 \times 90 = 180$ $3 \times 60 = 180$ $4 \times 45 = 180$ $5 \times 36 = 180$

$6 \times 30 = 180$ $9 \times 20 = 180$ $10 \times 18 = 180$ $12 \times 15 = 180$

So, the factors are {1, 2, 3, 4, 5, 6, 9, 10, 12, 15, 18, 20, 30, 36, 45, 60, 90, 180}.

Remember: Factors always come in pairs.

Do not use a calculator for this exercise.

1 Write down the first 5 multiples of each of the following.

   a 4   **b** 9   **c** 12   **d** 25

2 From the list of numbers below, write down those that are:

   a multiples of 3.   **b** multiples of 5.

   c multiples of 4.   **d** multiples of 12.

3	7	8	13	14	15	18	24
36	39	45	48	64	69	90	120

3 Find the largest number less than 50 that is:

   a a multiple of 3.   **b** a multiple of 8.

   c a multiple of 7.   **d** a multiple of 6.

4 Find the largest number less than 50 that is:

   a a multiple of 3 and 4.   **b** a multiple of 5 and 9.

   c a multiple of 3 and 5.   **d** a multiple of 2 and 7.

5 Write down all the factors of each number from 2 to 20.

6 **a** Which of the numbers from 2 to 20 have only 2 factors? Use your answers to Question 5 to help you.

   b What are these numbers called?

7 Write down all the factors of each of the following.

   a 48   **b** 52   **c** 60   **d** 75   **e** 100   **f** 130

8 Find the common factors of each of the following pairs of numbers.

   a 15 and 24   **b** 18 and 24   **c** 15 and 25   **d** 28 and 42

9 Copy the grid on the right.

Shade in, or cross out, the number 1.

Leave the number 2 blank and then shade in, or cross out, the rest of the multiples of 2.

Leave the number 3 blank and then shade in, or cross out, the rest of the multiples of 3. Some of them will have already been shaded in or crossed out.

Leave the number 5 blank and then shade in, or cross out, the rest of the multiples of 5. All but 3 of them will have already been shaded in or crossed out.

Leave the number 7 blank and then shade in, or cross out, the rest of the multiples of 7. All but 1 of them will have already been shaded in or crossed out.

1	2	3	4	5	6
7	8	9	10	11	12
13	14	15	16	17	18
19	20	21	22	23	24
25	26	27	28	29	30
31	32	33	34	35	36
37	38	39	40	41	42
43	44	45	46	47	48
49	50	51	52	53	54
55	56	57	58	59	60

The numbers that are left are the prime numbers up to 60.

Squares, square roots and powers

Example 16.7 ▷ Calculate: **a** 22^2 **b** $\sqrt{289}$ **c** $\sqrt{600}$

    a You can either use the square button on your calculator or calculate 22 x 22.
        $22^2 = 22 \times 22 = 484$

    b Using the square root button on your calculator, $\sqrt{289} = 17$

    c Using the square root button on your calculator, $\sqrt{600} = 24.5$ (rounded to 1 decimal place)

Example 16.8 ▷ Calculate 7^4

Using the power button on your calculator, $7^4 = 2401$
Remember $7^4 = 7 \times 7 \times 7 \times 7$

Exercise 16D

Do not use a calculator for Questions 1 and 2.

1 Write down the value represented by each of the following.
    a 7^2 **b** 9^2 **c** 11^2 **d** 13^2 **e** 15^2

2 Write down the value represented by each of the following.
    a $\sqrt{36}$ **b** $\sqrt{64}$ **c** $\sqrt{100}$ **d** $\sqrt{144}$ **e** $\sqrt{196}$

You may use a calculator for Questions 3–6.

3 Find the value of the square of each of these numbers.
    a 19   **b** 24   **c** 25   **d** 32   **e** 53

4 Calculate each of the following. Round your answers to 2 decimal places.
    a $\sqrt{40}$ **b** $\sqrt{80}$ **c** $\sqrt{120}$ **d** $\sqrt{500}$ **e** $\sqrt{900}$

5 Calculate each of the following.
    a 4^5 **b** 12^3 **c** 13^4 **d** 21^3
    e 6^6 **f** 7^5 **g** 8^3 **h** 2^{12}

6 Work out the value of each of the following. What do you notice?
    a **i** $5^2 - 4^2$ **ii** 3^2
    b **i** $13^2 - 12^2$ **ii** 5^2
    c **i** $25^2 - 24^2$ **ii** 7^2
    d **i** $41^2 - 40^2$ **ii** 9^2

Do not use a calculator for the rest of this exercise.

7 $\sqrt{2} = 1.4142136$, $\sqrt{20} = 4.472136$, $\sqrt{200} = 14.142136$, $\sqrt{2000} = 44.72136$

Use this pattern to write down the value of each of the following.

   a $\sqrt{20\,000}$ **b** $\sqrt{200\,000}$ **c** $\sqrt{2\,000\,000}$

8 Work out the value of each of the following.

   a **i** 1^4 **ii** 1^8 **iii** 1^9

   b **i** $(-1)^3$ **ii** $(-1)^4$ **iii** $(-1)^5$

9 Use your answers to Question 8 to work out the value represented by each of the following.

   a 1^{23} **b** $(-1)^{10}$ **c** $(-1)^9$ **d** 1^{43}

Decimals in context: addition and subtraction

Think about where you may have seen decimal numbers recently.

The most obvious example of decimals in context is money. Prices in shops are usually given to 2 decimal places.

Speedometers in cars and weighing scales increasingly have digital displays involving decimal numbers and nutritional information on food packets, such as cereal, often involves decimal numbers too.

Nutritional Information per 100 g		
ENERGY	1600 kj	280 kcal
PROTEIN	4 g	
CARBOHYDRATES	90 g	
of which sugars	40 g	
starch	50 g	
FAT	0.7 g	
of which saturates	0.2 g	
FIBRE	0.9 g	
SODIUM	0.45 g	
VITAMINS:		(%RDA)
VITAMIN D μg	4.2	(85)
TIAMIN (B₁) mg	1.2	(85)
RIBOFLAVIN (B₂) mg	1.3	(85)
NIACIN mg	15.0	(85)

The next two lessons look at decimals in real life situations.

Example 16.9   Over the course of the year Mr Smith's gas bills were £125.23, £98.07, £68.45 and £102.67. What was the total cost of Mr Smith's gas for the year?

This is a straightforward addition problem:

```
   £125.23
   £ 98.07
   £ 68.45
 + £102.67
   £394.42
```

Example 16.10 ▷ Asif earns £2457.82 in a month. From this £324.78 is deducted for tax, £128.03 for National Insurance and £76.54 for other deductions. How much does Asif take home each month?

This is a subtraction problem. The easiest method to solve it, is to add up all the deductions and then subtract from his total pay.

Deductions

```
  £324.78            ¹ ¹⁴¹ ⁷
  £128.03          £2457.82
+ £ 76.54        − £ 529.35
  ───────          ─────────
  £529.35          £1928.47
```

Exercise 16E

1 Work out each of these.

a 1.8 + 6.9	**b** 6.63 + 7.2	**c** 9.05 + 5.92
d 7.5 − 2.9	**e** 5.67 − 1.87	**f** 7.83 + 1.26 − 7.48
g 9 − 3.7	**h** 12 + 2.36	**i** 8.02 − 1.27 − 2.34
j 12 − 3.47	**k** 8.07 − 2.68	**l** 15.32 − 4.1 − 2.03

FM 2 A businesswoman pays five cheques into her bank account. The cheques are for £1456.08, £256.78, £1905.00, £46.89 and £694.58. How much did she pay in total?

FM 3 Bert booked a holiday to Portugal over the Internet. His return flight cost £118 and his hotel accommodation cost £135.67 in Faro and £165.23 in Lisbon. He also spent £48.80 on train fares to travel between Faro and Lisbon. How much did his holiday cost him in total?

FM 4 At the local shop Mary bought 2 tins of soup costing 57p each, a packet of sugar costing 78p, a loaf of bread costing £1.05, a packet of bacon costing £2.36 and a box of chocolates costing £4.23. What was her total bill?

FM 5 Five books are placed on top of one another. The books are 2.3 cm, 15 mm, 3.95 cm, 1.75 cm and 18 mm thick. What is the total thickness of the pile of books in centimetres?

FM 6 A cake was made using 132 g of butter, 0.362 kg of flour and 96 g of sugar. What is the total weight of these ingredients in kilograms.

FM 7 Misha's bank account has £467.92 in it. She writes cheques for £67.50, £42.35 and £105.99. How much money will be left in Misha's account after these cheques have been cashed?

FM 8 A new car has a list price of £6995.99. As part of an offer, a delivery charge of £109.80 and a discount of £699.59 are taken off the list price. How much will a customer pay for the car?

9 A quadrilateral has a perimeter of 32 cm. The lengths of three of the sides are 8.23 cm, 3.48 cm and 12.96 cm. What is the length of the fourth side?

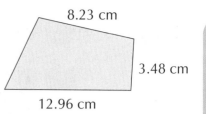

8.23 cm

3.48 cm

12.96 cm

FM **10** William pays a standing order of £55 for fuel each month. Of this £55, £32.78 is for electricity, £12.61 is for gas and the rest is for heating oil. How much does William pay each month for heating oil?

FM **11** Mr Brown's pay slip shows that he is paid a basic wage of £356.78 each week. In addition to his basic wage, he gets a bonus of £102.45. He has £67.82 tax, £34.80 National Insurance and £6.78 health insurance deducted from his pay. How much does Mr Brown take home each week?

Decimals in context: multiplication and division

Example 16.11 One chair costs £45.76 and a table costs £123.47. How much is a dining suite consisting of six chairs and a table?

This is a multiplication and addition problem:

Chairs cost	45.76	total cost	123.47
	× 6		+ 274.56
	274.56		398.03

Hence the total cost is £398.03.

Example 16.12 Eight litres of petrol and a can of oil together cost £8.95. If the can of oil costs £2.59, how much does one litre of petrol cost?

This is a subtraction and division problem:

Petrol costs

$$
\begin{array}{r}
8.\overset{8}{9}\overset{1}{5} \\
-\ 2.59 \\
\hline
6.36
\end{array}
$$

$$
\begin{array}{r}
0.795 \\
8\overline{)6.3\overset{7}{6}\overset{4}{0}}
\end{array}
$$

Hence one litre of petrol costs 79.5 pence.

Exercise 16F

1 Work out the following.

a	17.8	**b**	6.07	**c**	76.32	**d**	18.95
	× 6		× 12		× 25		× 54

FM **2** A packet of four AA batteries costs £4.15. How much money would you need to buy 9 packets of four AA batteries?

(3) John bought five tins of cocoa costing £1.12 each and seven jars of coffee costing £2.09 each. What was his total bill?

(4) To make some shelves Mr George orders seven pieces of wood 53.4 cm in length and two pieces of wood 178.5 cm in length. What is the total length of wood ordered by Mr George?

(5) A crystal decanter costs £56.32 and a crystal wine glass costs £11.58. How much will a decanter and a set of six wine glasses cost?

(6) Calculate each of the following.

    a $68.4 \div 6$ **b** $8.36 \div 8$ **c** $27.5 \div 11$ **d** $32.5 \div 26$

(7) A table and four chairs are advertised for £385. If the table costs £106, how much does each chair cost?

You may use a calculator for the last three questions.

(8) The distance from London to Leeds by train is 317.5 km. If a train takes 2 hours and 30 minutes to cover this distance, what is its average speed?

LEEDS
317.5 km

(9) A man earns £27 746.40 a year. How much does he earn each month?

(10) A holiday for 2 adults and 3 children costs £967.80 in total. If the cost per child is £158.20, what is the cost for each adult?

Long multiplication

You have already met several ways of doing long multiplication. Two of these are shown in the examples below. You may use any method you are happy with for Exercise 16G.

Example 16.13

Work out 164×56.

This multiplication could be done using the box method, as shown below.

×	100	60	4
50	5000	3000	200
6	600	360	24

```
  5000
  3000
   200
   600
   360
+   24
  9184
```

Example 16.14

Work out 238×76.

This multiplication could be done using the standard column method, as shown on the right.

```
      238
   ×   76
     1428
      2 4
    16660
      2 5
    18088
      1
```

Use any method you are happy with for the following questions and show all your working. Check your answers with a calculator afterwards.

1 Work out each of the following. Remember to show your working.

    a 157×24 **b** 324×33 **c** 513×32 **d** 189×23

2 Work out each of the following.

    a 258×34 **b** 276×47 **c** 139×62 **d** 126×39

3 Work out each of the following.

    a 637×28 **b** 377×44 **c** 265×75 **d** 753×63

4 Work out each of the following.

    a 207×14 **b** 620×26 **c** 805×63 **d** 199×99

Long division

You should remember meeting two different ways of doing long division. These are shown below. You may use any method you are happy with to answer the Exercise 16H questions.

Example 16.15

Work out $858 \div 22$.

This division could be done using the standard column method, as below.

Step 1: Start by asking how many 22s there are in 8. There are none of course. So, include the next digit, which is 5, and ask how many 22s there are in 85. Working up the 22 times table (22, 44, 66, 88), we can see that there are 3. Write the 3 above the 5.

Step 2: Work out the value of 3×22 (= 66) and write it underneath 85. Then subtract 66 from 85 to find the remainder of 19.

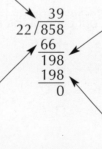

Step 3: Bring down the 8, next to the 19, to give 198.

Step 4: Now ask how many 22s there are in 198. Once again work up the 22 times table: 22, 44, 66, 88, 110, 132, 154, 176, 198. So there are exactly nine 22s in 198. Write the 9 above the 8.

As there is no remainder we can stop. The answer is 39.

Example 16.16 ▷

Work out 938 ÷ 36.

This division has been done below, using repeated subtraction or 'chunking'.

```
    938
  − 720    (20 × 36)
    218
  − 180    (5 × 36)
     38
  −  36    (1 × 36)
      2
```

As the remainder is less than 36 we can stop.

We have subtracted 36 a total of 20 + 5 + 1 = 26 times, so the answer is 26 rem 2.

Exercise 16H

Use any method you are happy with for the following questions and show your working. Check your answers with a calculator afterwards.

1 Work out each of the following. These divisions have exact answers with no remainders. Remember to show your working.

    a 644 ÷ 23

    b 1224 ÷ 34

    c 522 ÷ 18

    d 868 ÷ 28

2 Work out each of the following. These divisions have exact answers with no remainders.

    a 840 ÷ 24

    b 2021 ÷ 47

    c 532 ÷ 38

    d 741 ÷ 39

3 Work out each of the following. These divisions will give remainders.

    a 637 ÷ 28

    b 877 ÷ 41

    c 865 ÷ 25

    d 658 ÷ 33

4 Work out each of the following. These divisions will give remainders.

    a 407 ÷ 14

    b 820 ÷ 16

    c 915 ÷ 39

    d 799 ÷ 29

Long multiplication and division in real-life problems

Example 16.17 ▷

Mr Winston buys a car for £36 480. He agrees to pay for it in 24 equal, monthly instalments. How much does he pay each month?

First you need to identify that this is a division problem, then choose which method to use.

The calculation is done below using the repeated subtraction method. We can ignore the zero on the end of £36 480, as long as we multiply the final answer by 10.

The 24 times table has been written out on the right to help.

```
   3648
 − 2400   (100 × 24)
   1248
 − 1200   (50 × 24)
     48
 −   48   (2 × 24)   +
      0   (152 × 24)
```

$1 × 24 = 24$
$2 × 24 = 48$
$5 × 24 = 120$
$10 × 24 = 240$
$20 × 24 = 480$
$100 × 24 = 2400$
$50 × 24 = 1200$

Don't forget that we divided the starting number by 10, so the answer is £1520 per month.

Example 16.18 ▷

On checking his running diary, Paul finds that he has run an average of 65 miles a week during the last year. How many miles did he run in the year altogether?

You need to identify that this is a multiplication problem, recall that there are 52 weeks in a year, and then decide which method you are going to use.

The multiplication has been done below using the box method.

×	60	5
50	3000	250
2	120	10

So Paul has run a total of 3000 + 250 + 120 + 10 = 3380 miles

Exercise 16I

Work out each of the following, showing your working.

Check your answers with a calculator afterwards.

FM ① A typist can type 54 words per minute on average. How many words can he type in 15 minutes?

FM ② Small chocolate eggs cost 43p each. Mrs Owen wants to buy an egg for each of her class of 28 pupils. How much will this cost her?

(FM) (3) There are 972 pupils in a school. Each tutor group has 27 pupils in it. How many tutor groups are there?

(FM) (4) In a road-race, there were 2200 entrants.

(a) To get them to the start the organisers used a fleet of 52-seater buses. How many buses were needed?

(b) The race was 15 miles long and all the entrants completed the course. How many miles in total did all the runners cover?

(FM) (5) At a school fair, cups of tea were 32p each. The school sold 182 cups.

(a) How much money did they take?

(b) The school used plastic cups which came in packs of 25. They bought 24 packs. How many cups were left over?

(FM) (6) (a) A cinema has 37 rows of seats. Each row contains 22 seats. How many people can sit in the cinema altogether?

(b) Tuesday is 'all seats one price' night. There were 220 customers who paid a total of £572. What was the cost of one seat?

(FM) (7) A library gets 700 books to distribute equally among 12 local schools.

(a) How many books will each school get?

(b) The library keeps any books left over. How many books is this?

(FM) (8) The label on the side of a 1.5 kg cereal box says that there are 66 g of carbohydrate in a 100 g portion. How many g of carbohydrate will Dan consume if he eats the whole box at once?

(FM) (9) A first-class stamp costs 28p and a second-class stamp costs 19p. How much does it cost to send 63 letters first class and 78 letters second class?

(FM) (10) Twelve members of a running club hire a minivan to do the Three Peaks race (climbing the highest mountains in England, Scotland and Wales). The van costs £25 per day plus 12p per mile. The van uses a litre of petrol for every 6 miles travelled. Petrol costs 78p per litre. The van is hired for 3 days and the total mileage covered is 1500.

(a) How much does it cost to hire the van?

(b) How many litres of petrol are used?

(c) If the total cost is shared equally how much does each member pay?

AQA Question 1, Paper 1, June 2005

1 Here is a list of numbers:

17   28   36   45   57   68   72   86

From this list, write down:

a two numbers which have a total of 100

b two numbers which have a difference of 50

c the number which is a multiple of 7

d the number which is a product of 5 and 9

OCR Question 5, Paper 2, June 2004

FM 2 Jamie went out to a country park with his grandparents.

a In the café, his grandparents bought two cups of tea and a cola.
Grandpa had a slice of cheesecake and Jamie had a chocolate sundae.
They paid with a £10 note.

Calculate their change.

Café in the Park

Tea	£1.10	Cheesecake	£2.50
Coffee	£1.25	Scone & Jam	£1.25
Cola	99p	Chocolate Sundae	£2.99

b Postcards of the lake cost 32p.

How many postcards could Jamie buy if he had £1.50?

c The park information letter says that the distance around the lake is 3.5 km.
Grandpa said that he would only walk 2 miles.
1 mile is about 1.6 km.

Would Grandpa walk around the lake?

Show your working.

d A group did a sponsored run around the lake.
Each lap is 3.5 km.
Abbi ran for 4 laps.
She received £18 for every kilometre she ran.

How much money did she raise?

EDEXCEL Paper 1, 2005

3 Work out 286×43.

EDEXCEL Paper 1`, 2005

4 Here is a list of 8 numbers:

11   16   18   36   68   69   82   88

a Write down two numbers from the list with a sum of 87.

b Write down a number from the list which is:
   i A multiple of 9   **ii** A square number

c
| Cube | Square | Multiple | Factor | Square root |

Use a word from the box to complete this sentence correctly:

11 is a …… of 88

OCR Question 8, Paper 2, June 2004

5 The diagram shows a number machine.

INPUT ⟶ ×3 ⟶ −1 ⟶ OUTPUT

    a Work out the input when the output is:

        i 2   **ii** 0   **iii** 1.5

    b Work out the input when the output is 14.

OCR Question 7, Paper 2, 2004

6 **a** Write down all the factors of 12.

    b Write down a multiple of 12.

    c Work out $\frac{5}{6}$ of 12.

    d Write 12 out of 42 as a fraction in its simplest form.

AQA Spec B Mod 3 non calc, 2006

7 Calculate:

    a 456 + 346 + 75

    b 7.4 − 2.56

    c 6^3

    d $\frac{3}{4} - \frac{1}{5}$

EDEXCEL, 2005

8 Write these numbers in order of size. Start with the smallest number.

    a 76, 103, 13, 130, 67

    b −3, 5, 0, −7, −1

    c 0.72, 0.7, 0.072, 0.07, 0.702

    d 70%, $\frac{3}{4}$, 0.6, $\frac{2}{3}$

EDEXCEL Question 8, Paper 2, 2005

FM **9** The table shows the temperature on the surfaces of each of five planets:

    a Work out the difference in temperature between Mars and Jupiter.

    b Work out the difference in temperature between Venus and Mars.

    c Which planet has a temperature 30°C higher than the temperature on Saturn?

    d The temperature on Pluto is 20°C lower than the temperature on Uranus. Work out the temperature on Pluto.

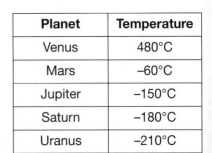

Planet	Temperature
Venus	480°C
Mars	−60°C
Jupiter	−150°C
Saturn	−180°C
Uranus	−210°C

10 a Put these numbers in order of size. Start with the largest number.

   0.786   0.09   0.8

   b Write 0.786 to 2 decimal places.

   c Convert $\frac{3}{8}$ to a decimal.

   d Work out 0.1×0.7.

11 Football teams are given points after each match they play, as shown:

Win	3 points
Draw	1 point
Lose	0 points

a Pam's team has played eight matches.

They have won four matches, drawn three matches and lost one match.

How many points in total has her team been given?

b Milly's team has played 10 matches and has been given 17 points.

Work out the **two** ways that her team could have been given 17 points.

First way:	**Second way:**
Number of matches won	Number of matches won
Number of matches drawn	Number of matches drawn
Number of matches lost	Number of matches lost

12 Glynn says that $\sqrt{(16 + 9)}$ is the same as $\sqrt{16} + \sqrt{9}$.

Show that Glynn is wrong.

13 Insert brackets on the left hand side of each of the following to make them correct.

   a 3 + 5 − 2 ÷ 3 = 2

   b 3 + 5 − 2 ÷ 3 = 4

FM The Eden Project

1 On a school visit to the Eden Project, children pay less than the normal entry fee.

It costs £24 for 6 children to enter the Eden Project.

How much does it cost for 10 children to enter the Eden Project?

2 Two families visited the Eden Project.

It cost the Brown family of one adult and two children £24.

It cost the Kahnaan family of two adults and two children £38.

How much does it cost Mrs McDonald and her three children to enter the Eden Project?

3 The Schools Visit Manager at the Eden Project estimates that the ratio of men : women : children visiting the project is 1 : 2 : 4.

On the first Wednesday in March, there were 7700 visitors to the project.

a How many of the 7700 visitors were children?

b Every person visiting that day was given a ticket with a number on, and one was chosen at random for a prize.

What is the probability that a child won the prize?

4 In the information centre, Joel saw this table showing the number of visitors to the Eden Project from 2000 to 2006.

Year	2000	2001	2002	2003	2004	2005	2006
Visitor numbers (millions)	2.0	1.9	1.6	1.7	1.8	1.8	1.8

a Draw a bar graph to show this information.

b Find the mean number of visitors per year.

c Find the median number of visitors per year.

d Find the mode of the number of visitors per year.

5 Anika did a survey while she was on a school visit to the Eden Project. She asked other visitors what the best part of their day was. Here are her results:

	Schoolboys	Schoolgirls	Men	Women
Inside Humid Tropics Biome	12	3	6	2
Inside Warm Temperate Biome	4	7	4	10
Looking at the buildings	7	7	6	2
Day off school	9	2	0	0
The weather	0	0	0	0
The food	1	0	0	0
Other	3	1	2	2

a How many boys said 'Looking at the buildings' was the best part?

b How many girls said they liked the inside of the biomes best?

c How many more girls were asked than women?

d Which was the overall favourite?

e Why do you think that no men gave 'Day off school' as their answer?

f What type of weather do you think it was on the day that Anika did her survey? Explain your answer.

g Anika wants to do this survey again. Write down one thing that she could do to make it better next time.

6 The Eden Project has its own outdoor amphitheatre which is used for plays and pop concerts.

It has a **total** area of 2282 m².

The stage covers 700 m² of the total area.

The remaining area is for the 2109 seats for the audience.

What area, in m², does each member of the audience get?

Round your answer to one decimal place.

7 The tallest biome is 55 m high. A type of bamboo, *bambusa gigantica*, can grow up to 45 cm a day.

If it continued to grow at this rate, how many days would it take a 3 m *bambusa gigantica* to reach the roof?

8 The thermometer on a wall in the Humid Tropics Biome shows 24°C.

Lorna remembers the formula she used in her science lesson last week to change a temperature in degrees Celsius to degrees Fahrenheit:

°F = 1.8 × °C + 32

Change 75.2°F into °C.

The greenhouses, or biomes, in the Eden Project are domes that are made out of hundreds of differently-sized hexagons and a few pentagons. The 'glass' is actually a transparent cushion made from three layers of tough plastic that is self-cleaning and should look good for about 30 years.

The next seven questions are about this amazing shape – the hexagon.

9 The most commonly used regular hexagon in the Warm Temperature Biome has a side measurement of 4.45 m.

What is the perimeter of this hexagon?

4.45 m

10 a Use the fact that the angles in a triangle add up to 180° to find the total of the interior angles in this regular hexagon. (*Hint:* Sketch a hexagon and draw triangles inside it.)

regular hexagon

b What is the size of each interior angle in this regular hexagon?

11 Use your answer to Question 10 to help you explain why regular hexagons tessellate and regular pentagons do not. (*Hint:* Find the size of the interior angle of a regular pentagon.)

12 Some of the hexagons that make up the very top of the biomes have parts that open automatically to stop the biggest greenhouses in the world getting too hot.

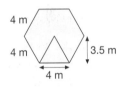
4 m
4 m
3.5 m
4 m

The diagram above shows one of those hexagons. Find the area of the triangular opening.

13 The largest hexagon used in making the biomes is 11 m across! The length of each side is 5.5 m.

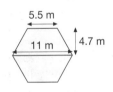
5.5 m
11 m
4.7 m

A hexagon can be made from two identical trapeziums.

The formula for the area of a trapezium is $\frac{1}{5}(a + b)h$.

Find the area of the hexagon above.

14 Part of the reason that a hexagon is so strong is that it has lots of lines of symmetry.

Draw a sketch of a hexagon and draw on it all of the lines of symmetry.

Remember to use dotted lines for your lines of symmetry.

15 Using a ruler and a protractor, make an accurate copy of this diagram of a regular hexagon.

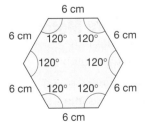
6 cm
6 cm 120° 120° 6 cm
120°   120°
6 cm 120° 120° 6 cm
6 cm

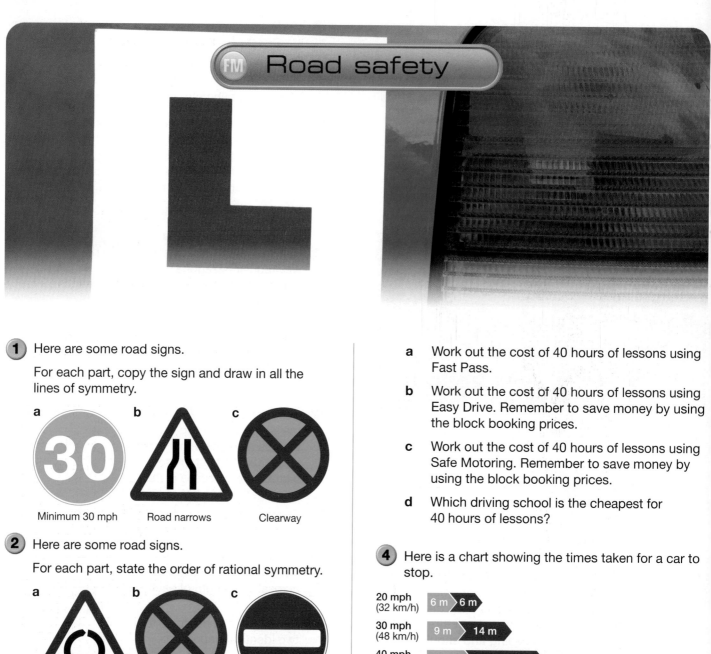

1 Here are some road signs.

For each part, copy the sign and draw in all the lines of symmetry.

a
30
Minimum 30 mph

b
Road narrows

c
Clearway

2 Here are some road signs.

For each part, state the order of rational symmetry.

a
Roundabout

b
Clearway

c
No entry

3 Here are three advertisements for driving schools.

Fast Pass
First four lessons £8 each
Then £20 per lesson
All lessons 1 hour

Easy Drive
Standard hourly rate £20
First five hours £60
Block bookings
10 hours £150
15 hours £225

Safe Motoring
First lesson free
Normal price £20 per hour
£2 off per hour for block booking
of 10 or more lessons

a Work out the cost of 40 hours of lessons using Fast Pass.

b Work out the cost of 40 hours of lessons using Easy Drive. Remember to save money by using the block booking prices.

c Work out the cost of 40 hours of lessons using Safe Motoring. Remember to save money by using the block booking prices.

d Which driving school is the cheapest for 40 hours of lessons?

4 Here is a chart showing the times taken for a car to stop.

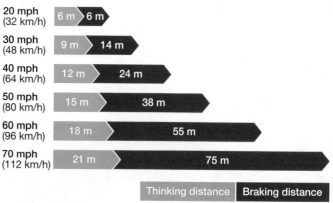

| | Thinking distance | Braking distance |

20 mph (32 km/h) — 6 m / 6 m
30 mph (48 km/h) — 9 m / 14 m
40 mph (64 km/h) — 12 m / 24 m
50 mph (80 km/h) — 15 m / 38 m
60 mph (96 km/h) — 18 m / 55 m
70 mph (112 km/h) — 21 m / 75 m

a Work out the stopping distance when travelling at 20 mph.

b By working out the stopping distance when travelling at 30 mph, show that a car would travel almost twice as far when stopping from 30 mph than 20 mph.

5 The table shows the percentage of casualties in road accidents for different age groups.

Age	Percentage
17–25 years	33%
26–39 years	28%
40–59 years	24%
60 years and over	15%

a Draw a pie chart to show this information.

b Give a reason why there are more casualties in the 17–25 years age group.

6 Research shows that it is safer for pedestrians to walk facing traffic than walking with their back to traffic on rural roads.

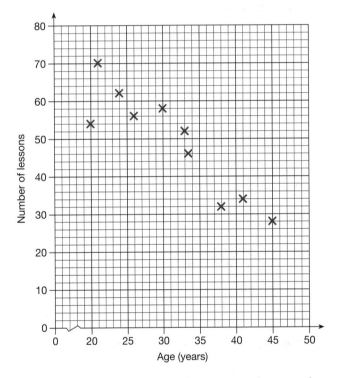

10% of those involved in an accident when walking with their back to traffic are killed or seriously injured.

5% of those involved in an accident when facing traffic are killed or seriously injured.

a If 2000 pedestrians are involved in accidents when walking with their back to traffic, how many of these are likely to be killed or seriously injured?

b If 2000 pedestrians are involved in accidents when facing traffic, how many of these are likely to be killed or seriously injured?

7 The driving test is made up of two parts: the theory test and the practical test.

A learner has to pass the theory test before taking a practical test.

In April 2008, the theory test cost £30 and the practical test cost £56.50 for weekdays and £67.00 for weekday evenings or weekends.

a Priya passes at the first attempt. She takes her test on a weekend. How much does it cost altogether?

b Tessa passes her theory test first time and the practical test on the seond attempt. How much more does it cost if the practical tests are taken at the weekend than if they are taken on a weekday?

8 A practical test lasts for 40 minutes and covers 12 miles. Work out the average speed in miles per hour.

9 The table shows the number of attempts that some drivers take to pass their driving test.

Number of attempts to pass	Number of drivers
1	16
2	9
3	7
4	4
5	3
6	1
	Total = 40

a What fraction of the drivers pass at the first attempt?

b Work out the median number of attempts to pass.

10 The scatter diagram shows the relationship between the age and the number of driving lessons taken by students at a driving school.

a Describe the relationship between the age of drivers and the number of lessons needed.

b Estimate the number of lessons taken by a 36-year-old person at this driving school.

c Explain why it would not be sensible to use the scatter diagram to estimate the number of lessons needed by a 50-year-old person.

FM Squirrels

Red squirrels are native to Britain. In 1870 some North American grey squirrels were released in the North of England. The grey squirrel thrived in the conditions in Britain and slowly took over the habitats of the red squirrel, reducing their numbers dramatically.

1 Today it is estimated that there are 180 000 red squirrels and 2.7 million grey squirrels in Britain.

   a Write 2.7 million in figures.

   b Write the ratio number of red squirrels : number of grey squirrels in its simplest form.

2 The population of red squirrels in England, Wales and Scotland is estimated as:

Country	Number of red squirrels
England	35 000
Scotland	120 000
Wales	25 000

Draw a fully-labelled pie chart to show this information.

3 A study on the body weights of squirrels gave the following data for red squirrels over a 12-month period.

Month	Jan	Feb	Mar	Apr	May	Jun	Jul	Aug	Sep	Oct	Nov	Dec
Average weight (g)	273	265	274	280	285	290	310	325	345	376	330	290

This graph shows the same data for grey squirrels.

a On a copy of the graph, draw a line graph to show the average body weight of the red squirrels.

b Why do you think the weights of the squirrels increase in the autumn?

c Comment on the differences in the weights of the red and grey squirrels over the year.

4 One reason that grey squirrels do better than red squirrels is that they are more aggressive feeders. This table shows how many of each type can be supported in different types of habitats.

Grizedale forest in Cumbria has an area of 2445 hectares. The table also shows the percentage of Grizedale forest given over to different habitats.

Type of habitat	Number of grey squirrels per hectare	Number of red squirrels per hectare	Land use (%) of forest
Broad-leaved woodland	8	1	65
Coniferous woodland	2	0.1	12
Agricultural	0	0	10
Wildlife management	10	2	2
Open areas	0	0	11

a How many hectares of Grizedale forest are broad-leaved woodland?

Give your answer to an appropriate degree of accuracy.

b Assuming that no red squirrels live in the forest, estimate how many grey squirrels the forest could support.

c Assuming that no grey squirrels live in the forest, estimate how many red squirrels the forest could support.

10 adult male red and 10 adult male grey squirrels are trapped and studied. This is the data obtained.

Red squirrels

	A	B	C	D	E	F	G	H	I	J
Body length (mm)	202	185	215	192	205	186	186	199	235	222
Tail length (mm)	185	164	198	175	182	173	162	184	210	203
Weight (g)	320	292	340	305	335	341	295	325	360	357

Grey squirrels

	A	B	C	D	E	F	G	H	I	J
Body length (mm)	272	243	278	266	269	280	251	272	278	281
Tail length (mm)	223	196	220	218	218	222	198	220	226	225
Weight (g)	530	512	561	512	542	551	520	530	558	564

5 a Work out the mean and range of the weights of the red squirrels.

b Work out the mean and range of the weights of the grey squirrels.

c Comment on the differences in the weights of each species.

6 The scatter diagram below shows the relationship between the body length and tail length of red squirrels.

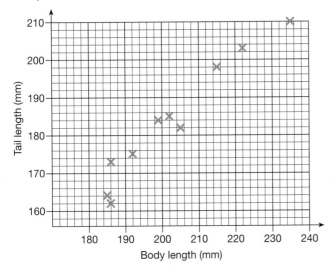

a Estimate the tail length of a red squirrel with a body length of 210 mm.

b Describe the correlation between the body length and tail length of red squirrels.

c i Using the data for grey squirrels, draw a scatter diagram to show the relationship between body length and tail length.

Use a horizontal axis for body length from 240 mm to 290 mm and a vertical axis for tail length from 190 mm to 230 mm.

ii Draw a line of best fit on the diagram.

iii Use your line of best fit to estimate the body length of a grey squirrel with a tail length of 205 mm.

iv Explain why the diagram could not be used to estimate the tail length of a young grey squirrel with a body length of 180 mm.

7 The normal diet of red squirrels is mainly seeds and pine cones with some fungi and plant shoots.

This table shows the percentage of each type of food in the diet of some red squirrels.

Food	Seeds	Pine cones	Fungi	Shoots
Percentage	42%	34%	14%	10%

Copy and complete a percentage bar chart to show the information.

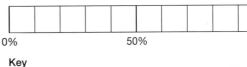

0%   50%   100%

Key

▨ Seeds   ☐ Pine cones   ▧ Fungi   ▦ Shoots

8 This table shows the number of baby red squirrels born in 100 nests.

Number of baby squirrels	Frequency
1	24
2	42
3	19
4	10
5	5

a Work out the mean number of baby squirrels per nest.

b The probability of a baby squirrel surviving to adulthood is 0.4.

How many of the squirrels in the table above would you expect to survive to adulthood?

9 This is an extract from a newspaper article.

> By 1998 on the Welsh island of Anglesey grey squirrels had almost totally wiped out the native red squirrels. Since then due to a policy of removing grey squirrels from the island the red squirrel population has recovered and in 2007 was 180. This is a 720% increase on the population in 1998. By 2010 it is expected that the grey squirrel will be completely removed from the island and the population of red squirrels to be over 300.

a What is the expected percentage increase in the red squirrel population between 2007 and 2010?

b Show that there were approximately 25 red squirrels in 1998.

10 Red squirrels are affected by the Parapoxvirus. A colony of red squirrels numbering 1260 was infected by the virus and lost 15% of its numbers. How many squirrels were left in the colony?

Mobile shop

Mobile shops were very common in the 1960s but as supermarkets started to open and people had access to cars, they fell out of favour. Nowadays, with people wanting fresher produce and concerned about driving long distances to shop, they are returning to some remote rural areas.

Jeff and Donna decide to start a Mobile shop in a rural area of North Devon.

1 This is a map of the villages they decide they will serve with the distances between villages shown.

The distances are in kilometres.

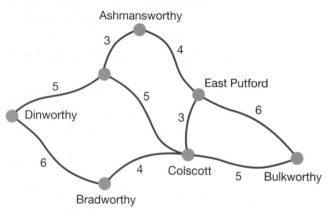

They plan this route: Ashmansworthy – Dinworthy – Bradworthy – Colscott – Bulkworthy – East Putford – Ashmansworthy.

a How many kilometres is this route?

b They plan a timetable.

They intend to be open for 30 minutes in each village.

It takes 5 minutes to pack all the groceries safely after they close before they can drive off.

It takes 5 minutes to unpack the groceries after they arrive and before they can open.

They know they need to allow 2 minutes per kilometre on the rural roads.

They intend to open the shop at 9 am in Ashmansworthy.

This is the timetable for the first two villages.

Copy and complete the timetable for the opening times at each village.

Event	Time
Open Ashmansworthy	9.00
Close Ashmansworthy	9.30
Leave Ashmansworthy	9.35
Arrive Dinworthy	9.51
Open Dinworthy	9.56
Close Dinworthy	10.26
Leave Dinworthy	10.31

c What time do they arrive back in Ashmansworthy?

2 Most mobile shops are often converted single-decker buses.

Jeff and Donna see this advert and decide to buy this bus.

> **1983 Leyland Tiger** – Mid engine, Plaxton Paramount 3200, Semi-automatic, 53 seats with belts, Air Door, Very clean inside and out. Drives well, MOT Jan 2008. Length: 12 metres, height 3.2 metres, width 2.5 metres. Price: £2500.
> For more photos please visit our website www.usedcoachsales.co.uk

They know that fitting out the bus will cost £5000.

Insuring and taxing the bus will cost £1500.

Buying the initial stock for the bus will be £2000.

They have savings of £7500.

a Show that the minimum they will need to borrow is £3500.

b The bank agrees to lend them up to £3500 at an interest rate of 7.5% per annum.

i How much will the interest be on £3500 for one year?

ii If they borrow £3500 and decide to pay the loan back over one year, what will be the approximate monthly payment?

3 Health and Safety rules state that they must have adequate lighting, hot water for washing hands, a fridge for storing chilled foods and heating for the winter. They consult an electrician who estimates the power for each item to be:

Lighting	500 W
Water heater	2 kW
Fridge	1 kW
Heating	kW

a W stands for Watts. What does k stand for?

b What is the total maximum power needed? Answer in Watts.

4 Before they go ahead with the plan, Jeff and Donna decide to do a survey of the villages to see if there will be enough business to make the venture worthwhile.

a Jeff says, 'We need to find out the population of each village and survey about 10% of the residents in each of them'.

Donna says, 'We need to find out how many households there are in each village and survey about 10% of them'.

Donna is correct. Explain why.

b The number of households in each village is given in the table.

How many households in each village should be surveyed?

Village	Households
Ashmansworthy	322
Dinworthy	178
Bradworthy	476
Colscott	150
Bulkworthy	483
East Putford	189

c This is one of the questions that Jeff prepares for the survey. Give two criticisms of this.

How much do you spend each week?

Up to £20 ☐   £20 – £30 ☐   More than £30 ☐

d This is a question that Donna prepares for the survey. Give two reasons why this is a good question.

Please tick the appropriate box.
How much do you spend each week on:

Item	£0 to £9.99	£10 to £19.99	£20 to £29.99	£30 or more
Meat				
Fruit				
Vegetables				
Cleaning products				
Other household items				

e This is one of the tables they compile after doing the survey of how much households spend each week on meat.

Amount, m, £	Frequency, f	Midpoint, m	$m \times f$
£0 ≤ m < £10	48	5	
£10 ≤ m < £20	97	15	
£20 ≤ m < £30	38	25	
£30 ≤ m < £40	17	35	
Total		Total	

Copy the table and work out the mean amount each household spends on meat each week.

5 The bus is 12 m long and 2.5 m wide. This is a scale drawing of the bus with 1 cm representing 1 m.

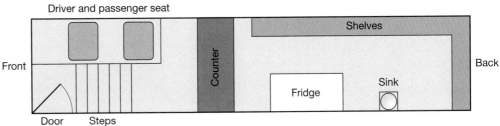

a What is the total area of the bus?

b What is the actual width of the counter?

c The area behind the counter is the 'shop area'. The back of the counter is 6.5 m from the back of the bus. Show that the shop area is 54% of the total area to the nearest percentage.

d The fridge is $1\frac{1}{2}$ m high. What is the volume of the fridge?

6 Donna uses the following formula to work out the profit the shop will make each week.

P is the profit. T is the total amount taken over the counter in pounds in a week.

$$P = \frac{T}{5} - 150$$

a Explain how you can tell from this formula that the basic running costs are £150 a week.

b What is the profit if the weekly takings are £1600?

c Jeff says that they need to make a weekly profit of £400. Show that they need to take £2750 each week to do this.

d They apply for a grant to the European Union community fund who agree to subsidise them by 10% of their takings each week. How much profit do they make when their weekly takings are £1800 and they receive a subsidy of £180?

7 A council survey shows that in a month the bus will drive about 1200 km with a CO_2 emission of 390 g/km. At the same time, the number of miles driven by people living in the village to travel to supermarkets will reduce by about 6000 km with an average CO_2 emission of 170 g/km. Estimate the saving in CO_2 emissions in a year if the mobile shop starts to operate. Answer in kilograms.

Index

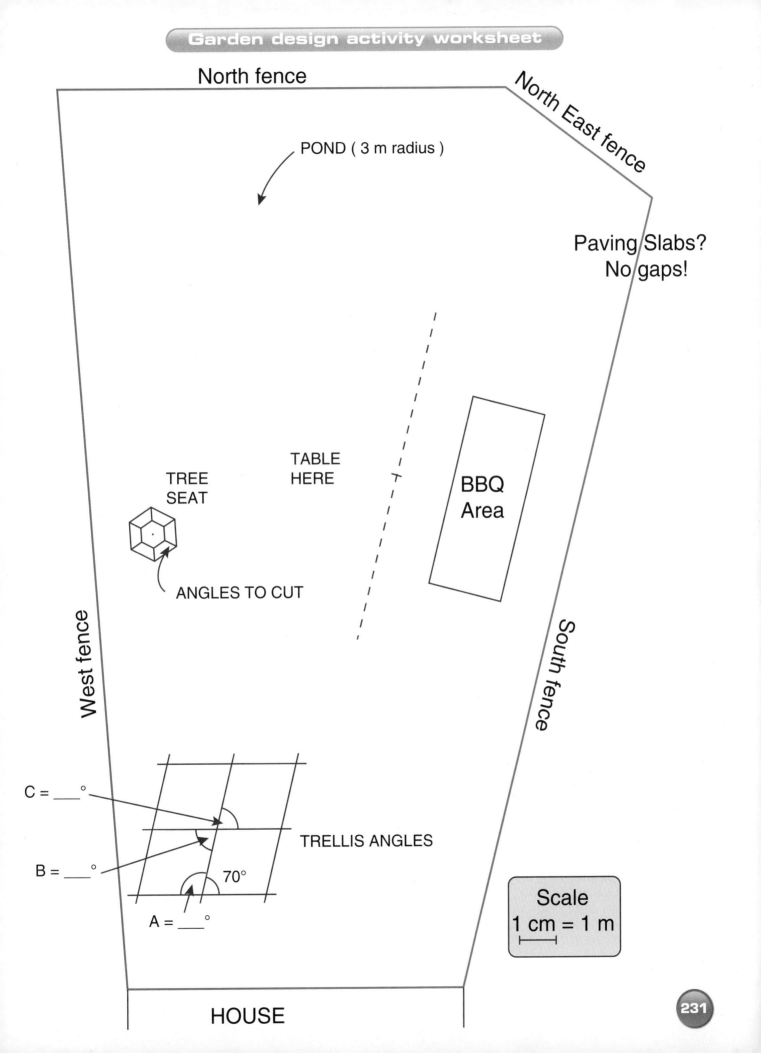

North fence

North East fence

POND (3 m radius)

Paving Slabs?
No gaps!

TABLE
HERE

TREE
SEAT

BBQ
Area

ANGLES TO CUT

West fence

South fence

C = ___ °

TRELLIS ANGLES

B = ___ °

70°

Scale
1 cm = 1 m

A = ___ °

HOUSE

231

William Collins' dream of knowledge for all began with the publication of his first book in 1819. A self-educated mill worker, he not only enriched millions of lives, but also founded a flourishing publishing house. Today, staying true to this spirit, Collins books are packed with inspiration, innovation and practical expertise. They place you at the centre of a world of possibility and give you exactly what you need to explore it.

Collins. Freedom to teach.

Published by Collins
An imprint of HarperCollins*Publishers*
77–85 Fulham Palace Road
Hammersmith
London
W6 8JB

Browse the complete Collins catalogue at
www.collinseducation.com

ISBN 978-0-00-726624-1

Keith Gordon, Kevin Evans, Brian Speed and Trevor Senior assert their moral rights to be identified as the authors of this work.

British Library Cataloguing in Publication Data
A Catalogue record for this publication is available from the British Library.

Extra Functional Maths material written by Greg and Lynn Byrd
Commissioned by Melanie Hoffman and Katie Sergeant
Project managed by Priya Govindan
Indexed by Michael Forder
Edited by Brian Ashbury
Proofread by Amanda Dickson
Design and typesetting by Jordan Publishing Design
Covers by Oculus Design and Communications
Covers managed by Laura Deacon
Illustrations by Nigel Jordan, Tony Wilkins and Barking Dog Art
Printed and bound by Martins the Printers, Berwick-upon-Tweed
Production by Simon Moore

Acknowledgments

The publishers thank the Qualifications and Curriculum Authority for granting permission to reproduce questions from past National Curriculum Test papers for Key Stage 3 Maths.

The publishers have sought permission from AQA, OCR and EDEXCEL to reproduce past GCSE exam papers.

The map on page 150 is reproduced by permission of Ordnance Survey on behalf of HMSO. © Crown copyright 2008. All rights reserved. Ordnance Survey Licence number 100048274.

The publishers wish to thank the following for permission to reproduce photographs:

p.16–17 (main image) © VisualHongKong / Alamy, p.32–33 (main image) © Gilbert Iundt / TempSport / Corbis and (inset image of flag) © Andrew Paterson / Alamy, p.64–65 (main image) © V. J. Matthew / istockphoto.com, p.80–81 (main image) © Brandon Alms / istockphoto.com, p.98–99 (main image) © Josef Philipp / istockphoto.com, p.112–113 (main image) © Elena Schweitzer / istockphoto.com, p.126–127 (main image) © Comstock / Corbis and (inset image of violin case) © Nancy Louie / istockphoto.com, p.138–139 (main image) © Laurence Gough / istockphoto.com, p.150–151 (main image) © Guy Nicholls / istockphoto.com, p.162–163 (main image) © Cornel Stefan Achirei / istockphoto.com, p.218 (main image) © Brian Kelly / istockphoto.com, p. 219 (bamboo image) © Ian Pettigrew, (biome image) © Kevin Jarratt / istockphoto.com, p. 220 (main image) © Chris Elwell / istockphoto.com, p. 221 (ambulance image) © Nick Free / istockphoto.com, p. 222 (main images) © Sharon Day / istockphoto.com, p. 224 (main image) © David Lyons / Alamy

Every effort has been made to trace copyright holders and to obtain their permission for the use of copyright material. The authors and publishers will gladly receive any information enabling them to rectify any error or omission at the first opportunity.